LURK ON THE
LOVE PLANET

A Romantic Odyssey

by
Larry Sherrer

Also by Larry Sherrer

Zigzag Men — "the Catch-22 of the Vietnam war"

This is a work of fiction. All incidents and dialogue, and all characters are products of the author's imagination and are not to be construed as real. In all respects, any resemblance to persons living or dead is entirely coincidental.

All rights reserved. No part of this book may be reproduced in any form or by any electronic or mechanical means including information storage and retrieval systems without permission in writing from the publisher, except by a reviewer who may quote brief passages in a review.

- - -

My apologies to the good folk of Kilgore, Idaho; I am certain my fictional characterization of you and your town is unfairly narrow.

BRASS BOOKS

Visit our website at www.brassbooks.com

- - -

- - -

Cover design by Larry Sherrer

Cover photo of the earth provided by NASA

- - -

Destiny is an absolutely definite and inexorable ruler.
Physical ability and moral determination count for nothing.
It is impossible to perform the simplest act when the gods say "no."
I have no idea how they bring pressure to bear on such occasions;
I only know that it is irresistible

Aleister Crowley in The Confessions of Aleister Crowley.

- - -

I happen to believe you make your own destiny. You have to do the best with what God gave you... Life is a box of chocolates, Forrest. You never know what you're goin' to get.

Winston Groom in Forrest Gump.

- - -

Follow the weasel.

Crazy Uncle Harold

Contents

Jerry Garcia Gustafson

First Step

In the beginning at The Planet of Love, Jerry had little more to do than perch on a stool behind a glass counter full of sexual paraphernalia from 10 am to 6 pm, waiting like a too-tall vulture for the day to die. It was an easy job; there were few customers and, so far, he'd never once had to sell a dildo. He had only to stay alert for shoplifters and collect cash from the infrequent sale of magazines, or lingerie, or any of the cute, kitschy shit comprising the store's inventory.

It was anxiety that kept him there. Jerry was fearful of doing anything that might jinx his inexplicable good fortune in being offered the position. He figured if he did nothing at all for eight hours, he could do nothing wrong.

He had no idea why Old Man Stamper had offered the job to him out of hundreds of likely job-seekers with actual retail experience. The man was clearly flirting with senility and otherwise a thoroughgoing mystery, so Jerry accepted his good fortune as something he might never understand.

While the job paid enough to buy the necessities, to his everlasting amazement, it also came with free rent in a little apartment over the shop. So, now he didn't have to endure the daily search for food and shelter on the streets of Seattle. This alone justified enduring the peculiar clientele that sometimes came through the door and the unreasonable anxiety that his long-dead Grandma (or some church-lady like her) would enter the shop and be horrified to find him working in such a place.

Over time, Jerry became less worried his recent good fortune would not hold. The nearly-idle time he spent watching the hours slough away from the clock over the door allowed him, for the first time, to look back and marvel at the protracted and chaotic odyssey that brought him to where he sat.

His trajectory toward The Planet of Love began from the lonesome, little, high-plains town of Kilgore, Idaho in the fall of the previous year, in what now seemed like another lifetime. Unlike Seattle, Kilgore sported one traffic light, one market, one café, dozens of commercial potato cellars, and two churches. Until he left, Jerry had lived nowhere else and had been no farther away from Kilgore than one bus trip to Boise to compete in the state finals of a high school track meet.

When he left Kilgore for good, he had no idea where he was going. He knew only, and with remarkable certainty, that the time had finally come to launch toward a more expansive life, one he had often imagined must be waiting for him somewhere, anywhere, other than Kilgore.

The peculiar certainty that it was finally time to leave came to him in an instant, triggered by an inconsequential mishap, little more than a private pratfall, notable only because it marked the precise end to the quiet order of his life and the beginning of a hectic odyssey involving wild turns of fortune.

If there had been any witnesses, they might have found his pratfall funny.

In the natural way of things, the chaos would abate over time and sweet order would return to his life, but it was to be an order different from anything he had known. Once established in orbit around The Planet of Love, he would discover that life in Kilgore had been lacking more than he ever imagined.

- - -

It all began in the back office of Kilgore's branch of the Clark County Library. Jerry had been working there off and on since high school as a sort of librarian's assistant and handyman, reshelving books and doing odd jobs. There were even times (whenever Ms. Nervan was beset by her "monthly migraines") that he found himself managing the whole operation, acting as the librarian. The job offered little money and no benefits at all beyond ample opportunity for reading, the only activity for which anyone might have described Jerry as passionate. The good citizens of Kilgore were more likely to have described him as reclusive or standoffish, or even (already at his young age) eccentric.

It was after-hours. The library was closed. Ms. Nervan had left for the day and the place was empty and quiet. Jerry stayed to commune with familiar, musty books rather than retire to his apartment. Confident no one would disturb his indolence, he adopted his customary, after-hours reading position, his feet on Ms. Nervan's desk, tipping her old-fashioned, wooden desk chair to the edge of stability. In one hand he held, as it happened, an ancient paperback copy of *Stranger in a Strange Land* (an example from his favorite genre that he was rereading for at least the third time). His other hand cradled his otherwise empty head. In that precarious position (one his Grandma would surely have warned him about if she were still alive) and while in that vulnerable mental state, lost as he was in a strange land, Ms. Nervan's chair collapsed.

Jerry landed in a noisy flurry of arms and legs, both chair and human. The sharp crack of failed joinery, and Jerry's "whuff," as the air went out of him, accompanied an acoustic clattering of wooden chair parts and the sproinging ricochet of freed recliner springs. This was followed by the soft smack of the paperback's inelegant landing.

Jerry arose in shock amongst the ruins of Ms. Nervan's chair as if jerked to his feet, dangling like a marionette, without a cogent thought beyond the certainty that something more had happened than the simple failure of an old wooden chair. He felt as if something in him had changed, decisive as an over-center switch.

His life was reconfigured in that moment. He saw a merciless summation of it, all-of-a-piece and for the first time, a harsh revelation, a floodlit look at the big picture: He was alone, in every way, in the dim and dusty back room of an inconsequential, small-town library, stunned by the horrifying notion that in another twenty-five years, without willful intervention, he would be a fifty-year-old Librarian's Assistant and Handyman, reshelving the same moldy books, maybe having to repair another fracture of the same damn chair, perhaps even wistfully remembering this first time it had failed.

For a few thudding heartbeats, he did not know (as his Uncle Harold might have said) whether to shit or go blind.

- - -

It was Jerry's awakening from the pathetic torpor he had previously assumed was his assigned portion. It felt as if someone had snuck up behind him and kicked out his physical and metaphorical underpinnings. His brief existence in the known world had shrunk to sad insignificance, while the unknown world correspondingly expanded in all directions, well beyond his dizzy comprehension.

He knew he had to leave Kilgore. He was not supposed to be there. It was obvious that he'd been living in The Wrong Place all this time!

How this particular certainty was implanted in his febrile brain, or how a collapsing chair triggered its implantation, were mysteries he would carry with him all the way to The Planet of Love and beyond.

- - -

Though transformed, he did not move. What kept him upright and stable was his innate, plodding rationality. It was something that had always kept him steady-on through the harshest bumps in life, like a soul-centering gyroscope. It now served to moderate the mindless panic that might otherwise have sent him sprinting down the cold, two-lane road out of town toward Idaho Falls, or careening around the library like the snake-spooked monkey he had once seen in the Boise Zoo.

During those pounding heartbeats of catalepsy (his motor racing, but his brakes still on), while still astraddle the ground zero of Ms. Nervan's shattered chair, an onslaught of practical questions swarmed his thoughts:

Where would he go?

What would he do?

Did he have enough money?

How should he begin?

Then a fresh thrill of excitement began to riffle through the anxious swirl of questions. It felt like high, clear harmonies sparkling through the low notes of a dirge:

He could go anywhere!

He could do anything!

He wouldn't need much money!

He could begin right now!

The excitement reverberated in counterpoint with the anxiety, the two flushing through him, alternating allegro, making him feel as though his appearance might be changing like that of an agitated octopus.

Before surrendering to the urge for motion, Jerry looked down to inventory his body parts, half-expecting some radical change in appearance, a radioactive glow perhaps, or the prickling growth of pinfeathers, but nothing appeared to be different from the same gangly prospect he'd seen all his life. His long legs were spread and bent at the knees, ready to duck or run. Long-fingered hands were poised as if (unbeknownst to him) they'd undergone self-defense training. When he noticed the paperback, now lying on the floor at his feet, wings splayed, as concluded as his long-standing torpor, he resisted the compulsion to reshelve it as the old Jerry would have done. Instead, he stepped over it on his way out of the library.

It was the first step of his odyssey.

Walk-away

Jerry became a "walk-away," a term police use to describe certain missing persons, adults who walk away from their familiar world, disappearing without a clue as to where they've gone or why.

From his standing position in the epicenter of Ms. Nervan's devastated chair, he walked away from everything familiar, past the bookshelves he'd come to know so well, across carpeting he'd been vacuuming for years. He shut off the lights and locked the door behind him just as if it was a normal day. He dropped his library key in the book return slot and began to anticipate the mystery his disappearance would create. He liked the idea of it. Apart from the shattered chair, there was nothing out of place in the library except that old copy of *Stranger in a Strange Land* on the office floor. (Much later, he wondered if his "awakening" might have been triggered by repeated exposure to the patient tutelage of Robert Heinlein, finally making him able to "grok" his own situation there in Kilgore.)

Jerry walked down the library sidewalk (from which he had removed tons of snow) and through the empty, late-night streets of Kilgore, following, without thinking, the familiar path he had always taken to get to his pitiful apartment, little more than a rented room over Mrs. Tipton's garage. This time though, he realized there was a possibility he would never walk that path again and a fresh thrill caught his breath, a heady blend of excitement and fear. With every step, still in the dazzling afterglow of his epiphany, he began to see the library as a too-comfortable trap that had been closing around him for years. He felt lucky to be stepping away from it, and just in time. Walking through the surreal flashing yellow light of Kilgore's single, trafficless intersection, and into the bracing night breeze off the Tetons, he felt the exhilaration of the newly liberated; disoriented, but on the road to an undiscovered life.

Namesake

In his apartment, Jerry pushed the PLAY button on what had once been his crazy uncle's boombox. "Truckin" from *The Very Best of Grateful Dead* played while he sorted through his clothes, deciding what to pack and what to leave behind.

When he was small, his mother would dance to this music in her fluid, whirling style that seemed to fit any tempo. She would hold little Jerry on her hip with one arm and transcribe elegant finger swirls in the air with the other, encouraging him to do the same. Memories of his Deadhead mother were few and faint, but the songs on this one CD brought back many of them. The dancing was his favorite. A guitar solo by Jerry's namesake might prompt her to say, "That's my Jerry Garcia." Whenever this happened, she would smile happily and chuck him under the chin. Toward the end of her life (and as he got older and too big to carry as she danced) she would still catch his eye across the room during a favored solo, raise her eyebrows with her special happy look, point to the speakers, and then to him.

She played the music so loud it drowned all thought and disturbed the neighbors.

Jerry Garcia was her musical muse and Gustafson was her family name, so she had named her only child Jerry Garcia Gustafson.

Jerry's father was little more than a persistent mystery. His mother would never talk about him and took the truth of him to her grave when Jerry was five.

She met her death on a two-lane, country road just north of Idaho Falls, while riding in a car with a man engaged to another woman. Together, they crested a small hill at high speed and rear-ended a slow-moving tractor towing a piece of farm equipment called, appropriately, a harrow. She had long been notorious among her conservative neighbors for hitchhiking to attend any Grateful Dead concert within a thousand miles. The manner of her death did not improve her reputation.

After one of those hitchhiking trips to a concert in San Francisco, she returned pregnant. This was shocking to the locals on many levels, that she should hitchhike alone (or at all for that matter), that she should enjoy such awful music (and the company of the sort of people who did), and finally that she should come back pregnant, unmarried, and determined to raise her child alone, relying only on the support of her disapproving and now scandalized mother. Most exasperating of all to the town gossips was his mother's unwillingness to say anything about the father. It was rumored she didn't know who he was.

After his mother's scandalous encounter with the harrow, there were just three Gustafsons in Kilgore. Jerry lived with his Grandma in "the old Gustafson place," as the Kilgorians called it, while his mother's much older brother, universally (and unkindly) known in those parts as Crazy Harold, lived a separate, ascetic life in his own little shack outside of town. Then, when Jerry was sixteen, his Grandma died unexpectedly in front of the television. Jerry found her body when he got up in the morning. She was sitting in her favorite chair with a quilt over her lap, still staring at the TV, which was now displaying the morning version of last night's news. Though her eyes were empty and dry, they and her mouth were wide open, as if she had been horrified beyond continuing by something in a late-night broadcast. Since there was usually something on any nightly news to offend her antiquated sensibilities, it may well have been the news that killed her. The doctor said it was a heart attack, but Jerry would always believe the TV did it. So, just to be on the safe side, he stopped watching TV from that day forward; he did not want to fall prey to a deadly broadcast. (He had long before decided to give farm equipment a wide berth.)

His Uncle Harold hired an auctioneer to sell the old Gustafson homestead. Proceeds from the estate sale, which included the TV set and everything else in the house, were enough to pay for her funeral, burial expenses, and the services of the auctioneer. After his Grandma's death, Jerry was ostensibly in the care of his Uncle Harold, though his uncle returned to live alone in his cobbled-together shack at the edge of town. Jerry rented the room over Mrs. Tipton's garage because it was cheap and close to the library.

When Jerry was twenty, his crazy uncle shot himself, making Jerry the last of the Gustafsons of Idaho, an orphaned, bastard child, now somewhat reclusive, and evermore lost in books.

After his Uncle Harold pulled the trigger, Jerry arranged with the same auctioneer to sell the few remaining worldly possessions of the Gustafson clan. This amounted to his Uncle's old truck, the few appliances found in his shack, an eclectic collection of tools and yard maintenance equipment with which the man had sometimes taken on extra jobs, and the shotgun he used to shoot himself. Money from the sale was enough to pay his debts and his burial expenses. The sum total of Jerry's inheritance, all material possessions passed down from generations of the hard-working and now depleted Gustafson clan, was zero.

At that point, there was no one in Kilgore, or anywhere else, who might know, or care, what Jerry's middle name was. He'd never told anyone what it was and 'Garcia' appeared only on his birth certificate. Since his Grandma would have known nothing about a former member of a rock and roll band, she was likely to have carried to her grave the assumption Jerry's mysterious father was Hispanic. This despite the fact that the full-grown Jerry gave every appearance of being the last in a long line of blond, lanky, big-boned, Idaho potato farmers like his Grandpa, a man whom Jerry knew only from photographs in which the man always looked taciturn and defeated, as if he somehow knew all the money he would make from an exhausting life of hard labor as a small-time potato farmer would go into the little, two-story cube of a house that would have to be sold to pay for his wife's funeral.

Jerry had proven to be no better with money than his Grandpa had been; he'd continued to work in the library after his Grandma died, making only a few dollars more than it cost him to rent his room and to feed and clothe himself.

Jerry doubted his Grandma had learned anything at all about his father from his mother because the two women never got along well enough to share such confidences. They were so different it was hard for Jerry to believe one had come from the other. His Grandma went to church on Sunday and to every church function offered during the week by the tiny Presbyterian congregation of Kilgore. Other than caring for Jerry after his mother died, his Grandma quilted with a few of her neighbors, and watched television, mostly the news, soap operas, and evangelical programs.

After having been serially raised by these two different women, even though he'd had more years with his Grandma, Jerry felt most akin to his mother. His Grandma remained impenetrable to the end of her days, as much lost in her own little world as he was.

The people who mattered in Jerry's life were all gone. So far as he knew, he was the last of the Gustafsons of Eastern Idaho.

Jerry was not bitter about any of this, nor did he make any excuses for it; much of his circumstance in Idaho was his own doing. It was difficult for a lonesome, orphaned, claustrophobic, wise-ass, living in a state of torpor, to make friends in a small town, especially when, as he now knew, it was The Wrong Place.

Duffel

Jerry's packing involved winnowing through meager possessions and stuffing what would fit into his uncle's Army duffel bag and into a little daypack he'd always carried on hikes into the foothills of the Tetons. Beyond the bare essentials, he made room for the few precious photographs he had of his mother. He kept one of him standing beside his uncle (taken when Jerry was in his awkward teens and already a head taller), and the only photo he had of his Grandma, stringing beans into a bowl on the front porch. Photographs of Grandpa Gustafson were all awkward and out of focus, so he left them behind. Once the photos were packed away, he was done. The room looked as barren as it had on the first day he moved in. He'd made no mark on the place. There was nothing else to do. He would leave in the morning, defined by the duffel and its simple contents.

His crazy Uncle Harold had left the duffle to him, mentioning in a long and rambling suicide note that it was something Jerry was to inherit, treating it as a significant piece of property. "PFC Harold Gustafson" was stenciled in white paint on the duffel's green canvas side, along with his uncle's military service number. It was typical of his Uncle's Quixotic thought processes to be concerned for the fate of his duffle before aligning a shotgun to his forehead. As a result, Jerry's valuation of the duffel varied. It was sometimes worthless treasure and sometimes priceless trash.

Go With the Flow

Jerry slept little that night, disturbed first by hours of half-baked plans and then by bizarre nightmares involving shotgun-wielding hunters springing up to shoot down flying books, treacherous furniture, and (an old player in his nightmares) aggressive farm equipment. He tossed and turned, vacillating between relief for having averted what might have been and dreamy hopes for what might yet be.

Jerry was awake before first light, exhausted, but keyed up. The strange influence of the collapsing chair was still with him, making him feel snapped from the frazzled end of Fortune's cosmic crack-the-whip and now fueling a manic urgency to move. While nibbling a granola bar for breakfast, he retrieved his life's savings he'd kept in a cedar cigar box in the closet. He removed the rubber band from an impressive roll of bills and began to count. Most of them turned out to be ones. He counted them twice, both times coming up with $388. He re-rolled the money and stuffed it into the front pocket of his Levis, where it bulged obscenely, but would be most difficult to lose.

Knowing it was too early to hitch a ride into Idaho Falls, he puttered nervously around the apartment, basically organizing those things he planned to leave behind. He felt lightheaded, as if he'd been uplifted from some dank and moldy place and plunked onto the surface of life's sunny playing field, feeling now, finally, a participant in the big game.

All he had so far was an incontestable urge to move and a general sense something good would happen if he let himself "go with the flow." He wasn't sure what that meant in concrete terms, nor did he know if he was brave enough to let it happen if he should learn what it meant. A literal interpretation suggested he might use the watershed in those parts as a guide, the continental divide being just a few miles to the east of Kilgore, inside Yellowstone Park. Based on nothing more than that, Jerry concluded The Right Place he hoped to find must then be somewhere to the west of Kilgore, on the down-slope. It wasn't logical, or perhaps even rational, but he could think of no reason to choose any other compass direction. Having chosen to go west was a beginning. If he were to go in that direction long enough, he might get to see the ocean and satisfy that landlocked desire.

The decision to go west boosted his spirits. He now had a larger plan: He would hitch a ride into Idaho Falls, buy a bus ticket, and go west from there until he saw the ocean.

Many anxieties clamored for attention as Jerry shouldered his duffel and took one last look around, trying to imagine what he would later regret leaving behind. The room was dead and empty of sentiment. He left the key in the door and walked away, leaving without any sort of rulebook for the big game, without a map to tell him how to get to The Right Place, or where the dragons might be. Still, it was exciting to think that mysterious and unpredictable things were possible.

He left with a clear conscience; there was no one in Kilgore, or in all of Idaho for that matter, to whom he would wish to say goodbye, or to whom he might owe an explanation for his departure, or who, come to that, would much care he was going.

Willard

Outside it was still dark. A high-country overcast hid the stars, but Jerry didn't need any more to navigate than the still flashing yellow light above Kilgore's only major intersection. There were no signs of life anywhere; no vehicles moved and no windows glowed from the buildings in town. Apart from a few dingy porch lights, it was dark, cold, and quiet; a suitable place to be leaving.

At the intersection, he leaned his duffel against the wall of Ray's Café, still closed at that hour, and sat on the curb, waiting for any sort of traffic. He knew it was earlier than five o'clock because Kilgore's only stoplight, a single, four-sided antique that hung from a cable strung diagonally across the intersection, changed to flashing red at five (when there was a greater likelihood of two vehicles approaching the intersection at the same time). Waiting to hitch a ride, he was alternately in the utter dark of a moonless, starless night or sickly jaundiced on one side by the stoplight.

\- - -

Sitting with the humble sum total of his life condensed into portable form inside Uncle Harold's duffel, he was beset by an incongruous rising tide of anger. Like the converted of any stripe, he was angry with himself for having been so complacent. Why had he taken so long to awaken from his indolence? What had been wrong with all the previous moments in his life during which he might have chosen to move on? He was filled with something akin to righteous impatience, an urgency to get out of Kilgore and on with his life. He was also scared shitless. Nevertheless, under the angry surface chop of this fearful thinking, a calm swell of conviction had begun to form; he was doing the right thing. There was no joy to be had in Kilgore. There was nothing, and no one, to keep him in there.

\- - -

The cold of the curb had begun to penetrate before he heard a distant clanging of metal, a familiar sound that could only have come from the loading dock behind the feed store at the edge of town. He hoisted his duffel and walked that way, knowing it was probably Willard Stank. Jerry hadn't remembered Willard's regular morning milk run to Idaho Falls until he heard the clanging of milk cans.

Behind the feed store, a single blue-white security light revealed a bundled figure with a rounded back and sloping shoulders that could only belong to Willard. He was struggling to load a heavy collection of stainless steel, ten-gallon milk cans into the back of an ancient Ford pickup that had once been painted red.

"Hey Willard," Jerry shouted ahead, not wanting to startle him.

"Jerry. What the hell you doin' out here?" Willard asked, perhaps less startled by Jerry's sudden appearance behind the feed store at that hour than surprised to see Jerry anywhere other than the library.

"You going into Idaho Falls this morning?" Jerry asked, ignoring Willard's question.

"You know it. Ever damn day. Cows need milkin, milk needs haulin. Need a ride?"

"Got room back here for this bag?" Jerry said by way of an answer, standing his duffel upright among the milk cans.

Willard watched with obvious, unspoken curiosity while Jerry climbed onto the dock and began loading the next milk can. When he realized he was getting unexpected help loading and no explanation was forthcoming about why Jerry wanted a ride to Idaho Falls, Willard returned to the work at hand. Together they finished the job with nothing more than a few grunts between them, urging the heavy milk cans into place. When they were loaded, the two men climbed into the cab without a word and drove away.

On the road, the level of conversation was little improved. Willard and Jerry had almost nothing in common; Jerry was not involved with transporting milk and Willard never frequented the library. Willard had been several grades ahead of Jerry in school, so they hadn't associated then either. About the only thing they had in common was the teasing they had both endured through school, Willard for his name and Jerry for his long-boned awkwardness.

- - -

The heater soon blew warm air on their feet while the radio gave the farm report, the two sounds competing with the truck's many rattles.

When Kilgore could no longer be seen in the rearview mirrors, Willard turned down the radio until little could be heard about farm prices over the noises of the truck. Willard was marshalling his curiosity and trying to think of a way to ask why Jerry was out so early and carrying a duffle into Idaho Falls. It was generally considered rude by small town folk to pry into another man's business with a lot of questions, so Willard didn't ask for quite some time, not until they could begin to see the glow in the sky from the lights of what the locals called "The City."

"What you doin' in Idaho Falls?"

- - -

Jerry didn't answer right away; he knew how thin, sudden, and open-ended his plans were going to sound, but also because he didn't want to sully his clean getaway from Kilgore by leaving behind too many clues. (Jerry relished the idea of Ms. Nervan finding her shattered chair later that morning as the only trace of his disappearance, as if he might have been abducted with maximum prejudice by aliens.) He knew he would never see Willard again, but that was no reason to be rude; the man was giving him a ride after all. Instead of a direct answer, he decided to drop in Willard's ear one more clue to his disappearance. He knew it would be all over town as soon as Willard got back from his milk run and settled for breakfast at Ray's Cafe. What he said would give the Kilgorians something to ponder, and simultaneously pay homage to his crazy, departed uncle.

"I'm just following the weasel."

Willard gave him a curious, sidelong look, but graciously let it go at that.

Much later, Jerry realized his lone, strange clue had the added advantage (or disadvantage, depending on how long you thought about it) of furthering the odd reputation of the now vanished Gustafson Clan.

Dowsing

Jerry learned about following the weasel from his Uncle Harold, who had been, among other things, a dowser. The exigencies of daily expenses required that his Uncle Harold take on various low-skill maintenance jobs like landscaping, or ditch-digging, or small-engine repair, but he got few such jobs around Kilgore because it was well known Harold would abandon any local job to respond to a distant request to find water.

Dowsing was the perfect business for Harold Gustafson; all he needed was his pocketknife and his hat. He would climb into his old pickup and disappear from Kilgore, often for weeks at a time.

As a water-diviner, he had two divergent reputations: Wherever he found water, often in the dry country down in Utah or over in the Palouse, he was hailed as a marvel, a water savant, and farmers would recommend him to their neighbors. But, wherever he divined a dry hole, as he did several times in Wyoming, he was reviled as a charlatan, someone who ought to be run out of town, and just the sort of interloper about whom farmers warned their neighbors. The satisfied customers tended to stay home with their new wells, while dissatisfied customers were often so incensed by spending good money to be told where to drill a dry hole they would show up in Kilgore, vigilante style, looking for a piece of his hide. Somehow, Harold Gustafson was always somewhere else when the vigilantes were about. Wisely, he did no divining in the environs of Kilgore, where he was known as Crazy Harold, the man who talked to himself in public and claimed to find water with a stick.

- - -

Jerry was around twelve the first time his uncle tried to teach him how to dowse. He wasn't interested in learning how to do something that didn't have much science behind it, but Uncle Harold was insistent, evidently wanting to pass the family business on to the next generation and not believing someone who did little but read books could be prepared to make a living.

Young Jerry knew his uncle was right; all the reading he'd done had not prepared him for anything he could yet imagine. So, he tolerated his crazy uncle's desire to pass on the profession.

Jerry's first dowsing lesson began in Grandma's big backyard with a painstaking search for the ideal branch. Uncle Harold preferred to work with a long, thin, forking branch of a fresh willow, cut from the local area. He was scornful of those dowsers who claimed to find water using a pair of bent metal rods. Any fresh-cut branch was better than those metal rods. The branch had to be just so long and just so thick and, most importantly, had to fork just so. There were no willows in Grandma's backyard, but there was an old, overgrown Gravenstein that dropped far more apples each year than Grandma could bake into pies.

Uncle Harold found a branch he thought would do, cut and stripped it with his pocketknife, and showed Jerry how to hold it. It was like grabbing the top two branches of the letter Y, thumbs up, with the bottom of the Y pointing toward the ground. Then you had to tip your wrists out and back in a way that would bend the wood a little, and make the bottom of the Y point straight out, parallel to the ground.

After Jerry got the hang of how to hold it, Uncle Harold took it back, straightened himself, held the stick just so in front of him, and paced the width of Grandma's big backyard with Jerry trailing alongside. When he came to the edge of the property, he turned around, took a couple of big steps sideways, and began pacing back the other way. On the second pass, not too far from the apple tree, the divining rod began to wave up and down a little. He kept walking until the bottom of that Y bent straight down, as if drawn toward the center of the earth. He marked an X in the weeds with the side of his boot and then, for confirmation, made several approaches to that spot from different directions. On each approach, the stick pointed down in the same way and in the same location.

Uncle Harold marked the location for emphasis by clearing the ground with the heel of his boot, and announced, "Your Grandma could dig herself a well if she wanted to, right here, and have fresh water."

Over the years, Jerry had learned not to put much trust in his unpredictable uncle and was always skeptical of anything the man said. To Jerry's twelve-year-old eyes, it looked as if Uncle Harold was the force moving the stick. Plus, Jerry struggled with the image of his Grandma laboring with a shovel, especially on nothing more than Crazy Uncle Harold's say-so.

Even Grandma was conflicted about her oldest child, saying he had a God-given gift when he found water, but saying that divining was the devil's work when those out-of-town people came looking for him with fire in their eyes.

"Between 60 and 80 feet down," Uncle Harold declared, confident enough to predict even how far down Grandma would have to dig.

Jerry held the stick as he had been shown and walked back and forth over his uncle's same path, but even when he crossed "Grandma's well," the stick did not twitch.

Nothing.

"Son, you're not following the weasel," Uncle Harold said.

While Jerry didn't know *how* to follow the weasel on the day Uncle Harold divined Grandma's well, he knew what his uncle meant by that curious expression because it had been explained to him several times already.

The first time Jerry heard his uncle use the expression, he'd thought it was a reference to the monkey's chase around the mulberry bush, but Uncle Harold made it clear that following the weasel was a serious lesson, something quite real and not some damn nursery rhyme.

Uncle Harold kept himself in fine harmony with the weasel and followed it at all times. (The well was never dug, so Jerry never learned if Uncle Harold had been right about the water.)

All of his Uncle's coaching was wasted on young Jerry at the time. But, he remained impressed by the concept and he had no other father-figure to learn from. As he grew older, Jerry could still not conceive of a benefit to weasel-following, apart from the questionable art of finding water with a stick, but under his uncle's regular admonishments, he tried to learn what it meant. As near as he could tell, following the weasel meant subordinating one's will, listening for one's subtle, private drummer, all while avoiding conscious choice. How this related to a weasel made no sense to Jerry until, on one of his solo walks in West Yellowstone, he was fortunate enough to watch a weasel's frenetic hunting style. It left a convoluted trail through a snow-covered meadow, following subtle scents and sounds. Like the weasel, one had to tune the subtler senses, perhaps even the sub-senses, in order to pick up otherwise undetectable clues. Then one had to have faith in those clues and go, unhesitatingly, where they led.

Sometimes Jerry would pack a lunch and a book, hike high into the western foothills of the Teton Range, find an isolated meadow or a shelter from the wind among the rocks, and sit and read for hours. He liked being in wild, open spaces, and alone. Periodically, he would put the book down and raise his sails into the cosmic winds, listening for the music of the spheres, or a distant drumbeat. He tried to tune his senses to any intangible forces offering to move him one way or the other. Other than the hard rock, nothing told him to move.

Jerry's aforementioned internal gyroscope of rationality, like all gyroscopes, was good only for keeping a steady heading; it did not indicate which way to go.

He'd felt no strong need for guidance from the weasel until Destiny's mysterious epiphany goosed him out of Ms. Nervan's chair.

Now, he hoped to develop a weasel-following aptitude, something that could lead him to The Right Place.

Destiny's Delivery Service

Jerry continued to refine his cobbled-together plan for the rest of his life even as he waited in a blue plastic chair for the ticket window to open in the Greyhound Bus Depot in Idaho Falls. He decided that, once he saw the ocean, he would make his way to what he considered to be the last frontier of romance and adventure on the planet: Alaska. In his naiveté, he could imagine no better life than to be a bush pilot flying over the epic scenery during Alaskan summers and then, during the long winters, to be an author holed up in a remote cabin writing Science Fiction. He would have bought a ticket all the way to Anchorage if Greyhound went that far, but they didn't, so he had to decide on a penultimate destination to the west and within the range of his bankroll. As part of his middle-of-the-night planning, he had narrowed his choices to Seattle or San Francisco. Even as the ticket agent opened for business and Jerry stepped up to be first in line, he was still manically twirling his imaginary weasel-detecting antennae for guidance to choose between the two different fates he might encounter, one in Seattle and one in San Francisco.

The woman at the ticket window noticed Jerry's hesitation and graciously waited a moment before prompting him. "May I help you?"

Without guiding vibrations from the cosmos in choosing one city over the other, he was forced to decide on his own. San Francisco had a reputation for better weather and had been the home ground of his namesake (and the purported city of his conception, at a Grateful Dead concert), but Seattle appealed because it was closer to Alaska and had a reputation for being an aviation Mecca, which fit well into the balance of his sketchy dreams.

After a long, awkward moment, the scales of deliberation tipped ever so slightly. He said, "Seattle," and it was done. "One way," he added… a public commitment. Peeling the dollars off his bankroll left him a severely reduced fortune with which to manage in Seattle, while simultaneously eliminating any possible future life he might have had in San Francisco.

- - -

OLD MAN STAMPER

Travel Times

Old Man Stamper had been lonesome a long time. Years earlier, in grieving desperation after the last of his family died, he fled the memories in Sacramento to start a new life in Seattle. He came to the city with more money from the sale of his furniture business than he had inclination to spend, but he couldn't imagine retiring; he needed something to do, a small business he could manage himself. He started a copy shop. He called it COPY/COPY.

The distraction of change lasted a few years, but even in the middle of a big city like Seattle the lonesomeness returned. Although his copy shop kept him in daily contact with customers, such brief encounters offered little in the way of companionship. Customers didn't stay long; everyone was busy. The novelty of his nametag: "Old Man Stamper," prompted a few smiles, but little conversation. Stamper had been old so long there was nothing novel or amusing about it. He thought of himself as Old Man Stamper, referring to himself that way with customers, or even alone in the shop, narrating the tedium of his life: "Good morning Bertha," he'd say to the big copier. "Old Man Stamper is late again today... shouldn't have bothered with the birds so long."

He shuffled through the shop to the front door, flipped the CLOSED sign to OPEN, and switched on the lights. Behind the counter he checked for work orders. There were none. "Customers are staying away in droves." Stamper pushed the big copier's ON button, filling the shop with its usual hum. "You like it when I turn you on, don't you Bertha?" He patted Bertha's collator and settled onto the padded stool in the center of the little shop, lit his third (or fourth) cigarette of the morning, and leaned his elbows on the counter.

Old Man Stamper's first name was Barry, but no one had called him that since his twin brother died years ago. His wife had always called him Bee (and his twin brother Gee, for Garry), but she'd been dead even longer than Garry. Old Man Stamper's son, in his better moods, had called him Pop.

His son was gone too, killed in Vietnam.

When Garry died, Old Man Stamper was the last of his family.

The first act of his fresh start in Seattle was to purchase the building where he now lived and worked, and rarely left. There were two shops downstairs, the copy shop and the empty shop space next door that he used to store what was left of the business inventory from his brother's last hare-brained business idea. Upstairs were three apartments, now filled to overflowing with the excess inventory from his furniture business in Sacramento, pieces showing the craftsmanship he loved and could not bring himself to leave behind. It had taken three moving trucks to haul it all from Sacramento to Seattle. Old Man Stamper lived in the largest of those three apartments, in the small fraction of square footage not filled by his beloved furniture.

Work in COPY/COPY occupied his life, greasing the slide of years. Although business was steady at first, the work orders dwindled when he began having lapses.

- - -

At first, Old Man Stamper was merely forgetful. Anything not set to happen automatically was something he might forget. He might complete a copy job, but neglect some part of the work order, such as to bind it. He'd forget to make a timely order for more paper or ink and run out. He might forget to pay a bill. It was frustrating, often costly, and not well tolerated by his vendors or his customers.

Old Man Stamper was lonesome, but peaceful. He depended on his daily routines. He became detached, an objective observer of his own decline, reaching a point where he didn't worry about much at all. At times he even welcomed the stir of memory, however surreal. It was better than anything on television.

Lately, he'd begun to experience "travel times," as he thought of them, moments when he was somewhere else, or more accurately, sometime else. These lapses didn't bother him at first because they resembled nostalgia, vacant-headed journeys down memory lane, but over time they became more surreal. It was sometimes quite disturbing to remember what had happened in his travels, but he often couldn't. He had confrontations with people who died long ago, arguments and even fistfights with his brother, and contentious furniture dealings with childhood friends, people he hadn't thought about in years. The travel times were beyond his control and didn't make much sense, but they were so real it became difficult to trust the reality of the lonesome life he led. He was usually fine during the day, but small blocks of time could pass without notice. Most disturbing were the travel times after which he found himself in a different place with no memory of having moved, leaving him to wonder what he'd done on the way there. So far, no real harm had been done; he'd always been able to reorient himself.

His son Darren had been gone more than a quarter of a century, longer than any of his family except for his own parents. Old Man Stamper hoped Darren would show up in one of his travel times to give him one last chance to talk to his only child, to have an adult conversation without bickering over trivialities as they so often had. Many things had been left unsaid between them. It was a nagging regret in his long and eventful life. Perhaps one last visit could somehow make things right. It concerned him to think that Darren might have already appeared in one of his travel times and they'd talked. Or, perhaps they'd said nothing to one another again. He couldn't remember.

- - -

Surrounded on most days by no signs of life in the shop other than Bertha's hum, Old Man Stamper often rested his elbows on the counter and imagined letting go, just laying his head down and letting go. He'd never felt so deep down into the raggedy end of life. How long, he wondered, would it take for someone to find his body? It scared him to think of it ending that way. The fear energized him, prompting one of his more lucid moments. He had to act soon, to ready his affairs for the end of his control over them. "Being of sound mind and body…" was a rapidly closing window. He didn't have anyone to inherit his modest holdings, but he hated the idea of leaving his affairs a mess. He had to talk to his lawyer. And, he had to find someone to run the shop for him. In a moment of panic at the realization he would not always remember these were the two things he should do, he wrote them down. It was a short list, but he could think of nothing to add.

He addressed the first item on the list by calling his lawyer.

"Simon, I need to make an appointment to draw up a will." He listened for a minute, made notes on a calendar, said "OK, thanks," and hung up.

He read the second item on his list: Find someone to run the shop. Now he had begun, it was easier to keep going. He turned Bertha off, flipped the OPEN sign around, locked the shop, lit a fresh cigarette, and shuffled the few downhill blocks toward the main office of The Washington State Employment Security Department. He had to stop and rest often, so it took him the balance of the morning to get there. Once inside, he was so exhausted he sat in one of the chairs at the margins of the action. Hopeful people stood in lines, waiting for their turn at the agent's windows. Stamper wasn't clear any more on why he was there. He became too tired to deal with any of it, the constant chatter and crowded spaces. He just wanted to lie down. He struggled to his feet and shuffled outside to catch a taxi home. There was no other way he could make it back up the hill.

- - -

The next day, Old Man Stamper read that second uncompleted item on his list and made that long downhill walk again. He did it every day after that too. It became part of his daily routine, an end in itself, its original purpose forgotten for the most part. He would close the shop, puff down to the Unemployment Office, recover on the sidelines for an hour or two, and taxi back. This new morning routine meant the shop was closed for half the day, but that was better than leaning on the counter until he died in harness, and alone.

His resolve to find someone to run COPY/COPY always faded before he could act on it. Instead, he just watched, drifting back and forth from a crotchety study of the wildly inappropriate job-finding apparel he saw on the people waiting in line, to a foggy stir of memories brought on by their young, hopeful faces.

- - -

Back On the Bus

Life Plan

Waiting in the blue plastic chair, with bus ticket in hand and his long legs resting on a duffel footstool, Jerry wondered again what had happened to him the night before. What provoked that sudden implosion of his rutted life? He needed to have a name for it. Had he experienced a kind of epiphany, or was it some variation of a premonition, i.e., somehow knowing in advance he would eventually find The Right Place? Maybe he just had encountered an unforeseen lump in the space-time continuum that bumped him out of his rut. Or, maybe it was a less-than-subtle intervention by the weasel. There were many and various names for the forces that run counter to chance, so perhaps Destiny had tiptoed up behind him where he languished, had rolled up her terrible towel and snapped him to full alert. Or, Fate had flicked him with her famously fickle finger. Whatever its name, some beneficent karmic force had booted his bony butt and lifted him from his meaningless life for a second try. He'd been like a wind-up toy stuck in a corner, now given a rewind and a new heading. Even though terrified, Jerry was thankful for it.

Despite the sobering depletion of his resources, for better or worse, he'd made a commitment to Seattle. He felt good about his first conscious, proactive, life-altering decision. There was a little regret for having said goodbye to whatever life he might have found in San Francisco, because that city had only been in consideration because of his mother's purported romantic assignation. When Jerry was young, he had figured this meant his father lived in San Francisco. He got over that. The way people moved around, and especially the way Deadheads traveled from far and wide to attend Dead concerts, meant his father could have been from anywhere. By now, he might have moved to another state, or another country. With his Seattle decision, Jerry had severed the last and most tenuous of his roots. He would make his own romantic associations somewhere else.

He pulled a notebook and pencil from the duffel to work on his Life Plan. Previously, he'd had nothing resembling a Life Plan apart from vague, long-standing dreams of flying and writing. It was time to flesh them out. He put pencil to paper, trying in the best way he knew to make the dreams more real.

(1) <u>In the wide-open spaces of Alaska, I will work as a bush pilot.</u> During the Alaskan summers, I will fly the open skies, ferrying passengers and cargo between scattered settlements. I will be a free spirit, self-employed and self-reliant, living where eccentrics are commonplace, where it is significant to encounter another human, and where my claustrophobia will be as irrelevant as renter's insurance.

(2) <u>I will write Science Fiction novels.</u> During the long winters, I will hole up in a remote cabin to complete a series of otherworld novels, something like the *Dune* series by Frank Herbert.

Having his Life Plan on paper made it seem more doable. He'd just have to work on the details.

- - -

Kilgore's Library

The books in Clark County's library system had been Jerry's higher education. Despite its small size, it contained a considerable sampling of the world's thinking, though Jerry often thought he might be the only one in Kilgore much interested in how the rest of the world thought. Reading as much as he did was just one of several things that distinguished Jerry from the other eccentrics in the county. But, because the library's catalog was short on the classics and long on reference books, his education was spotty. The library contained everything there was to know about planting, growing, harvesting, and storing potatoes, but there was nothing by Shakespeare. There were dozens of books on the wonders of nearby Yellowstone, but little poetry.

Its fiction shelves contained an exhaustive selection of just two genres, Romance and Science Fiction. Most of the Romance had been ordered by Ms. Nervan in response to endless requests from the women in Kilgore for the latest bodice-ripper, but Jerry loved the Science Fiction. It was a mystery why there were so many novels and short-story anthologies from that genre in Kilgore's branch. He could only guess it had come as a donated collection. Not much of the collection was new, but "The Golden Age of Science Fiction" was well represented. He had long since read them all. Furthermore, he'd requested Science Fiction books from other branches of the Clark County Library System and read them all too.

Jerry was going to miss the library. He'd spent many more hours there than the county paid him for, most of them spent reading. It had always been a comfortable place for him, a welcome constant in his life, more home than his rented room.

- - -

As a result of his peculiar self-education, Jerry had yet to discover the many ways in which his Life Plan was naïve. Something told him (maybe the weasel?) he was not quite ready to go directly into the wilds of Alaska. He had no pilot's license, knew nothing about how to obtain one, and had never even been in an airplane. In fact, he had never been farther from the earth than the six foot eight inches he once jumped in a high school track meet. He assumed there would be little more to flying a bush plane than there was to driving a tractor, which he had done for several summers during the potato harvest. Since he had never been west of Boise, he had no idea what to expect in Seattle or where to begin when he got there. He knew nothing about finding work in a big city; he had gotten his job in Kilgore's library by hanging around so much that Ms. Nervan started paying him out of petty cash to do little jobs. And, while it was true he had written a few short Science Fiction stories, no one else had read them. What's more, he knew nothing about finishing a novel or getting it published. He assumed writing a novel would be the same as writing a short story except it would take longer.

However, he was not so naïve as to think either component of his Life Plan would be easy; becoming a bush pilot and a published author of novels would take time and money. He would need to address these lofty goals in stages. The first stage would be to find a job in Seattle so he could pay for a room and for flight lessons, and then, maybe next summer, he'd travel on to Anchorage, prepared to earn a living.

As it would turn out, he was not even ready for the wilds of Seattle.

- - -

MARILYN GLADKOWSKI

Leaving Oceanside

Marilyn Gladkowski came into orbit around The Planet of Love when she abandoned her life in Oceanside, California. She left her father's duplex in NCO Housing at Camp Pendleton for the last time without having planned beyond what was required to make a clandestine departure. This was not like her at all. She worked in a travel agency and was very good at her job; planning was in her nature and traveling was something she'd done most of her life, at least to the various military bases where her family had been stationed. She arranged every detail of travel for other people more carefully than she planned her own escape from Oceanside.

She was not driven to leave by her brutish, largely absent father, who was all that was left of her family. (Her mother was dead and her three older brothers, who were just like dear old dad, were now stationed in various Marine bases around the world.) Nor did she leave to escape the pervasive militaristic atmosphere she'd always known and didn't like. She left to get out of a relationship with a young Marine whom she had once hoped might be different than he turned out to be.

She'd first noticed Coby when she stepped into the weight room at Gold's Gym to stretch out and cool down from her Zumba class. He was powering through an impressive workout regimen that rattled the place, clanking and slamming the free weights. Sweat dripped from his smooth blocky torso as if he'd just stepped from a shower. She could not help but stare and ended up cooling down longer than normal. When Coby finished and began toweling off the sweat, he flashed a knowing grin her way that made Marilyn blush.

And so, it began.

- - -

Coby was a vain young man, proud of his lifelong accumulation of muscle mass and of being the shortest Marine at Camp Pendleton. His face was as square and blocky as the rest of him, but still handsome, despite a frequently broken nose. He attended to every detail of his impressive body, even to the point of shaving body hair from his tanned skin, as if always in preparation for show time on a bodybuilder's stage.

A Marine of his height could not afford to be anything less than the hardest ass among hard-asses.

In the beginning, he lavished Marilyn with attention and with feigned affection in order to get her, first on his arm, and then into bed. He liked attention from women, especially those as pretty and petite as Marilyn. She looked good in her leotards and was even shorter than he was. Coby's height had always been an issue, so he did not associate with women who were taller.

Coby's goal from childhood was to be a Marine. He began lifting homemade weights before he was old enough to join a gym. He bulked up, but he didn't grow taller. He had perfect posture, but he could only do so much with that. He became so muscular that, prior to his induction physical, on the advice of the marine recruiter, he cut back on his weight training and managed his diet for two months lest he be rejected for being overweight relative to his height.

Unlike many of the other recruits, Coby could easily handle the physical demands of basic training and was mentally tough enough to endure the special harassment brought on by his lack of height and cocky manner. Having been on the defensive his whole life, Coby also knew when to assert himself and when to stand and take it. Boot camp was difficult, but he endured, earning a reputation as a tough little sonofabitch. He would only tolerate being described as "little" if that word was bracketed by the words "tough" and "sonofabitch."

- - -

Marilyn, like Coby, was a bundle of energy, economically wrapped. Having been a small female in a male-dominated world, and bounced from base to base, she needed to feel accepted. In a home atmosphere prizing self-discipline, she pushed herself hard with everything she did. She threw herself into her job at the agency with the same fervor she displayed in her Zumba class.

Marilyn lost her mother while in her early teens, so she grew up seeking the attention of her often-absent father, a lifer Marine Supply Sergeant, and of her three much-older brothers, who wanted nothing to do with her.

Supply Sergeant Gladkowski always left the duplex early each morning to report for duty at the base. When off duty, he met his cronies at the NCO club. On weekends, he left the duplex early to play golf and then met his cronies at the NCO club. He came home late each evening full of beer and capable of nothing more than watching TV until bedtime. He had no idea how to relate to a young daughter born so late in his life. She displayed a preference for frilly things, especially in pink, and was a tiny little thing, not Marine material at all. There was little love lost between them.

When Marilyn was old enough for her body to begin attracting attention, she looked for love in all the wrong places. Soon she stopped looking. Out of high school, she took a few junior college courses in business administration until she got the job in the travel agency. Except for her bus rides to and from work, and her regular side trips to Gold's Gym, she kept to herself.

- - -

At first Marilyn thrilled at Coby's attention. He was a remarkable man, charming in his own way, self-assured and capable. In time, she would learn he was also capable of deception. When she began to see through Coby's charm facade, the man she discovered was ugly, and nothing like the kind of life-partner Marilyn dreamed of finding.

Their problems began when Marilyn made it known she was looking for more from their relationship than energetic sexual marathons. Coby considered Marilyn's emotional "neediness" as a weakness. He became ever more verbally abusive and rough in bed. Marilyn tried not to irritate Coby with her need for affection. She circumvented his volcanic disapproval by complying with his sexual demands, but her lack of enthusiasm pissed him off. Even when he took her to a dance or a dinner party, they were routine, halfhearted, one-sided affairs at which she was merely an accessory to impress his comrades.

Marilyn wanted romance, a desire born of her need for acceptance. She had never been in love; had never felt the singular, uncritical acceptance she thought might come from true, reciprocal love. Deep in her bones she knew such love was out there somewhere and her bones told her it wasn't in Oceanside. Hers was an abiding hunger Coby could not understand. It was simply not in his emotional rucksack.

As their relationship worsened, Marilyn began trying to avoid Coby, but it was too late. Coby had become cozy with Marilyn's father, one Marine to another. Coby learned when she could be found at home alone.

Once Marilyn realized Coby was unavoidable, she began to fear him.

Coby *was* different from the other men in Marilyn's life in that he felt no compunction against using his strength to get what he wanted. Marilyn's desires were irrelevant to Coby. There was no trace of mutual give and take; Coby gave it to Marilyn whenever and however he chose and Marilyn had no recourse but to take it. The physical abuse became routine. He would not stop at "no" and she could not keep away from him. Sex had become rape.

Getting Away Clean

Marilyn's only defense against further abuse was to disappear, to vanish without a clue. Even if she could get away clean, there was still the fear Coby would find her. He was prideful, stubborn, and possessive. Even though she was really nothing more to him than a plaything, an extension of his profound ego, he would consider her leaving to be a personal affront and would not let it go.

The first step in the furtive planning of Marilyn's escape was to call her Aunt Irene in Seattle.

"Can I trust you to keep a secret from my father?" Marilyn asked.

"Love," Irene said, "I'm happy to keep anything at all as far away from that old man of yours as I possibly can."

"Aunt Irene, I'm very serious. I need you to promise not to tell my father or anyone else about this conversation. This is very important to me. I don't want him to know where I've gone, but even more, I don't want my ex-boyfriend to know."

"I won't tell a soul, Love," Irene promised. "What's up?

"If my father were to find out where I went, Coby could wheedle it out of him with a few beers."

"Coby being the ex-boyfriend?"

"I'm leaving home and I don't want to be found," Marilyn said. "I want a clean break from everything and everybody in Southern California."

"Are things getting mean down there?"

Marilyn didn't want to get into that; she was having enough trouble keeping it together for the phone call.

When Marilyn didn't answer, Irene didn't press. "It's about time, Love; I'm sorry your Mom ever got involved with that crowd."

Marilyn believed Aunt Irene would keep her promise of silence because it was clear from the few times her aunt came to Oceanside, first to help her sister through the divorce, and again to attend her sister in the hospital, that she genuinely hated Marilyn's father.

"I have enough money for a train ticket to Seattle," Marilyn said. "I'd like to stay with you, if that's OK, just long enough to find a job and a place of my own. I know it's a lot to ask, but you are the only family I can trust. I want to get as far away from Oceanside as I can."

"No problem, Love. You're welcome to stay in my spare bedroom as long as need be. It'll be crowded because I store all my extra junk in that room, but there's a bed and dresser in there you can use."

"Oh, wonderful," Marilyn said, near tears with relief. "Thank you so much. I didn't know where else to turn."

"Love, I'm just glad to see you get away from that barbarian father of yours."

"I have a few more things to get done before I can leave, but I'll let you know my arrival time as soon as I can."

"This'll be fun," Irene said. "We can share a bottle of wine and have some girl talk."

- - -

If Coby were to find her in Seattle… well, she didn't want to think what he might do. As soon as he realized she was gone, Coby would quiz her father and bully acquaintances in Oceanside for information about where she'd gone, so she was scrupulous about leaving no evidence. At the end of her last shift at the travel agency, she left a sealed note in her boss's in-basket saying she quit, was sorry for the short notice, and wouldn't be back.

She'd never mentioned her Aunt Irene to Coby, so he would have no reason to suspect she had fled to Seattle, but her father might guess Marilyn had gone that way and share his guess with Coby. To prevent that, she laid a false trail. She packed her bags in secret, waiting until she heard her father leaving for work before calling a taxi to take her to the train station. She pinned a brief goodbye note to the headrest of his recliner, where she knew he would find it. She wrote little more than that she was leaving for a job opportunity in Sacramento and wouldn't be back. Marilyn would not regret leaving her father and knew he wouldn't miss her, except for her cleaning and cooking, but she didn't want him to think she had been kidnapped and call the MPs. When the taxi arrived, Marilyn had one last look around, tossed her house keys onto the living room floor, and closed the door behind her.

Seattle by Train

Marilyn was exhausted at the end of the long, tedious trip to Seattle, but relieved to see her Aunt Irene waiting to greet her. They hugged rather tentatively, made small talk while waiting for Marilyn's bags, and then wrestled them into Irene's old Ford.

"Thank you sooo much," Marilyn said when they were in the car. "I didn't know where else to turn."

"No problem at all, Love," Irene said, pulling into Seattle's traffic. "You're smart to get away from that old drunk. Does he know you're gone?"

"I left him a note. He'll know I'm gone for good, but he won't know where. He probably won't see the note until he gets home from the NCO club tonight."

"That's good; you wouldn't want him to think you'd been abducted,"

"You mustn't tell anyone I'm here," Marilyn could not help but remind her aunt.

"I know. I won't, Love. Don't you worry. If anybody asks about you, I will happily lie through my teeth. I hope you never go back there."

"I can't see why I ever would. And, I promise I'll find my own place as soon as I can get a job."

"You just settle in as best you can and don't worry about that. I'll be glad for a little company."

Irene worked long hours as an office manager at Kenmore Air Harbor at the north end of Lake Washington, so Marilyn had the tiny two-bedroom apartment to herself most of the day. She kept the doors locked and the curtains drawn, imagining Coby had tracked her down and was about to kick down the door. She tried to convince herself she was a long way up the west coast from Oceanside, that Coby wouldn't have the time, inclination, or opportunity to come looking for her and that he wouldn't think her worth the trouble. She had long conversations with herself, to "get a grip" and "get over yourself," but she couldn't shake her fear. She settled into one corner of Irene's spare bedroom, living out of her suitcases, dreaming of the day when she could afford her own apartment.

Irene was always tired after work, so there wasn't much socializing just when Marilyn was hungry for company. They shared some wine on the weekends, exchanging Marilyn's complaints about her father and Coby, with Irene's complaints about her job. Their only common ground was Marilyn's mother, which was a topic neither seemed inclined to resurrect.

During the day, Marilyn read the want ads and worked on her resume, trying not to address why she'd walked away from her last job. It would be a problem explaining her sudden departure from the travel agency in an interview. The question was certain to be asked. She'd been hoping to capitalize on her travel agency experience, but was afraid to use the reference, since Coby might question her old boss. She'd have to get by without using that reference, focus on her business training courses instead. Travel agencies seemed to be downsizing anyway.

If Marilyn ever got an interview, she'd have to confront her fear of going anywhere. She'd figured out the bus schedule and studied maps for the location of the downtown unemployment office, but she'd done it all without leaving Irene's spare bedroom. She'd ironed her lucky job-finding outfit, a rose-pink linen skirt and matching jacket, which she would wear over an ivory-colored blouse. Every morning, she told herself this was the day, but the pink outfit hung unworn for a very long time.

- - -

EMMA

Can you run a copy machine?

Each morning, Old Man Stamper settled into his favorite chair close to the main doors at the Washington State Employment Security Department. He would light a fresh cigarette, in obvious violation of prominent No Smoking signs, and wait to catch his breath. His morning walks down the hill had helped a little to clear his thinking, but he still didn't often remember he was looking for someone to run the copy shop. He studied the endless parade of the unemployed, trying to imagine their stories, the work they'd done, the work they wanted, letting their faces remind him of people he had known when he was younger, when life had been a grand, hopeful adventure.

On one such morning, Emma walked in.

Emma!

At the sight of her, Stamper felt like a man electrocuted. He gripped the arms of his chair, almost dropping his cigarette, and leaned back as far as he could, as if to get further away from the apparition of his young wife.

She came in boldly, radiant in her rose-pink business suit. She stood in the middle of the big floor, looking all around, reading the signs, before finally joining one of the already well-formed lines.

It *was* Emma. He was sure of it. It was more than mere resemblance; it *was* the same young woman he had met and married forty-six years ago. Everything about her, her profile, her skin, her petite body, even the way she stood, had him gasping for breath. His old heart pounded. He searched for some evidence it *wasn't* her. Maybe her hair was just a little curlier than he'd ever seen it, and he couldn't remember Emma ever having worn such a brightly colored outfit, but that was it. In every other way, it *was* Emma. Then, when the young woman happened to turn his way and saw him staring at her, Stamper saw Emma's eyes, big, brown, and clever, a sight he had not seen since Emma's mind started to go and the fire left those big, brown eyes he'd loved so much.

- - -

Marilyn was aware of the old man staring at her from across the room, his head clouded by cigarette smoke, in clear defiance of signs posted everywhere. His staring made her uncomfortable, so she faced him boldly, turned her head toward the No Smoking sign on the wall nearby, and then looked back at him.

The old man looked at the sign and back at her with no change of expression. He continued to stare as he sucked in and released another lungful of smoke, letting it drift out his nose and slack, half-open mouth.

Marilyn decided the man was a pervert. She would put him out of her mind. To make that obvious to the scrawny old fart, she turned her back on him.

- - -

Old Man Stamper realized he must be in the middle of another delusion, though it was far more real than any he'd had before. While his heart told him to walk over to the young woman and fold her into his old, wrinkled arms, he wasn't yet so far gone he didn't know such a move would end badly.

He tried to remember when young Emma's hair might ever have been that curly, or when she had ever worn such bright pink things.

He wanted to believe this *was* his Emma.

But, he could not.

He reveled in the flood of memories undammed at the sight of this woman, prompting a strange mix of joy and sorrow, but it wasn't really Emma. As he waited for his hammering heart to slow, he remembered he had a job to offer. Could this Emma possibly be interested in managing COPY/COPY? What a wonderous thing it would be to have her living in the apartment across the hall from his own, to be able to see her every day.

It was worth a try.

He had to take his time though; he was too emotional at the moment to approach her; he wasn't even sure he could speak. The line she was in didn't appear to be moving, so there was time. He continued to stare. He would make his move when his heart beat more normally.

The long unmoving line ahead of Marilyn began to erode her enthusiasm. She was proud of herself for having made it this far, but her confidence was wavering. Then she heard a raspy voice close behind.

"Missy..."

The scrawny old pervert was standing right behind her. He was even older than she'd first thought, wrinkled of skin and clothing, his chin covered with a stubble of neglect. He smelled of tobacco. Long, gray, Einstein hair stuck out at odd angles from his head. He might have once been tall, but now stood so hunched that his baggy, red eyes were level with hers.

"Can you run a copy machine?" he asked.

Though Marilyn *could* run a copy machine, she was hesitant to share that information with an unkempt pervert, or even to speak to him.

"I don't believe we've been introduced," she said, feeling silly as she said it.

"Oh, sorry," he said. "I'm Old Man Stamper." He pointed to his nametag, still pinned to his faded, flannel shirt.

"Mr. Stamper, I'm Marilyn Gladkowski."

He nodded uneasily, looking in her eyes, straining as if to distinguish something he might recognize through his dirty glasses. After an uncomfortable moment, he asked again, "Can you run a copy machine?"

Marilyn looked at the long, unmoving line ahead of her before she nodded her head to admit she could.

Stamper pulled an overstuffed wallet from his baggy pants. His crooked, tobacco-stained fingers shook as he began a prolonged search through the stacks of miscellaneous paper in the wallet. It was such an awkward process that Marilyn had to resist reaching out to help the old guy. Finally, he pulled out a business card, curved from long storage in the wallet. He handed it to her and began struggling to get the wallet's contents back in order.

"I may have a job for you," he said while he worked on the mess of paper. He shrugged one bony shoulder as he said, "It doesn't pay much, but it comes with an apartment."

Marilyn looked up from the card and met Stamper's sad gaze. He then pointedly looked at the long line ahead of her and back, raising his shaggy eyebrows, "Come by any time."

Marilyn watched the old man shuffle toward the exit through the crowd. Strange. It was as if he'd selected her from the crowd and had no more business in the place. She put the curved business card in her purse and stayed in line for most of an hour, sticking to her original plan. She brought the card out of her purse several times to read again, as if it might tell her more than an address and phone number. Was it a scam of some kind, some perverted trap?

COPY/COPY. It looked innocent enough.

- - -

Once Old Man Stamper got outside the Unemployment Office, he was too wobbly to take another step; he had to lean against a bulletin board near the front door. Being so close to Emma/Marilyn had shaken him profoundly. He felt like a man coming to the surface from a great depth. He took deep breaths of the fresh salty air, pulled out his Zippo, and lit up. The cigarette smoke made a wiggly stream upwards from his trembling hands.

He could not yet process what had just happened. Had that been real? The businessman in him was having second thoughts too. What had he done? It was stupid to offer a job to someone based on nothing more than her uncanny resemblance to his young wife. Plus, he hadn't mentioned what he could pay, or anything about the work or the apartment. He really was pathetic. Still, he hoped she would come by.

He felt older than he'd ever felt before. He fought off the weight of it, mumbling out loud to himself, "Of course you feel old, you old fart, you're older than you've ever been." He recognized this as something Emma might have told him. Maybe it was Emma sending him a reassuring thought.

He walked to the curb and hailed a taxi. Once back on his stool in COPY/COPY, Old Man Stamper continued to tumble the events at the Unemployment Office around in his mind. Had he been visited by a reincarnation of his young wife, or had he just offered a job to a perfect stranger? Should he feel blessed or depressed? After a time, he couldn't think about it anymore. Alone on the stool, exhausted, and with no customers to interrupt him, Old Man Stamper laid his head on his forearms and let sleep take him.

COPY/COPY

Marilyn left the building after deciding that any job she was likely to find there probably wouldn't be better than what Old Man Stamper offered... if it was real. She sipped a latte at a nearby Starbucks, lost in thought. If the job was simply running a copier... no problem. It wasn't what she had in mind, but it was a job, and *with an apartment*. The idea of moving out of her aunt's spare room appealed to her; any sort of apartment would be better than the corner of a storage room. The morning's anxiety of venturing out of seclusion was all but forgotten. She had to check this out. "Come by anytime," the old man had said. She pulled the card out of her purse again to memorize the address. Then she pulled out her map of Seattle bus routes.

The bus rolled into the margins of the city, through progressively worse neighborhoods, with frequent empty storefronts, vacant lots overgrown with weeds, and everything tagged with graffiti. When the bus passed COPY/COPY and came to a stop down the block, she hesitated to get off. The shop was small and cluttered, its front windows obscured by posters and overlapping flyers. It was nothing like the orderly offices she had quit in Oceanside and its lights offered the only tattered signs of life in the shoddy neighborhood. The other half of the same building looked unoccupied, a mirror image of the copy shop except for the padlocked front door and blacked-out windows.

Mindful of her current accommodations, she marshaled her courage, swallowed her anxiety, and got off the bus.

- - -

The steady, whirring chunka—chunka—chunka of Bertha and the tink—tink—tink of paper dropping into wire collating racks combined into a complex drone inside the shop. Old Man Stamper, eyes closed, dozed on the stool behind the counter and didn't respond to the tiny brass bell over the door announcing Marilyn's entrance.

She took in the scene while standing just inside the door. The copier chunked away as the proprietor slept. This wasn't much of a business. She might have turned away and left it all behind if the copier hadn't finished its job in that moment. The final chunka led to the final tink and the sudden silence roused Old Man Stamper. He began pealing a ream of paper to add to the feeder tray, oblivious to Marilyn's presence.

"Mr. Stamper."

He jerked at the sound of her voice, but at the sight of her, his jaw dropped, his face turned a deathly pale. He almost dropped the ream of paper, but braced himself against the counter and struggled to return to the stool.

"Sorry," Marilyn said, "I didn't mean to startle you. Is that job still open?"

Stamper rallied. He smiled weakly, showing his tobacco-stained teeth. "You bet, Missy," he said, searching the countertop as if to find what to do next. Marilyn, she'd said her name was Marilyn. "Come on over here Marilyn and I'll show you how to work this thing."

- - -

Old Man Stamper struggled to keep control of himself; she seemed skittish and he didn't want to scare her away. He kept telling himself it was just like training a new employee. No big deal. He'd trained dozens for his furniture business over the years. She moved closer, but still kept the counter between them.

"This is Bertha's control panel." He patted Bertha out of habit. "She's a big old girl, but she can crank 'em out." Marilyn didn't seem reassured by his beginning, but he persisted through the detailed workings of the machine, all the while trying not to look at Marilyn because he found it difficult to talk sensibly when their eyes met.

"Your job sheets are over here," he said, indicating a stack of forms, "your paper is back there on the shelves, and you put the finished jobs on these shelves, arranged alphabetically." He indicated a large set of shelves holding one lonely finished job. Stamper looked around for anything else Marilyn might need to know.

He was feeling panicky; he had to get away for a while to recover. It was just too intense to be in the presence of someone who looked so much like Emma. "The number to my apartment is by the phone if you have any questions." He gestured toward the telephone on the counter, then turned and headed for the back of the shop, planning to leave her alone so he could calm down and she could feel more comfortable.

"But we haven't even talked about this," Marilyn said in response to the old man's presumption. "What are the hours? What does it pay? And what about the apartment you mentioned."

"Oh, yeah." Stamper heaved a heavy sigh, upset with himself for having handled things so poorly. He fished a ring of keys from his baggy front pocket and kept his eyes down as he worked to remove a key from the ring. "I'll start you out at minimum wage. After a month or so, if we're both still happy, I can bump it up a couple of dollars. Open at 9:00, close at 6:00. I'll spell you an hour for lunch."

He offered her the key. "That sound OK to you?"

Marilyn hesitated.

Mr. Stamper pointed straight up with the key. "Apartment's up there."

Marilyn looked at the ceiling.

"Come on, I'll show you," he said and shuffled toward the back of the shop, down what appeared to be a dead-end aisle of storage shelves.

- - -

Marilyn held back. Where the hell was he going?

At the end of the aisle, Stamper opened a door out of an apparently solid back wall of the shop. It was like a secret passageway, only a faint crack transected the wainscoting trim to reveal the presence of a door, no doorknob, no frame, and no apparent hinges. He left the door open behind him, and began struggling up steep wooden stairs. By the time he'd climbed out of sight, Marilyn had worked up the courage to follow him, telling herself she could handle a scrawny old man if she had to. Still, she followed what she hoped was a safe distance behind.

All the way up the dark, narrow stairwell, Marilyn worried that it all seemed too easy, too good to be true. The pay was OK, but a free apartment, if it was livable, was worth a great deal. But, why had it been so easy? He didn't know anything about her. Why was he offering the job?

On the second-floor landing, Stamper inserted the key, pushed the door open, and reached in to switch on the light. While Marilyn walked into the center of the room, Stamper stood back at the entrance, giving her space and time to look it over.

"I'll get all this extra furniture out of here, move it into my apartment across the hall. You can keep any of it here if you like."

Old Man Stamper could see Emma again. His frail old heart melted at the memory. He would offer this woman, this Emma/Marilyn, whatever she wanted. He longed to have any sort of female influence in his life; it was an essential part of what he'd been missing since Emma died. But more than that, Stamper felt forty years younger with Marilyn close by.

"I'm sorry about the pink walls," he said. "It was like this when I bought the place."

"I like pink," Marilyn lifted a lapel to prove her point.

- - -

Marilyn was delighted by what she saw. It was small, but well configured with a kitchen/living room combination, one little bedroom, and a small bathroom with a tiny shower stall, but it was much bigger than Aunt Irene's spare bedroom. Plus, it was crowded with jumbled stacks of beautiful, wooden furniture. And, he'd said, "You can keep any of it here if you like."

"Can you start today?" Mr. Stamper asked, looking like he would much rather take a nap than to do any more copy work.

"No," Marilyn said, "but I can start tomorrow."

- - -

Marilyn was on the first bus out of Kenmore the next morning, bags in tow, and the security and independence of an apartment key in her purse. She arrived too early. The building was dark, the door to COPY/COPY was locked, and there was little sign of life on the whole street. She had a key to her new apartment, but no way to get to its front door. She towed her bags another two blocks to a small café where she sat and drank coffee until COPY/COPY was scheduled to open. Then she had to wait on the weedy sidewalk for another twenty minutes before the lights came on.

"I'm sorry, I overslept," Old Man Stamper said when he opened the door.

"Good morning," Marilyn said.

"I should have given you a key to the alley door too. Again, I'm sorry. Here, let me help you with your luggage. It's best to go around this way."

Stamper adopted one of Marilyn's bags, towed it down the sidewalk and around the corner of the building into the alley. Marilyn followed close behind. He led her to a heavy door in the center of the building, fished out his ring of keys, and worked the lock. He huffed and wheezed her bag up the stairs to the familiar landing, where Marilyn had been the day before. When Marilyn caught up, he was leaning against the wall, struggling to breathe. His old hands trembled as he worked an extra key to the alley door off his key ring for her.

"When you get settled, come on down and I'll get you started." He said this over his shoulder, already descending the inside stairwell back to the shop.

Marilyn let herself into the apartment, wove through the maze of furniture, and laid her suitcases on the bed.

She stood there for a time, listening to the quiet. It felt good. She could see lots of things that needed doing, cleaning, curtains, furniture to sort through, and maybe a little paint, but there would be time enough for all that.

She hung her pink jacket in the closet and went down the inside stairwell to begin her first day at COPY/COPY.

\- - -

Old Man Stamper watched her work. She took control of Bertha and processed the first work order with no hesitation. She placed the finished job in a paper bag, filed the work order, and then looked to him and smiled. That smile was enough to convince him he'd been right to hire her; he would be better off having that smile to brighten his days. He nodded his approval and she picked up the only remaining work order. Marilyn wasn't going to need much training. He realized he should leave.

"Looks like you got it under control, Missy."

She smiled again.

"Don't hesitate to call my apartment phone if you have a question." He would have preferred to spend the day watching her, but he knew doing so would prove awkward, and he needed a nap.

\- - -

Old Man Stamper paced a tobacco cloud between his apartment phone and the birdcages. He said to an attentive crowd of finches, "Big news today, babies; we have a *neighbor*." He was feeling good about the marvelous morning he was having; Emma/Marilyn was just downstairs! He was almost excited. Maybe he didn't need a nap. He should stay alert in case she called.

The birds eyed his pacing.

"Her name is Marilyn. Maybe I'll invite her over someday soon to meet you. The amazing thing, wait till you see her, she looks exactly like Emma. Exactly!"

He stopped his pacing to rummage in the kitchen cabinets for the birdseed. "Well... just like Emma looked when she was that age... when we first met."

While he filled the feeders, he admitted to the birds, "I'm losing my grip; sometimes I think she *is* Emma." He finished filling the feeders, checked their water, and sat down by the biggest cage.

"She's smart too, sharp as a tack. She had Bertha humming right away."

He lit a new cigarette with the old one and leaned forward to confide in the birds. "It's nice to have Emma back," and his rheumy eyes filled with tears.

Old Man Stamper sat and smoked and watched the birds, pondering life with his new neighbor. "How can I make her happy here?" he asked the birds. "Maybe if there were more people around... someone near her age..." He began shuffling again between the phone and birdcage while he thought about it. He stopped. "I could open the other shop." He sat down with the birds to sell them on the idea. "It wouldn't cost much to open, just incidentals, cosmetic stuff... I could finally put Garry's crap to work." He chuckled at some memory of his twin and then went quiet for a long time. "It couldn't be another girl though, not for a shop like that."

- - -

The copier was older than anything Marilyn had ever used, and larger, but it wasn't too complicated to operate. She soon had the orders finished, but she could see lots of other things that needed doing. She began by organizing the paper stock and then went on to clean the dust off things.

At noon, the hidden door in the back of the shop opened and Old Man Stamper emerged with a sandwich.

"I'll watch the shop each day at noon, while you have your lunch. I hope you like turkey."

"Oh, thank you! I'm starving." She'd been too nervous for breakfast.

Stamper fished two twenties out of his wallet. "Here's an advance, so you can buy what you need to make a lunch for yourself tomorrow. Louie's Market's just a few blocks east of here. Payday is Friday. How's it going so far?"

"Good… I think; no real problems. I even took a new order." She hesitated before adding, "It was from a Ms. Moody. She wanted to know if you had died."

"Hah! She's always surprised I'm still kicking. Tell her I'll let her know when I'm dead."

Marilyn never found the right time to ask why he had chosen to hire her out of the crowd the way he did. She could only guess it must have been her lucky job-finding outfit.

- - -

Old Man Stamper hired movers to relocate the furniture Marilyn hadn't chosen to keep into his apartment. Some of it had to go into the third apartment over the spare shop, wherever they were able to find room for it. Marilyn was delighted with the furniture she chose to keep and that made him happy.

Two weeks after Marilyn came into his life, he resumed his mornings at the unemployment office, this time looking for someone to set up, and then perhaps to manage, a second store in the spare shop downstairs using the inventory stacked in there, all the stuff left over from his twin brother's last misguided business venture. He wasn't sure what sort of fellow might work in such a place, much less how to identify him. As a result, he spent his time at the unemployment office watching the people, unable to begin a proactive search. The longer he sat, the drowsier he became, but he was always careful to return by noon to watch the copy shop so Marilyn could break for lunch. He then got to see her again at six o'clock each day when he would appear through the magic door in the back wall to count the till. Marilyn's brief, smiling summary of her workday was the highlight of Old Man Stamper's day.

The daily take was already growing, surpassing anything he'd seen in a long time. People seemed to like having their copies made by an attractive young woman who didn't forget things. Before he left the shop each day, he took time to notice and comment on all the extra things she'd done to clean and organize. While it was true she had the place spotless and better organized, he did it mostly to stay in her presence a little longer.

Like the shop, Old Man Stamper felt rejuvenated. His daily walk to the unemployment office, followed by a good, solid nap in the afternoon, (instead of attending to Bertha) left him more energetic and perhaps better connected to the moment. Stamper's morning walk became more than simply a search for a second employee. It was a campaign to slow the decline of his condition, and he thought it might be working. He still forgot things and experienced a lot of surreal dreaming, especially during the long nights when he couldn't sleep, but there was nothing as unsettling as the "travel times" he'd had before finding Marilyn. He could now more easily make it all the way downhill to the unemployment office if he walked slowly and stopped halfway to rest and light another cigarette. Once there and inside, he sat in his lucky chair to recover, the same chair from which he'd found Marilyn, and from which he could watch through the window the crowds outside, milling around the bulletin boards. On most days, he would sit there until time to taxi back for Marilyn's lunch break, watching people queue up for their turn at the next available agent, overwhelmed by the hopeful bustle all around him, and giving little thought to finding someone to run a second shop.

- - -

Jerry Had a World in Mind

Carpe Diem

He responded to the call for boarding and was first in line, fidgeting with excess energy, eager to get farther away from Kilgore and on down the road to the proverbial Right Place. Yet, Jerry was dreading the ride. Getting on the bus was going to be difficult, but staying on the bus would be the real challenge. Bus rides had always been the worst sort of torment for him, requiring that he sit in a confining space without hope of stepping outside for depressurization when he felt the inevitable rising need to move. He was anxious to get a seat near a door, any door, or at least a window. Even as a child, Jerry had always felt better near an exit anytime he was prevented from being outdoors and alone, his preferred circumstance. He avoided crowds and crowded places. Until that chair collapsed, the high ceiling of the library had made it one of the few indoor places where he was comfortable. Despite his dread of the long bus ride ahead, he was giddy as a game show contestant about to spin the big wheel.

In order to endure the long, grueling ride ahead of him, he planned to nurture his excitement and use that energy to distract himself from thoughts of confining spaces. He intended to focus on one of the major components of his new Life Plan: writing.

In the hours ahead, he planned to start his first, full-length novel!

Why not? What better time than now? And after all, he had resolved not to waste any more of his life.

He would have to do it all in his mind, to visualize the organization of the story in his head, remember it all, and then write it out when he got to Seattle. (His steno pads were inside the duffel bag, now being secured in the cargo compartment of the bus.) Jerry was confident he could do it that way; in his earlier writing efforts, he had been able to assemble whole short stories in his head without making any notes. This would be similar. He could work out the details, the storyline, the action, and the interplay of his characters. Then, as soon as he found a place to stay in Seattle, he could begin the actual writing of his first, full-length manuscript by recording his mental notes in the steno pads. With his mind thus preoccupied with writing, the hours on the bus would roll by more easily and, as a bonus, he might accomplish a substantial beginning for his novel by the time he got to Seattle, perhaps even before he was out of Idaho!

Jerry was so excited about this new resolve he became convinced his claustrophobia would not be an issue. He would delay no longer! He would start to live his dream; the time had come to act. *Carpe diem*, by God! He would seize the day and wring its little neck.

Yoda said:

Do, or do not. There is no 'try'.

Jerry's Protagonist

There was never any question Lurk would be his protagonist; Lurk was Jerry's earliest fictional character and seemed to have always been a part of his life. Lurk was already in attendance while Jerry patted together summertime mud towers in the "sandbox" of Grandma's backyard or rolled up improbable snowmen dioramas in the winter.

Right from the beginning, though, Jerry had kept Lurk's existence a secret from everyone, especially from Grandma, who didn't have a playful bone in her body. While still very young, Jerry had sense enough never to talk to Lurk when anyone else might hear. There was already enough peculiarity in the Gustafson family with Uncle Harold around.

By the time Jerry started school, Lurk's character was well-formed and firmly under Jerry's control. He no longer found it necessary to talk to his imaginary companion, even when he was alone. Lurk became a presence, the friend Jerry imagined coming to his rescue when he was forced to endure the unpleasantries of the playground, as the older boys made fun of his bookish ways, or called him Bones, or toyed with how his young beanpole frame could be made to look awkward. Lurk could never actually come to his rescue, of course, but he was a great solace and good company after the unpleasantries were over. Together they would revel in how it might have gone with Lurk's intervention.

As puberty rumbled through Jerry's world, Lurk matured too, becoming a replacement for the missing men in his family, something like a silent, invisible, big brother. When Jerry began to write short Science Fiction stories, Lurk evolved once again, this time into a literary character, poised to leap into any conflict Jerry created for him, slaying this or that monster, discovering this or that secret world, taking incredible risks without a second thought, and in general, have the adventures Jerry could not have in Kilgore.

- - -

Jerry wrote his first Science Fiction story in grade school. *The Flying, Floating Feather-Slooper Eaters* was not well received. In it, Jerry created a minimalist ecology on an ocean world, populated by a frail species of feathered, hooked-beaked, pterodactyl-like creatures that lived on the wing above an endless sea. They cruised along just above the waves and used their hooked beaks to snatch an occasional Floating Feather-Slooper from the water's surface. The Floating Feather-Sloopers bobbed on the surface like upside-down mushrooms with long sticky tongues, surviving on a diet of feathers they slooped with their tongues from the water's surface around them. The feathers, of course, fell from the wings of the Flying, Floating Feather-Slooper Eaters. Reading that strange, Seussian story in front of the class produced a memorable assortment of reactions from the serious-minded children of potato farmers and cemented Jerry's place in the community; it was obvious to one-and-all the peculiar Gustafson gene had taken him over.

No one in his school, or in all of Kilgore, shared Jerry's predilection for Science Fiction. He endured the puzzled looks from teachers and the hoots of derision from his classmates whenever he was forced to read yet another improbable yarn in front of the class. In time, he learned to keep his Science Fiction stories to himself. He began to scribble them into green, spiral-bound steno pads he bought from Pinkston's, Kilgore's single little "Mom and Pop" grocery store (owned and operated by the Pinkstons). He kept the fiction-filled steno pads squirreled in his room where Grandma wouldn't find them, just as if they were a shameful stash of pornography.

As Jerry's efforts became more sophisticated, he attempted to write in the style of whatever author was his current favorite. One month he did his damnedest to write like Isaac Asimov. The next month he might decide to emulate Ray Bradbury, or Frederik Pohl, or Arthur C. Clark, or any one of the dozens of great writers he had come to know from the library's impressive collection of Golden Age science fiction.

- - -

While Jerry's short stories allowed him to soar beyond the bland lands of Idaho and to probe outside the muffled confines of his self-imposed torpor, they were merely subconscious practice for his true aspiration, which was to attempt something on the order of the classic, full-length, "other-world" novels of the masters. Jerry wanted to create a world, populate it with his own characters, and then let it evolve.

Lurk had long-since become formed in the heroic mold as a literary character, with the nuances of his persona as familiar to Jerry as those of an older brother. Lurk had all of the qualities Jerry wished he had himself. Lurk was a skilled pilot, qualified in several aircraft types and able to repair anything he flew. He was an adventurous entrepreneur with a history of exploring the latest world where man had learned to live. He was an experienced lover too, his mere presence having a magical effect on women. He was tall and tan, and strong as an ox.

Jerry had just one of those things in common with Lurk: He was tall.

Now, with Jerry having leapt into an unknown world himself, it was time to give Lurk a planet to conquer, to let Lurk do what Lurk would do. Jerry couldn't wait to see what would happen.

Jerry had a world in mind too. He had noticed much of interplanetary Science Fiction involved overcoming hostile environments in order to obtain whatever the planet offered. Jerry wondered about the literary possibilities of life on a planet well-suited to humans, one with an agreeable climate and an accommodating ecology, but otherwise without apparent intrinsic value for its resources. What he had in mind for Lurk was a planet just the opposite of Arrakis, the famous spice planet portrayed in Frank Herbert's classic series of otherworld novels. Jerry had read the whole *Dune* series several times. Arrakis was so arid that water was treasured above all else. People off the planet of Arrakis valued only the mysterious spice, mined from the sand of the planet's vast, worm-infested desert. He was especially intrigued by the "power word" Herbert had chosen to arm the Arrakis fighters. The word was "Maud'Dib." So, by modifying the word a little, Jerry created a name for his planet, a name that would be a subtle tribute to his beloved *Dune* series.

The name of his planet would be Mowdabb.

Jerry didn't imagine most readers would notice the homage (assuming there would someday be readers), but he liked knowing it was there.

Mowdabb would be wet and warm, moderate in every measure, an accommodating environment for the peaceful existence of humans, but a place that was otherwise worthless. It would give humans everything they needed to live, but nothing to mine or export, nothing for anyone living off the planet to covet, and thus nothing over which to fight. How this environment would lend itself to adventure was not yet clear, but with Lurk's help, Jerry planned to work it out.

Getting Started

Being first in line, Jerry got the seat he needed. Since his legs had never fit in the space normally allotted for legs, he had always sought the front seats of the bus where he could extend his legs and look out the big glass windshield to calm his claustrophobia.

He extended his left leg like a fallen tree limb into the aisle and made a big show of retracting his leg for each new passenger, trying to make obvious his need for extra room, hoping everyone would pass on by and no one would sit beside him.

First up the stairs behind Jerry was a tiny, well-laundered family he guessed might be Guatemalan. They looked like the migrants he'd worked with during fall potato harvests. They occupied the first two rows across the aisle, just behind the driver. The father and son shared the first seat, the father wearing a white straw Stetson, a pearl-buttoned shirt, and bolo tie. The small boy wore a superman t-shirt. The mother and daughter shared the second seat, their black, braided hair contrasting with their matching white embroidered dresses. The children sat next to the windows.

Behind the Guatemalan family came a parade of sun-roasted farmers and their tired housewives, threadbare migrant workers, and road-weary hippies wrestling daypacks. Single moms lugged their kids and all the kiddy paraphernalia they hoped might keep things peaceful for the long ride ahead.

Jerry was so involved in his needy display for personal space that he hadn't noticed the queue outside the bus, so the last four people to enter were each, in their own way, a surprise. The first two surprises were twin teen-aged girls, cute, with short, blond hair. They bounced up the steps, jabbering with each other and the driver, moving past Jerry, each one, in their exuberance, flashing identical smiles his way and suppressing a giggle apiece at the sight of him.

He was disarmed by their twinness, by their cuteness, and by the fact that they each suppressed a giggle as they passed. What had made them giggle? Was it his long-legged predicament or his too-obvious bid for an oversized quotient of legroom?

Jerry was spared having to dwell on it because his attention was diverted by the arrival at the top of the bus steps of the most beautiful woman he had ever seen. She was a tall and slender brunette with flawless, milky-white skin. She paused at the top of the steps to study the busload of humanity. She did so with consummate self-assurance, as if deciding whether she wanted to be part of such a group. She carried herself with easy grace, taking the time to look at everyone as she passed, including Jerry. He stared back open-mouthed. She left a delicate wake of some exotic perfume that suggested expensive hothouse flowers and something musky. Like him, everyone on the bus watched the brunette as she past. Then, row-by-row, they turned their eyes forward, so they were all now staring at Jerry's slack-jawed trance. The brunette settled into what appeared to be the last empty seat, near the back of the bus. Now even the brunette was looking at Jerry. Then, in perfect synchronicity, all their eyes shifted to look beyond Jerry, at the last person up the stairs. He turned to face the embodiment of every bus rider's nightmare.

It was an obese woman carrying large, overfull shopping bags on each arm. She blocked the light coming in the front windshield. Jerry retrieved his leg from the aisle, folding most of it onto the empty seat beside him. He knew she would need all available space to pass and was still hoping there might have been one last, empty seat behind him he hadn't noticed. She surveyed the long aisle ahead, wheezing from the climb up the steps. Her smile labored to hold up splotchy red cheeks as she turned to look down at Jerry. She took one step forward, her paper bags unseating the Guatemalan's Stetson, and rotated her bulk 90 degrees in the narrow aisle, turning her broad back to Jerry. She held that position for a moment, as if to contemplate the dumbfounded Guatemalans who, all together, would not have outweighed her. They were trying, unsuccessfully, not to stare. Then she ceased her struggle with gravity and landed in the seat Jerry had been trying to save with his left leg only milliseconds before. The impact rocked the entire bus and left Jerry folded against the window with his knees under his chin, as if the force of her landing had blasted him there.

Like an elephant seal getting comfortable on the beach, the woman wriggled to settle herself and her belongings into place, rotating to face forward with her bags lined up in the aisle.

Her undeniable usurpation of Jerry's personal space left him just short of voicing the keening, claustrophobic panic that now threatened to overtake him. He was stuck in place, wedged against the side window like a bullfrog corked in a pint jar, immobilized and without hope of jumping to freedom.

Oblivious to Jerry's problem, she lifted a shopping bag onto her lap and began to sort through its contents. The taut pink ham of her upper arm squished against Jerry's bony shoulder with every inexplicable readjustment of what Jerry decided (from the smell) must be her long-overdue laundry. He guessed she must be taking her laundry to Boise, where the machines might be large enough. As she sorted, she hummed tuneless songs. His attempts to avoid bumping against her relentless encroachments, forced him ever nearer a fetal position.

The bus was stoppered full with the fat woman's entrance and the driver started the engine. Jerry considered making a desperate leap for the stairs just beyond the partition in front of him, but did not act before the bus began to roll. There would be no possibility of escape until the next stop, which was, unfortunately, hours away in Boise.

Beginning to Write

For every swaying, tire-humming mile and through every persistent stanza of the fat woman's maddening medley, Jerry coveted the wide-open countryside passing his window. He imagined himself to be a grenade whose pin had been pulled, but for whom there was too little space to allow the release of his spoon. This imagery may well have been all that prevented his detonation.

"Just bump my shoulder one more time…" he thought. "Just start one more song…"

And, she always did.

Why-oh-why, Jerry lamented, hadn't he paired up with someone before boarding, someone small? Or, why hadn't one of the twins chosen to sit with him, or even the brunette? Why had he chosen to ride the express?

He hugged his knees and wallowed in black, claustrophobic bile, imagining himself engaged in a heroic struggle against kicking out the side window and leaping into open air, or alternatively, against clambering forward over the partition that now restricted his folded legs and then plastering himself against the windshield. He resisted doing either by means of a tumultuous internal struggle involving a complex dance of two different partners: One rocked stoically in place while chanting "This too shall pass." The other screamed obscenities and slam-danced against the frantic need to find an exit. The dance eventually exhausted him, weakening his urge to get out of the dark tomb of the bus and allowing him to fold in upon himself like the closing of a flower. His mind turned inward and became quieter, letting him focus at last on an imagined world — Lurk's adventures on Mowdabb.

This then, was how he began to write his first novel. The first section of it came together in his head while he glowered out the side window of a miserable Greyhound bus rolling through the bland lands of eastern Idaho, through Pocatello, Twin Falls, Mountain Home, and beyond.

- - -

Unfortunately, it was many days before Jerry had occasion to write down Lurk's story. The big city offered unforeseen difficulties. Through it all, Jerry persisted. He carried his duffle, and the notebooks inside, with him at all times and added to the story whenever he could.

In time, he came to treasure those battered notebooks, not only because they were the original incarnation of his novel, but also because they functioned like a journal of Jerry's odyssey.

From the very first notebook:

Preflight

Lurk Rydgyd walks around the hovercraft, making his slow, preflight inspection. He is moving deliberately because he intends to inspect both the ship *and* the Doublemint Twins belted into the back seats. Just for show, he briefly studies various non-essential latches and fasteners on the outside of the ship. Then he opens the passenger door to preflight one of the twins. First, he pretends to inspect the fresh-air nozzles over each of their blonde heads, swiveling them gently, as if they might be critical components (even though the fresh air blower has never worked). All the while, he is breathing in the sweet female perfumes filling the back seat. Then, he pops and resets a few circuit breakers on the central console between the twins. He does this for no reason other than that the circuit breakers are just inches from their two sets of nubile knees. When he has popped and reset them all, he shows the nearest twin his pearly-whites, says "Pardon" and, with trembling hands, begins to inspect the security and proper positioning of her lap belt, shoulder straps, and quick-release buckle, to make certain her tan little torso will not fall out.

"Wouldn't want to lose you, would we?" he says to her, giving her the tamest leer he can manage.

When he has finished inspecting her restraints (and taxed his own), he walks around to open the other door and inspect the other twin.

"Pardon," he says as he begins an identical inspection. "Wouldn't want to lose you, would we?"

The first twin giggles.

They are identical, like mirror images of one another, about twenty years old and dressed for the commercial they are about to make in the ruins. They wear cute little T-shirts displaying the Wrigley's logo and short white shorts against the constant heat.

Lurk feels intoxicated. There's a fresh sheen of sweat on his forehead after finishing the inspection of the second twin. He's been on Mowdabb a long time and it's been even longer since he's seen anything as delectable as the twins. He recovers his poise somewhat, enough to give each of them another big smile and a thumbs-up through the window as he closes the passenger door. He is thrilled to see what, in his intoxicated state, he interprets to be pure animal fascination on their faces.

Lurk *is* a magnificent specimen, taller than most men, raw-boned, and well-muscled, with big, work-roughened hands and broad shoulders. Months in the Mowdabbian sun, and, before that, years working under various suns on the frontiers of planetary exploration, have left him bronzed, with his hair and eyebrows bleached almost white. His rugged face, with heroic chin and pearly-whites, is flawed only by his eyes, which, though striking in their pale-green contrast to his tan and peering out from under a bushy blond fringe of overhanging brow, they are perhaps a tiny bit too close together.

Lurk might have been able to manage more sophisticated behavior around the women neatly buckled into his airship if he hadn't spent so much of his life on the frontiers of planetary exploration, where there was never enough of them.

All the way back to the pilot's seat, he is pummeled by an onslaught of erotic fantasies, obsessing about the parts of the women he cannot see, wondering if the twins are identical in every way. He is revived by the smelling-salt growl of their female manager, already belted into the other front seat.

"Quit ogling the girls, Jerkoff," she says. "The only services we need from you are as pilot and guide."

Lurk flashes his pearly-whites and proudly quotes the company slogan. "The Rydgyd Flying Service, 'Better than the flaccid ones.'"

Even though the manager rolls her eyes in naked disgust, Lurk is pleased with himself. He buckles into the pilot's seat and begins the pre-takeoff checklist. He finds it difficult to concentrate because of the manager's black halter-top, a structural marvel working to full capacity. Though scaled a bit larger than the twins, the manager's proportions appeal even more to Lurk's hungry eyes. She is a tall and stunning brunette who handles herself with consummate assurance. What's more, Lurk cannot help but notice she is blessed with the flawless, milky-white skin that has proven to be his undoing in the past. Though older than the twins and perhaps more sophisticated, she is non-the-less beautiful in her own way.

She's 'Amazonian' he decides happily.

Damn! Three beautiful women and a whole planet to himself. Lurk's spirits soar even before he gets the hovercraft off the ground.

Destiny Smiled Back

As the bus entered the outskirts of Boise, Jerry formed a plan for the possibility the fat woman might not get off there. If she stayed in her seat, he was going to stand up (as best he could underneath the overhanging luggage compartment) and put his right foot on the partition in front of him. With that leverage, he thought he could pull his body up and swing it around the chrome pole at the end of the partition, over the woman's copious lap, and into the aisle. He visualized then bounding down the exit steps and into the terminal. Once inside, he would skip and dance and whoop and swing his arms until the authorities came to hold him down.

He was spared the embarrassment of a failed attempt to leap the fat woman's lap, because she heaved her bulk to the vertical, collected her laundry bags, and got off the bus.

Jerry spent all of that forty-five-minute layover in Boise circling the terminal like a wild animal. Now that he'd begun moving away from Kilgore, he could not abide delay. He did not skip or dance or whoop, (for fear of possible incarceration and the resultant delay in his journey), but he did swing his arms and stretch his stiffened muscles, taking up as much space as he could. He watched the twins surround a grandfather-type and jabber their way out of the terminal and into the parking lot, never to be seen again. The exotic brunette hung around the terminal, talking on her cell phone, waiting like Jerry for the bus to continue to Seattle.

Since it looked like the bus would be full again, he was lined up early for boarding and first up the steps. He chose the seat behind the driver this time, for the added legroom without the restricting stairwell partition and for the comforting view out the windshield. He smiled at all the smaller people boarding after him, hoping one would choose to sit with him. Destiny smiled back; a little old lady wearing a maroon wool suit and matching pillbox hat returned his smile and hesitated slightly. Jerry scrambled to his feet and indicated the seat next to him, the one by the window. Apparently impressed by his energetic display of courtesy, she settled into the seat. She smiled once again at him and then, while still sitting upright in the center of her seat, lowered her chin to her chest and fell asleep. He'd gone from the worst possible traveling companion to the best.

The bus bore its human cargo westward through Meridian and Nampa, across the Snake River, and into the brown and rolling monotony of eastern Oregon. The diesel's drone seemed to help Jerry lose himself in Lurk's story, which unfolded like the passing landscape, assembling itself easily in his mind.

The Ruins

Lurk holds the ship at a steady hover while checking the instruments. When satisfied all systems are go, he tips the nose down and they leave behind Mowdabb's only airfield and the crude building serving as the hanger/office of the Rydgyd Flying Service.

They skim across the rolling terrain on a layer of ground-effect from the big fans, bobbing over the endless green hummocks of moss like a boat on the swells of an invisible sea.

Viewed from orbit, Mowdabb is a homogenous, monotonous, featureless sphere of dense unbroken green, without mountains or bodies of water. Viewed from an altitude of several meters, Mowdabb looks much the same.

It is a planet of moss.

Lurk sets a heading toward one of the exceptions to the vast green sea, one of the many scattered islands of dark, weather-rounded rock. First spotted from orbital surveys, they appear every kilometer or so all around the planet with apparent randomness. They are never more than a few meters above the green and wouldn't have caused the sensation they did in the scientific community, if they weren't covered with carvings. Whomever, or whatever, once inhabited the planet, had covered almost every vertical surface of exposed rock with strange, rounded, and deeply cut carvings. There is nothing recognizable in them, nothing representational, not even any discernable patterns, as if they were done merely for decoration or to satisfy some alien need to carve. Some of the larger islands of rock also have mysterious, cave-like openings that have received little study so far, due to the staggering cost of conducting such research.

The "ruins," as they are described (though they are not ruined in any way), generated such a sensation throughout the galaxy when the planet was first discovered, they prompted an onslaught of scientific types, all clambering for permits to explore. No one has yet come to Mowdabb to study the moss; they all came to study who, or what, had created the ruins, and to learn what might have happened to them. Did they die or did they leave? No one has yet found a clue about the former inhabitants, no bones, no statues, and nothing resembling a tool. Whoever built the ruins had gone away, or gone extinct, such a long time ago that only remnants of their monolithic architecture survived.

So far as anyone knew, there is nothing living on Mowdabb except the moss.

Lurk had established The Rydgyd Flying Service to make his fortune from the transportation problems presented by the moss. There is no relief from it. Different varieties of it appear everywhere in symbiotic combinations, ranging in size from microscopic to massive. Tangled mats of it cover every square kilometer of the planet. It is dense, many meters deep in places, rough-fibered, and always wet. Sometimes the green, growing part of the moss is held above the dense layers of ancient humus sediment moldering underneath, by woody, gray-green stems, like groves of bamboo. None of it is really moss, but moss is the nearest earthly analogue to it and no one has ever called it anything else. It is nurtured by heavy, daily precipitation and by dense, frequent fogs, making it daunting to move anywhere on the planet, either flying, walking, or riding in any conventional land vehicle. However, visibility permitting, transportation over the moss is easy by hovercraft, the ideal vehicle for Mowdabb. Hovercraft function well in the dense atmosphere and are cheap to fly and maintain on such a remote planet. On Earth, a hovercraft at full power can maintain an altitude measured in inches, but, in the heavy, humid, oxygen-rich atmosphere of Mowdabb, and in the planet's lighter gravity, even the overloaded collection of spare parts comprising Lurk's one-ship fleet is able to get several meters above the surface.

Lurk had been one of three, small, competitive, hovercraft operators to establish on Mowdabb. He was now the last remaining; all the others folded after the initial surge of scientific interest. Lurk had survived the competition because he could run the entire operation alone, the flying, the maintenance, and the paperwork. When the big-money expeditions came back, he would be their only option.

It is a monumental undertaking to coordinate an expedition of any size to such a remote planet. Scientific institutions are always slow to respond and under-funded. On the other hand, commercial institutions, such as advertising agencies, are organized for quick response to ever-changing trends in the market and to the latest buzz in popularity. And, they are willing to invest any amount of money in anything that could make them more of it.

Lurk and his passengers are heading toward a particular concentration of carved islands he has seen before. It is a place where the manager can have a choice of dramatic backdrops for her photo shoot. He thought the Doublemint commercial was a hare-brained idea, but they'd paid his brazen price. The money would be enough to keep the Rydgyd Flying Service in business until the next big expeditionary contracts came in.

Lurk begins a slow right turn, banking the ship toward the nearest scattering of ruins to give the manager a good view out the passenger side. He points across the cockpit. "There they are!" he says proudly, as if he owns them, "The Ruins of Mowdabb."

"Where?"

Lurk leans a little farther her way, to point again. "There," he says. "Those wet, dark brown rocks poking up through the moss."

Lurk enjoys the clean soapy smell of her and the softness he encounters with his shoulder. "*How do women do that?*" he wonders. "*Even on Mowdabb, they manage to smell good.*" Lurk will maintain this pleasant turn for as long as she wants.

"They look to me like every other goddamn dark brown rock in this hell-hole," she says, demonstrating her easy resistance to his charms.

"A little farther on, they get a lot bigger," Lurk assures her, "big enough we could make a landing on top of one of them. You can't really see the carvings and hieroglyphics this far away, but once we're on the ground, you'll have all the photogenic backdrops you could want."

"Yeah, all right. Slide over, you big ape." Lurk's broad shoulders are taking up too much of her cockpit space.

He centers himself in his seat, returns to their original heading, and taps the glass of his radio compass. "We just need to keep this heading for a few more minutes," he says to get her talking. Her only response is to give him a look. "We're heading 'Downtown'," he adds with enthusiasm. Again, there is no response. Lurk abandon's further attempts at conversation, but his enthusiasm is undeterred.

No one knew anything about the former Mowdabbians beyond their approximate size (from the many arches and openings into the buildings) and their propensity for building with native rock, burrowing and carving with a single-mindedness that, in itself, made them alien. If they had been preoccupied with such human failings as money and religion, "Downtown" might once have been their market or spiritual center, but it was all just guesswork. The peculiar fact that an uninhabited planet provided so few clues about the former inhabitants made Mowdabb a sensation throughout the galaxy when it was discovered and convinced Lurk that many more research expeditions were to come.

When their hovercraft reaches "Downtown," they are also approaching the range limit of Lurk's performance-challenged hovercraft, especially with a full load of passengers and camera equipment. They are also near the broadcast limit of the navigational radio transmitter back at the airfield. Lurk has to monitor the signal strength carefully so as not to veer out of range and diminish chances of a safe return.

Lurk's radio compass is a crude navigation system using a radio receiver to point the way back to the transmitter at the airbase. Without the radio beacon transmitting from the airbase, navigation would be impossible. Conventional magnetic compasses don't work on the planet because of its dense and magnetically complex core. Visual flight navigation is not reliable over the featureless green landscape and in the constant haze of Mowdabb's humid atmosphere.

Lurk has overflown "Downtown" a few times, but when he recognizes the cluster of pyramids emerging through the haze, he can also see another grouping just a little farther on, one he hadn't noticed before. Impulsively, he decides to check it out. Upon reaching the new cluster, he sees yet another through the haze, at the limit of his vision. "Downtown" begins to look like the beginnings of a beltway of Mowdabbian development. Lurk persists down the beltway despite flirting with both the limits of his signal range and his fuel supply. He is from pioneer stock, so he cannot resist the impulse to explore. Besides, he wants to find a site for this photo-shoot that will impress the hard-nosed businesswoman in the seat beside him.

The signal begins to fade. The compass needle swings idly. Lurk decides he cannot delay further. He makes a quick visual survey of landing sites large enough to accommodate them. Even from his moving vantage point, he can see all the buildings are heavily carved, a little taller and more elaborate than any he has seen before. They reminded him of Mayan step pyramids on Earth, but there are also various rock cubes and rectangular blocks, several with low, rounded openings visible.

"OK. Where would you like to land?" Lurk asks the manager.

"How the hell do I know? You're the goddamn guide, you pick a spot."

"Let's see if I can find one that serves cold beer," Lurk says in a silly effort to ease her anxiety.

She glowers up at him, but has no time for a scathing remark because the twins begin coughing in the back seat. Lurk looks back over his shoulder, but the twins are not coughing; they are motionless, looking back at him with identical, startled-doe expressions.

The engine!

Lurk turns back to check the gauges. Everything is wrong! Oil pressure is down. Engine temperature is up. Instinctively, he increases the power, but to no avail.

They are going down.

Reaching Seattle

After eighteen laborious hours on the bus, Jerry was delivered to Seattle, feeling little better than any newborn must feel after a difficult delivery. He had been awake most of the night on Mowdabb. Sleep had finally come as the bus droned down the western slope of the Cascades. He woke when it left the freeway and came to the first stoplight in Seattle's suburbs.

Once off the bus and inside the Greyhound depot on the corner of Eighth and Stewart, Jerry watched the brunette leave arm-in-arm with a handsome black man who was even taller than Jerry and much better dressed. Jerry had never seen anything like either one of them.

Jerry shouldered his duffel and stepped, for the first time, into big-city bustle, taking his first lungfuls of fresh ocean air. Revitalized, he began to walk, going with the flow of foot traffic, but still tending down-slope and westward, determined to persist until he reached sea level.

His path through the city was aimless and convoluted, finally more like that of a weasel. Wherever he turned there was something interesting. There was more activity in each city block than he had ever seen in all of Kilgore and the human diversity wherever he looked made the good citizens of Kilgore seem like members of the same family. When he caught a distant glimpse of ocean blue between the buildings he was drawn toward it immediately.

At the waterfront, he leaned against the boardwalk railing and stared across Puget Sound, soaking in the vista of open water. The expanse of the Sound was different from the expanse of Idaho and even different from the expanse of Yellowstone Lake, the largest body of water he had previously seen. There was energy in the salt water, and variety. It was both calming and busy. Ferries and tour boats roiled the waterfront, while the clouded Olympic Mountains provided a serene backdrop.

He loved it and he did not want to get far away from it ever again.

- - -

He asked several tourists for directions to the YMCA, before finally learning what he needed from a heavily tattooed coffee vendor. Jerry rented a room at the Fourth Avenue YMCA, left his duffel there, and returned to walk the streets, excited by the big city and too wired to do anything else. Prompted by a growling stomach, he stood in line for a Big Mac and returned to wandering the streets, munching his burger as he walked, moving without direction or purpose, exploring whatever interested him, sidetracked by wondrous things in shop windows. He consumed another Big Mac. (There was no McDonald's in Kilgore.) He watched the people, especially the abundance of Beautiful Young Women (another Kilgore rarity).

In a state of exhausted euphoria, the whole world seemed new. Unlike the dry brown world of eastern Idaho in the fall, Seattle was clean and green and wet from recent rains. Sunbeams panned over the city, directed by fast-moving clouds. They spotlighted one amazing vista after another.

While Jerry goggled at the sights like the rube he was, he didn't notice the clouds edging closer together, pinching out the sunbeams, and forming a solid overcast. The wind picked up, bringing with it a fishy, saltwater smell. The temperature began to drop and made him regret lightening his load by leaving his winter coat back in Kilgore.

The city transformed rapidly. Amid a cold breeze and scattered raindrops, pedestrians scurried for cover. People who had nowhere else to go, sought shelter in abandoned buildings, overhanging entryways, and under freeway overpasses. Some hunkered behind dumpsters, propping the lids for makeshift roofs, or covered themselves with cardboard or garbage bags, anything to keep out the damp wind.

Jerry was soon wet and chilled, but he continued to walk. He'd left his windbreaker in his duffel back at the Y, but that was now far away and wouldn't be enough even if he wasn't wet. He was shaking from the cold when he turned into an Army/Navy surplus store just uphill from the waterfront. He grabbed the warmest-looking thing on the racks, a full-length, arctic-weight, Army-green field jacket with rabbit fur trim around the hood. Standing in front of the three-panel mirror, not yet warm and still shuddering, he struggled to zip and snap himself into it. When he pulled the rabbit-fur-lined hood over his head, he hardly recognized the bloodshot, red-rimmed eyes looking back at him. He had a strange new look of manic uncertainty about him, like a tousled druggie, or a cold-blooded flasher.

Despite his seedy appearance, he didn't want to take it off. He pulled the damp roll of bills out of his front pocket and made a show of peeling off the necessary cash for the clerk who had obviously been doubting Jerry's likelihood as a serious customer. While he enjoyed the clerk's surprise, he tried not to show his alarm at how much the peeling had shrunk his bankroll.

What had he gotten himself into?

What would he do tomorrow?

When would the money run out?

When he didn't have enough for the Y, would he be homeless?

- - -

Street Life

A Fool and his Money

Hunched into the comfortable warmth of his new coat, he left the Army/Navy surplus store and returned to walking the street. The weather had worsened. The overcast was solid. Trash and leaves blew up off the streets. He knew the general direction to the Y, but not which streets to travel. He took a bearing on a building he recognized and began walking toward it in the same way he'd used distant landmarks to hike the hill country west of the Tetons. While this technique maintained the right direction, it took him down streets a wiser man would avoid. People in dark clothing squatted in entryways, huddled against the wind. Jerry shoved his hands into his coat pockets and glared straight ahead from under the rabbit fur hood, avoiding eye contact, trying to look large, worldly, and prone to violence.

Despite his efforts, he was approached by a skinny girl who looked about fourteen. "Sir, could I use your phone?" She wore a dirty pink tank top thin enough for Jerry to see she was feeling the cold. Greasy black Levis rode her jutting hipbones. "I got caught in the rain. I need to call my mom so she can come get me."

One side of her head was shaved, making it easier, Jerry supposed, to appreciate the array of silver rings piercing every available space around the curve of her ear. Her remaining hair was dyed black and combed straight over to cover her opposite ear. She carried her head tipped toward the side with the hair, perhaps to balance the heavy load of metal. She looked malnourished and, with her head thus cocked, a little demented.

"I'm sorry, I don't own a phone." Jerry was ready to help, but anxious about the situation. Something didn't seem right. The people in dark clothing were watching him.

"OK," she said. "How about a couple of bucks for some food?"

"Well, sure. I could do that." She looked in dire need of a warm meal, so Jerry pulled out his now tiny roll of bills.

The girl saw the money and gave him a quizzical look. She jerked her chin towards him in a puzzling gesture that set her silver swinging.

The effect was an uncomfortable mix of defiance, contempt, and maybe reluctant admiration. "You're a kind-hearted bastard, aren't you?" she asked, pegging him on her first try, her hard, young eyes daring him to deny it.

Jerry didn't know what to say; he'd never seen anyone like her. He peeled off two ones and held them out to her. Before he could wonder where two bucks would buy a warm meal, she accepted them and snatched the bankroll from his other hand. She was twenty yards up the street before Jerry could overcome his surprise.

"Rape!" she yelled, pointing back at Jerry. "He tried to rape me."

The people in dark clothing stood up, their eyes focused on Jerry, threatening, awaiting his next move.

He was stopped cold. The young girl disappeared around a corner with the last of Jerry's fortune.

If he chased her, they would stop him. The situation was hopeless. He carefully turned the opposite way she'd gone and continued his walk.

- - -

He was far, far away from the familiar cocoon of Kilgore, a gullible blockhead alone on a dark and windy street, hunkered down inside his hooded mega-coat, and now penniless.

The wind died down and a soaking rain began to fall in earnest, flooding the gutters and rushing, hell-bent, for lower ground. The heavy drops splashed up a dense layer a few feet above the street, robbing Seattle of detail.

He'd heard about the rain. He had no excuse. It was just more proof he was foolishly ill-prepared.

Jerry stepped into the vacant entryway of a closed upholstery shop to wait out the downpour, but it smelled of urine. He'd rather brave the rain. He sloshed on down the street, his stride laden by worries of empty pockets and by the growing burden of his now-heavy, non-waterproof coat.

He conducted a desperate review of recent events, looking for something he might have done right since leaving Kilgore. All he could come up with was that he'd paid in advance for one night's stay at the Y.

- - -

The next morning, Jerry's pulled on his new coat, still damp and now misshapen from having hung all night on a coat hook. He shouldered his duffel and left the Y, bumping through the morning crowd, scanning the storefronts for Help Wanted signs or for anything that might be interpreted as guidance from the weasel.

Things were tight everywhere. Every job possibility had prerequisites, if he could drive a forklift, or had a car, or had his own tools, or had any previous experience as a cook, carpenter, welder, salesman, etc. No one seemed to need a former part-time assistant librarian and/or handyman.

As evening approached, Jerry began looking for a place to lie down; the duffel was heavy. He was struggling through a variety of uncomfortable positions on a too-short park bench in the Pioneer district, when a wild-looking drunk with a large purple nose showed up to insist the bench belonged to him. There was a brief, ugly squabble, but Jerry had the advantage because he was soberer, taller, younger, and already established on the bench. In a final bid for 'his' bench, the drunk unzipped and pissed on one leg of it, as if to mark it as his own. Despite the awkward situation and the uncomfortable nature of the bench, Jerry was too tired to give it up to look for a better place. Having played his ace, the drunk lost focus on their conflict and passed out in the dirt under a nearby rhododendron, where he spent the night.

In the morning, stiff from a long, cold night on a short, hard bench with nothing more than a damp coat for a blanket, and with his arms around his duffel (out of fear the drunk would wake up and steal it), Jerry gathered himself to resume walking, driven now more by hunger than anything resembling optimism. Around lunchtime, he saw a chubby little girl abandon a half-eaten burrito outside a taco stand. After looking all around for potential witnesses, and remembering how upset his Grandma got by wasted food, he snatched the burrito and scurried away.

- - -

Jerry slipped into an anxious life of competition for food and shelter with those already living on the street. Since he preferred walking to standing or sitting, he spent most of each day on the move. He ranged the streets of Seattle, experimenting with various ways to carry a duffel. He savored the occasional glimpse of salt water at the far end of a busy street or the breath-taking appearance between clouds of the Olympic Mountains across Puget Sound, but there were few Help Wanted signs.

Whenever he became less hopeful in his job search, Jerry turned his thoughts to the one bright prospect on the horizon of his thinking, his novel. He contemplated life on another planet as his long legs covered the miles on this one. When he grew tired in the afternoons, he'd find a quiet place to transcribe his thoughts into the notepads he carried in his duffel. Rather than dwell on the inaccessible warmth and wealth all around him, or on the sordid realities of his life on the street, Jerry escaped to the planet Mowdabb, focusing instead on his storyline and the realities crashing down on Lurk.

From the notebooks:

Shelter

There is no time to react. All Lurk can do is slow their plunge and avoid anything made of stone.

They land flat on the moss, like a Frisbee on a lawn. A solid, teeth-jarring WHUMPH leaves them sunk to the windows between two, large pyramids.

Lurk checks his passengers. The manager appears to be unconscious. She's bumped her head against the door jam, but the skin is not broken over the small blue knot on her forehead. The twins clutch one another, their startled-doe expressions intact.

Lurk tries the door, but it is wedged shut by the impact and by the wall of moss pressing against the side windows. He raises one big boot and kicks out the front windshield.

Once outside, he clambers around the fuselage and raises the engine cowling, looking for leaks that might catch fire. Everything is dry, but the hovercraft is damaged beyond repair. The entire airframe has been warped by their crash, the aluminum skin wrinkled by the impact, making the wreckage appear to be melting in Mowdabb's heat.

Lurk crawls back inside and reaches into the backseat to unbuckle the twins. He helps them into the front seat and then boosts their firm little butts out the front window. With the twins helping from the outside, Lurk lifts out the still-unconscious manager. By the time they have her outside and laid out on the damp, dense moss, she begins to come around.

"Woo," she says.

"Yes," Lurk says, "that was a woo."

The twins nurse the manager, pressing damp moss on her forehead. When they have her sitting up, she becomes her normal, nasty self.

"Now what, Tarzan?" she says, packing the words with disgust.

"Under the circumstances, Jane, I think you should call me Lurk."

"Under the circumstances," she comes right back at him, "I think I'll sue your incompetent ass for every dime you or your simian ancestors have ever made."

He smiles down on her; he is beginning to like this woman. She shows remarkable spunk, a quality that, experience has shown him, is necessary in a woman if she has any hope of lasting long in his company. Also, since he doesn't have much money, or now any flying service, and since they are a long way, in time and space, from any lawyers, her threat is empty.

"You ladies rest up here," he tells them. "I'll scout around."

"Yeah, right, Tonto," Jane snarls, "find us a goddamn taxi."

Lurk heads for the nearest pyramid, sinking to his thighs in the stiff, dense moss. It is like walking in damp green Styrofoam chips.

When he reaches the pyramid, he pulls himself up onto the first layer of rain-worn, chocolate brown stone. Each successive layer is shorter, like a domed layer-cake. The smooth upper surface is clear of moss, but every vertical surface is deeply carved, which provides hand and toe-holds to aid in climbing from one layer to the next. From the top, he can see similar pyramids and smaller square structures scattered about, some with cave-like openings.

Thinking a cave might offer shelter, Lurk orients himself to one of the closer openings before starting back to the women. Once off the pyramid, he finds it easiest to step in the same holes he made in the moss on his way there. He hurries because darkness is not far off, and on Mowdabb, the nights are dark, cloaked by dense, settling fogs.

Lurk leads the women toward the nearest cave opening, forging a trail through the moss. The going is slow. They follow in Lurk's footsteps, comical in their efforts to match his big strides. A warm fog begins to fall like a heavy velvet curtain, impenetrable, almost a drizzle. After ten, wet minutes, they arrive at the cave, where their safari stalls. The women, drenched now anyway, wait outside in the fog to let Lurk explore inside.

Entering the Cave

The stone bracketing the low, dark cave opening is worn by time and the constant rains, resembling a rounded mouth in the stonework. Despite its ominous look, and because nothing appears to have disturbed the surrounding moss, Lurk ducks inside. He remains crouched near the opening, stooped because he cannot see the ceiling or anything else. He listens for sounds as his eyes adjust. The cave is silent and emits the same dank odor of rampant chlorophyll that pervades the whole planet. In time, he can make out a barren, rectangular stone room with a ceiling too low for him to stand upright.

The interior walls are stacked with what he first thinks are stones, but on closer examination discovers to be something else, dark brown organic shapes like thick axe heads, but with a hard, ridged texture. Someone, or something, had collected them and neatly stacked them up the walls with orderly precision.

The cave is mysterious, but benign, shelter for the night. Lurk moves back to the opening and motions the women in, out of the increasing drizzle.

Jane does not hesitate to follow, but the twins need to have Jane coax them inside. The three women, soaked and shivering, huddle in one corner of the room for warmth and a sense of security. They soon fall asleep, entangled like a litter of worn-out puppies.

Lurk sits in the opposite corner. It is late and the ordeal of the day has left him exhausted, but he fights sleep, standing guard against the unknown.

He wonders about the objects on the shelves. Could they be tools? Weapons? Seeds? Eggs? But, the cave is so peaceful, he slips into a sound sleep.

Faint Hope

In what seems like only a moment, he is awake. The first hint of light spreads inward from the cave opening. Lurk feels refreshed despite the shortness of the Mowdabbian night and the vivid memories of incredible erotic dreams involving a surreal amalgam of high-tension halter-tops and nursing puppies.

Lurk crawls out into the morning light, careful not to wake the women. The night's fog is gone and everything glistens with billions of drops of water. He explores the immediate area, struggling through the dripping cushions of moss, lifting his feet high with each step. It takes almost twenty minutes, but he makes it to the top of the largest pyramid in the neighborhood, double the height of the one he climbed after the crash. He is not pleased with the view. As far as he can see through the damp atmosphere, at every point of the compass, it is the same, hummocks of green moss that softens every rocky edge, homogenizing the landscape.

It would take them a month to walk to the edge of what he can see, and years to cover the distance they flew from the airfield.

Even more sobering, Lurk doesn't know which way to go. The radio compass was lost in the crash.

There is little hope of rescue. Lurk's last competitor left the planet a few weeks earlier, leaving him a transportation monopoly, but also leaving the planet with no rescue vehicle. The only hovercraft on the planet is now junk, doomed to be overgrown by moss.

It would be at least three months before anyone with the necessary search equipment would be back on Mowdabb to look for them, by then it would likely be assumed they must already be dead.

And, they might be. If they were going to survive long enough to enjoy that faint hope of rescue, they would have to discover how to do it quickly, before they starved, and within a few kilometers of where he now stood.

Lurk feared they would be consumed by moss long before then.

- - -

FINDING THE BUDDHA

Being Invisible

Jerry lived day-to-day, place-to-place, and meal-to-meal in Seattle, lonesome despite the crowded streets. He began to yearn for human contact. He stayed as presentable as possible in his reduced circumstance, but many citizens would not meet his eye. He was becoming invisible.

"Hi. Beautiful day."

No reaction.

"Good-looking dog you have there."

No response, but at least the dogs saw him.

Conversations with street-people, the non-citizens, were problematic. The majority existed inside a private, hostile world requiring Jerry to relate to their desperation or their dementia. A few were menacing, but most of them were harmless. One sad fellow adopted Jerry as his new best friend and followed him for days, talking a steady stream of gibberish. Jerry missed the easy, idle conversations of Kilgore, even though at the time he'd considered them too boring to justify the oxygen they consumed.

Jerry almost gave up talking. He went for days without saying a word, feeling ever more invisible. Then, on the sort of day that made him abandon his usual Seattle ramble, with a faint drizzle blowing sideways on a steady breeze, he found conversation. He was looking for shelter from the damp wind under the elevated spans of Interstate 5 where it wound along the hillsides near downtown. He walked from one likely spot to the next, hoping to find an unoccupied place in the dry dust where he might be alone to transcribe his Mowdabb musings. He came upon a young man sitting cross-legged, in what might have been a semi-lotus position, using a worn-out tire as a meditation cushion. This erstwhile Buddha, positioned between two massive concrete columns supporting the north and southbound lanes of the overhead freeway, was briefly highlighted by a sunbreak. He was reading a paperback held low on his folded legs. He wore thick, wire-rimmed glasses and a yellow raincoat that might have been a saffron robe. His skin was pale and smooth over a round, peaceful face. His hair was a uniform half-inch stubble all over his head, including the sparse patch on his chin. He read with serene, downcast eyes, his mouth open, lost in the story in his hands, and oblivious to the constant thrum and slap of tires overhead. Before the sun break faded, the otherwise motionless Buddha turned a page with practiced ease.

Jerry might have respected the Buddha's serenity and paused only long enough to appreciate this strange apparition, except that the young man was reading one in the series of *Riverworld* novels by Philip Jose Farmer, a Science Fiction classic by one of Jerry's favorite authors. He'd read them all. Jerry was compelled to speak. He cleared his throat, so as not to startle the Buddha, indicated the book, and said, "One of the greatest premises in all of Science Fiction."

The Buddha looked up through dusty, thick lenses, watching Jerry lower his duffel and take a seat on a nearby, empty Washington apple crate. The Buddha did not go back to his reading, or react in any way for a long interval of perfect, neutral intensity.

When at last he spoke, he said, "Short on science."

Matching the young man's reflective approach to conversation, Jerry took his time to reply. "Yes," he said. "But the author's intent is to imagine impossible conversations. The science is secondary."

Philip Jose Farmer's *Riverworld* was a place where everyone who has ever lived wakes up simultaneously on the shores of an immense river circling a planet. This fanciful construction allowed Farmer to use characters from different periods of history or even fictional characters from the work of other authors, engaging them in philosophical conflict. The *Riverworld* novels *were* short on science, but they did provide a setting for some interesting conversations.

After further contemplation, the Buddha asked, "What's your favorite?"

The question was clearly a test, a challenge to Jerry's knowledge of the book, so he thought about his answer. "Conversation? I'd say Sir Richard Francis Burton and Hermann Göring."

The Buddha nodded slightly, inscrutably, still focusing his thick, dirty lenses on Jerry.

"Have you read *Venus on the Half-Shell*?" the Buddha asked, supplying the next test question.

This was perhaps Farmer's most outrageous use of another author's character. *Venus on the Half-Shell* was published as having been written by Kilgore Trout, a *fictional* Science Fiction writer created by Kurt Vonnegut and a frequent character in Vonnegut's novels. Farmer wrote *Venus on the Half-Shell* in such a perfect imitation of the Vonnegut style that most people thought Vonnegut had written it, despite his vigorous denials. Vonnegut originally authorized Farmer's use of his fictional writer character, but later became annoyed with the situation. He expressed concern that confusion over the book could hurt his literary reputation, prompting Farmer to retort that the book could hardly do more damage to his reputation than several of Vonnegut's own books had done.

"Farmer had me fooled for a while," Jerry admitted, "but the book was just too outrageous, even for Vonnegut."

The Buddha nodded his appreciation of Jerry's admission of having been fooled, and then took another long, inscrutable moment to ask, "What's your favorite Vonnegut?"

"That's a tough one," Jerry said. "I like them all for different reasons. *Hocus Pocus* is my favorite of the newer ones, but none compare to *Slaughterhouse 5*."

The Buddha nodded again, already in apparent contemplation of his next question. And so, the conversation continued.

They talked for hours on that first day, and often thereafter. The testing nature of their dialog abated, evolving into wider-ranging conversations (though always somehow related to Science Fiction). The Buddha's knowledge of Sci-Fi was encyclopedic, even greater than Jerry's, and he always carried an evolving collection of the genre with him. Jerry had never before found anyone who shared his love of Science Fiction, so he looked for the Buddha's yellow raincoat wherever he wandered. They were not exactly friends, but always stopped to talk when they met. They joked they were the only two members of the SSSFFC, the Seattle Streets Science Fiction Fan Club.

If anyone else came within earshot of their conversations, the Buddha became quiet and inscrutable, responding to Jerry's prompts with a shrug, his signature contribution to any topic outside of Science Fiction. Jerry wondered if the Buddha was trapped in his own peculiar sort of torpor, akin to Jerry's condition in Kilgore.

When Jerry ask the Buddha his real name, the answer came so softly Jerry asked him to repeat it. The Buddha leaned forward slightly, as if to avoid having to say it much louder. "Leif," he said, as if it was a password.

The Wildly Romantic Weekend

The duffel Jerry carried everywhere was boldly stenciled with his dead uncle's name and rank. So, when he showed up out of the darkness around the glow of a tiny cook fire, those in attendance saw his trademark duffel slung over a shoulder and assumed he was a recently discharged PFC named Harold Gustafson. When they called him Harold, or PFC, and shared a bite of whatever was cooking, Jerry could see no advantage to correcting them. He was not proud of this inadvertent deception, but he did nothing to dissuade them. Survival skills come in all forms.

The war stories he heard around those cook fires were always a strange mix of grief and fond memories. Jerry was especially fascinated by them because of his Uncle's refusal to talk about his time in Korea and because it was reputed that Jerry's father had been a soldier in the Army in Vietnam.

The notion that Jerry's father had been a soldier was a small part of the romantic tragedy his Grandma wove for Jerry after his mother died. But, since his Grandma lived in a perpetual religious haze and often had a tenuous grip on everyday events, Jerry doubted every bit of it.

Jerry knew nothing for certain about his father.

Grandma's sketchy, romantic story of Jerry's father was as follows:

Jerry's mother met his father at an Army Special Services dance and they fell in love at once. He was a young soldier enjoying a last weekend in San Francisco before shipping off to war in Vietnam. They were together every moment for two glorious days and one fateful night following a music concert. After their wildly romantic weekend, after promises to write, and after a tearful departure, they went their separate ways, him to overseas deployment and her back to Kilgore. Since he was never heard from again, and their love had been true, Jerry's father must have been killed soon after he arrived in Vietnam.

It would have been difficult for his already-scandalous, concert-hitchhiking, Deadhead mother to raise an illegitimate child in a small town like Kilgore. Her ultraconservative mother would have wanted to spin the story to make the already eccentric Gustafson clan look more respectable. She would likely have embroidered her daughter's romantic fling (or carnal interlude) to make it more palatable in the telling. So, any 'facts' about Jerry's father that came through Grandma's filter could not be trusted.

Jerry's suspicion about the "wildly romantic weekend" was more prosaic: His young mother may have been as gullible and foolish in a big city as Jerry had proven himself to be. His father was likely to have woven any sort of tale to get in his mother's pants. Jerry had heard stories about the drugs at Grateful Dead concerts, so he believed his conception was probably a single stoned quickie, an anonymous bump in the night.

Jerry had given up trying to learn more about his father. He only hoped his mother had at least one wildly romantic weekend before she died, but he would never know.

Humble History

After Uncle Harold's death cut the last tenuous cord tethering Jerry in Kilgore's backwater and Destiny shoved his dingy into the mainstream, he drifted the streets of Seattle without direction or purpose, rudderless, no horsepower and no sail, behaving like a single-celled organism drifting with the tide, blindly flailing his flagella.

He did not yet realize he was an *incomplete* creature; he thought he was merely alone.

While still working in the library, Jerry had read and reread *The Last of the Mohicans* by James Fenimore Cooper, hoping to find something in that sad ending to guide him into the future. All that translated into his life was a vague reinforcement of his nascent romantic inclinations to seek adventure and to do the right thing.

Jerry was not bitter about his humble history; the fact he was an orphaned, bastard child and the last of the Gustafsons of Kilgore was not his doing. He was not to blame for his father's irresponsible impregnation of his mother or her lack of a wedding ring. He could not have prevented his mother's collision with the harrow, his Grandma's murder-by-television, or his uncle's meditation with a shotgun. His blamelessness comforted him. It made him philosophical about his lot in the world and determined to work with the hand he'd been dealt.

On the street, Jerry held tight to his cowboy ethos of quiet self-reliance as best he could. He avoided the shelters and soup kitchens. He never once asked citizens for spare change. Instead, he lived on the wasteful excesses all around him, and on the occasional kindness of others.

Romantically, Jerry was no worse off in Seattle. His only romantic involvement in Kilgore had been a casual, short-lived, on-again-off-again affair that ended when Karen said good-bye (to him and to her other boyfriends) and joined the Air Force. When she was gone, he realized the insignificance of their relationship and how unlikely Kilgore was to offer a better one.

On the plus side of Jerry's life, his novel flourished while he was on the street. He had lots of time. When his supply of steno pads became full, he wrote on whatever he could find, a partially used, wire-bound notebook gleaned from an office tower dumpster, a lost diary found in the weeds and containing only a few pages of wisdom from a girl named Becky who was uneasy about starting the fourth grade. These and more he filled with successive pages of Lurk's plight on Mowdabb, adding them to his increasingly overstuffed duffel.

The pages from this time of Jerry's life, reflect the concerns he shared with Lurk's clan regarding issues of food and shelter.

Scavenger Hunt

Jane is not happy.

"Three months!" She says it like it is forever (which it might as well be) and like it is all Lurk's fault, which, of course, it is. "Three months HERE!" she says, extending her arms to indicate the relative nothingness that surrounds them.

"That's not the worst of it." Lurk says.

The women look at him with horror, perhaps trying to imagine what could be worse than being stranded with Lurk for three months. "Well, what? What's the worst of it?" Jane yells at him.

"We've nothing to eat," Lurk says. "And nothing is known to be edible on Mowdabb. There is a lot of organic material around here, obviously, but it hasn't been tested. The bottom line is: We eat what's here or we starve."

The twins start to cry. "I knew this commercial was a stupid idea," one of them says through her tears.

"Ahh, pull yourselves together," Jane snaps at them. She turns back to Lurk. "Well, what do we have to do? Let's get started."

Lurk is impressed by her pluck.

"OK... It's going to take a lot of time and luck." Lurk's tone says they won't like what he tells them. "If we are lucky, we will only get very, very hungry, but there's a good chance we could get very, very sick, or worse."

"Just lay it on the line, Tarzan. What are we facing here?"

"Lurk," he says.

"What?"

"My name is Lurk."

"Your name is Lurk?" She seems to find this difficult to comprehend and pauses for one quick shake of her head, as if to jiggle this oddity into place before she can continue. "Whatever. OK, 'Lurk,' tell us what we need to do."

Lurk is pleased. She is looking to him for leadership and, quite obviously, she is softening, falling under the spell of his many charms.

"OK, Jane. First we do a survey of what looks like it might be edible."

"Wait," Jane says, "my name is not Jane. Stop calling me that."

Lurk does not respond. He just stares at her, one eyebrow raised, and waits.

"OK," Jane says, "I started it. I'm sorry I called you Tarzan."

"Very well, apology accepted. What *is* your name?" Lurk asks.

"It's Eve," she says.

Lurk re-raises his eyebrow at her, figuring she's being somehow sarcastic, or is setting up some elaborate joke to play on him, something he won't be able to follow.

"Evelyn actually," she admits, "but everyone calls me Eve."

At the end of a half-hour scavenge for potential foodstuffs in the immediate area of the cave, Lurk's clan reconvenes to dump their resultant collections on the stone entryway of their shelter. The pile is both meager and unsavory. Only the crisp little spheres that look like a cross between gooseberries and gelatin capsules have the appearance of being edible. There are a few other things, analogous to the 'gooseberries,' but with slightly different shapes. All of them were found dangling inconspicuously from the underside of various types of moss. There are a few fibrous components in the pile, leaves and roots no one can imagine chewing. The gooseberry juice feels slightly oily and does no immediate harm to the skin. Overall, nothing looks like it could keep them alive very long.

Lurk holds up one of the moss fruits that is a little different, a shiny, dangling, cone-like thing about an inch long. One of the twins holds a pair of them up near her twin's ears. "Earrings!"

Lurk thinks they look beautiful.

The most unusual find is a fuzzy, brown pod, like a small, flattened coconut, brought in by one of the twins who stumbled over it while struggling through the deep mulch under the moss. The shape reminds Lurk of something, but he cannot place what it is. It seems unlikely they can eat it, though, since it is hard as a rock.

Lurk found two things during his foray for edibles he did not bring back. One was a tiny green mound of protoplasm that might have been a drop of mint jelly except that it recoiled when he touched it. The other was similar, but more slug-like (in that it was bilaterally symmetrical and had a likely head and tail). It was about an inch long, gray-green, and looked utterly unpalatable. He would wait until they were desperate to mention them.

They decide the first thing to be tested is the gooseberry. They draw moss stems to see who goes first. Eve loses.

"Put a drop of the oil on your tongue," Lurk suggests, "wait a few hours, then try a little larger dose."

Eve has her own method: She pops a whole gooseberry in her mouth, crunches it up, and swallows. The twins adopt their startled doe expressions as if expecting to see her begin flopping on the ground.

"If we're going to have to live on this stuff," Eve says, "we're going to have to consume a lot of it and I don't plan to starve to death waiting on the results of a taste test."

She smacks her mouth a few times, executes a crooked little shrug. "Tastes like olive oil with maybe a hint of dandelion." She turns to one of the twins, "Look, love, my hair is driving me nuts in this heat. Do you have something you could use to give me a haircut?"

The twins welcome the distraction and begin to rummage in their personal effects. All they can find to use is a tiny pair of cuticle scissors.

"If we're going to have to live like this for three months," Eve says, shaking her hair loose and turning her back on the twin holding the scissors, "you'd better make it short."

An hour later, Eve's heavy brunette locks lay in a heap. "Oh, that feels wonderful!" she says, running her hands over the inch-long stubble on her head. Lurk thinks she looks like a prisoner of war, but has enough sense not to say so. Eve turns to face him. "Well, Lurk, I didn't die. Shall we try some more gooseberries?"

They all eat gooseberries and nothing else for two days. There are no ill effects apart from mild diarrhea and a strong craving for something more substantial. In that time, the twins give each other identical POW haircuts.

After the second day, Lurk takes a small bite of one of the 'earrings.' As soon as the juice of it hits his tongue, he spits it out immediately.

"Spicy!"

It has the papery crunch, texture, and fire of a mild Jalapeno. Aside from a mild burning sensation that soon fades, there is nothing else to stop him from trying another. This time he chews it up and swallows.

"Spicy celery."

While they wait to see if Lurk will begin flopping on the ground, one twin volunteers to give him a haircut.

While his hair is already quite short, he appreciates the attention and accepts the offer.

There are no ill effects from eating the spicy 'earrings' either, so, for the next two days, Lurk and the women eat gooseberries and earrings. Complaints of mild diarrhea continue.

Further explorations for edibles result in the discovery of a translucent, pale-green globe about the size of a cherry that they call marbles. They have a melon-flavored juice and a delightful euphoric kick. Lurk and Eve each require about five marbles to feel the full effect. The twins begin to get silly after three.

Lurk salvages what he can from the wreck. There isn't much; a first-aid kit, the seat cushions, a few pieces of metal that might prove useful, seatbelt straps, some pieces of glass from the instrument housings, and other odds and ends, including Eve's camera equipment.

Their hunger is soon unrelenting. They begin to lose some weight and strength. Lurk begins to dream of meat. Fortunately, before Lurk and his clan become too weakened by their limited diet, another option presents itself.

Popnuts®

Lurk is awakened by a muffled 'pop' in the middle of the night, followed immediately by Eve's scream. She comes rolling across the cave floor into Lurk's corner. The twins scramble to join Eve. It is the first time the women have been in his half of the cave and Lurk is pleased, even under the extraordinary circumstances.

What happened? he asks.

"I don't know," Eve says, with obvious anxiety. "Something hit me in the stomach while I was asleep."

While the three women huddle in Lurk's corner, he crawls across the floor to where Eve had been sleeping. There is so little light he is almost on it before he sees it. It is motionless, about the size of a softball, and lighter colored than the dark stone floor. Lurk pokes it with one finger. It wobbles a few inches across the smooth floor and stops. He pokes it a few more times with the same result.

Lurk leaves it and crawls back to his corner.

"What is it?" Eve asks.

"I can't tell. It feels like a giant piece of popcorn."

"Then how the hell did it hit me in the stomach?"

"I don't know, but I don't think it's alive."

"Oh my God!" Eve says. "It's that damn nut/pod thing the twins dug up; I'd been rubbing the fuzz off it and still had it in my hand when I went to sleep."

The next morning, Eve volunteers to taste the puffy heart of the popped nut. She likes the oatmeal flavor and shows no ill effects. So, in the afternoon, she tears the white-textured 'meat' away from the remains of the hard shell and eats the whole thing. She chews it with great satisfaction. As nightfall approaches, there have been no ill effects from the meal and she announces it has cured her long-standing diarrhea. They begin searching for nuts.

While everyone else is digging in the deep compost under the moss where the twins found the first nut, Lurk is distracted, haunted by the notion he is missing something. When his hand closes on the hard, round shape of a nut deep in the soft, damp litter, he knows what it is: He has seen the shape before, on the shelves of their cave! They aren't fuzzy like the one in his hand, but they are the same otherwise. If the smooth ones packed on the cave walls will pop like Earth popcorn, and expose its edible center, they are living in a food storehouse!

Lurk smashed one with a rock and dismissed the shattered mess. It took Eve's warm belly to discover the right way to open a Mowdabb nut: Warm it above 96 degrees for about four hours to crack it open,

That night, they all sleep with one clutched against their bellies, accepting the rude awakening as a small price for their first satisfying food since the crash. Everyone stuffs themselves with the dense heart of Popnuts®.

It was not until later they learn how to pop the nuts by focusing the heat of the sun.

(In later years, off planet, Popnuts® [*also called Mowdabb nuts*] will command astronomical prices for they can be made to grow nowhere else in the known universe and because they are an essential ingredient of the Mowdabb Diet®.)

- - -

PLANET-RISE

Hope

Only after he'd been sufficiently bumpered, flippered, and tilted in the pinball game of Seattle's streets, was Jerry ready to collect his bonus round. Street-life restructured his preconceptions and prejudices. He'd seen the variety in the human species and learned to tolerate it. Having become more introspective, more careful, and skeptical, and thus less vulnerable to the myriad street cons.

He'd previously looked down on those who were grossly self-indulgent, particularly those who ate more than was good for them and, as a result, commanded more than their fair share of the world's dwindling spaces (as in the case of space allotted for one bus passenger.) He'd previously felt superior to those who couldn't express a complete thought without saying "like" or "you know," or those who watched TV all day instead of reading anything more enlightening than the ads for Wal-Mart. While he still believed that too many people were self-involved and criminally negligent of the world's written treasures, he had almost lost his need to feel superior.

A necessary edge had been honed onto his personality. Without it, Jerry wouldn't have been prepared for the next, extraordinary phase of his life. The prickly element of his nature remained intact, though now reserved for self-preservation rather than for self-entertainment, as it had been when tail-plucking self-important ducks in Kilgore's little puddle or teasing Grandma about her conservative, church-lady ways.

Essentially, the rube had been shaken out of him.

Jerry honed his weasel-following skills on the street too, though the effort was unconscious. Often while his mind was traveling to Mowdabb, his body would be walking on its own, as if for the sake of walking. Through all of it, he listened to hope's relentless tunes.

Hope... the thing with feathers—

That perches in the soul—

And sings the tunes without the words—

And never stops—at all—.

Emily Dickinson - Hope - The Complete Poems, no. 254

He had no reason to believe he would ever find a job or an end to his wandering, but he remained blindly hopeful. No matter how interminable the cold, wet night, a shiny new hope would invariably spring from the dead ashes of each morning and accelerate his heartbeat. He never doubted his luck would turn when the time was right, when the weasel thought he was ready, when the music of the spheres attained their full harmonic resonance, or some damn thing. He *would* get his plan back on track. He would learn to fly. He would finish his book. And, he would move on to Alaska.

At this point in his life, Jerry had not read any Shakespeare, so did not yet know what the Bard of Avon had to say about that:

The miserable have no other medicine

But only hope.

Claudio, in Measure for Measure, act 3, sc. 1.

Eternal hope was Jerry's daily elixir.

- - -

Cold hopes swarm like worms within our living clay.

Percy Shelly - Adonais, st. 39.

Jerry emerged from his latest nightly nest behind overgrown landscaping at the lower-end of the Pike Place Hill-Climb with cold hopes swarming within his cold, living clay. Stretching out the stiffness, brushing away the rhododendron litter, and shouldering his duffel, he warmed himself with a climb up the cascade of staircases linking the waterfront to the market.

For breakfast, he found a bruised pear in a garbage can behind a row of fruit stands on Pike Street. It was still sweet and juicy. He scrounged an unfinished bag of French fries from a pile of serving trays inside the door of a hamburger shop. He resisted a half-eaten ham and cheese sandwich in a garbage can, waiting for something fresher, like the Whopper with one bite missing he found three trashcans later. For the un-squeamish, food was never a problem. A little more walking found him sipping half a milkshake through a fresh straw.

He moved on with no particular destination, perfectly open to guidance by the weasel. On this morning, the weasel led Jerry uphill toward the Broadway district. The sun had burned through the morning fog by the time he reached the top, where the streets leveled out. Sated by his garbage breakfast, Jerry began people-watching, which he did most mornings.

He would select someone interesting to follow, perhaps a Dharma bum distributing religious cards and soliciting donations, or a tattered fellow on a three-wheel bike, leading a one-man parade, saluting passersby. He might follow someone carrying a musical instrument in hope of hearing a song. Sometimes he would discretely shadow one of the Beautiful Young Women that graced the city, though they usually dipped but briefly into the motley crowd like delicate dragonflies dimpling the surface of a stream. On any morning, he might cross a street in whatever direction offered a green light, or amble only on the sunny side of the street. On crowed sidewalks, or when tall buildings loomed, he might choose a lesser-traveled side street, uphill if he had not climbed it before or downhill if he was tired.

This morning's weaselly route plunged Jerry deep into the diversity of Seattle's Broadway district, the most diverse district in a city known for diversity, a good place to exercise one's tolerance. Even at this early hour, he encountered more exotic examples of the human menagerie than he would in a lifetime in Kilgore, or possibly in all of Idaho. Two saffron-robed Hare Krishnas danced by in a blissful jig, one pounding a goat-skinned drum while the other clinked finger cymbals. A gaggle of tattooed and black-leather-jacketed teenagers moped around a Starbucks, sipping overpriced caffeine and posing. Two gay men outside a hair salon embraced in a full-body hug and passionate goodbye kiss. A purple-haired dominatrix, wearing a blood-red tube top, vinyl skirt, and chain-mail vest, parted the sidewalk flow, leading an older, gray-haired man by a leash. Though likely more accustomed to a business suit, the man endured his public humiliation promenade wearing tight, leather pants with a cup laced in place over his genitals.

Extremes in the human condition no longer shocked the worldly Jerry Garcia Gustafson; they were merely unique zoological adaptations to a niche. He enjoyed them, often following prime examples for blocks; they made him feel perfectly normal.

Striding with great purpose through this menagerie, were the typical business types, briefcased and suited in grays and tans, probably no different from what filled sidewalks in every large city at that hour. The business types peacefully coexisted with those who were indifferent to appearance and those who aggressively displayed their eccentricities.

Also within this pedestrian mix, were bewildered tourists, organized into colorful clusters by nationality or language. They discussed tourist literature, pointed out the sights to one another, and flowed through the sidewalk traffic like colorful schools of fish. They seemed to prefer pinks and blues and were often short-sleeved, having been deceived by the bright morning sun.

A few in the rush hour cavalcade were like Jerry, aimless and meandering, largely invisible, and carrying all they owned.

An Agent of the Weasel

What might have been an agent of the weasel appeared while Jerry waited on the sidewalk for a traffic light, standing within the malodorous pall emanating from the men on either side of him, one a skeletal man wearing black clothes and Alice Cooper makeup, the other an emaciated hobo wearing clothes shiny with dirt. He could distinguish sweat, tobacco, beer, and urine. This made him feel particularly good, like a model of cleanliness beside them. His red flannel shirt and Levis were recently scrubbed. His arctic-weight, Army-green field jacket was intact and as clean as could be managed, though now faded from constant use. It also sported an accumulation of indelible stains and a mangy, fur-trimmed hood. Rather than carry it, he rarely took it off.

In that moment, he became aware of a shrill voice in the distance somewhere behind him. It was yelling "aaaaaaaahhhhhhh." The sound mixed with street noises, echoed off buildings, and died away. Next the yell came from a few feet behind, so loud he flinched.

"AAAAAAAAHHHHHHH"

A skinny, shirtless man with unruly, red curls hurried in Jerry's direction with his arms over his head, not walking on the sidewalk exactly, but only on the curb, teetering side-to-side to keep his balance, like a monkey on a tightrope. People moved aside to give monkey-man plenty of space, as did Jerry.

On a whim, perhaps a nudge by the weasel, Jerry decided to follow monkey-man, curious how he would deal with red lights and crosswalks.

Whenever monkey-man's way was blocked by someone, or by a car door opened onto the sidewalk, or by anything that frustrated his path down the curb, he would load his lungs and yell again,

"AAAAAAAAHHHHHHH," expelling every molecule of his frustration, startling everyone within fifty feet. With the obstruction removed and his face bright red from yelling, monkey-man would continue, or, if necessary, hop around any obstacle that had not moved, and then back to the curb, as if everywhere else was burning coals.

Monkey-man's focus appeared absolute, his purpose urgent, and his intensity deranged, like an amped-up version of the gray- and tan-suited business folk hustling toward their urgent purposes.

At the next red light, Jerry stood close to monkey-man as they waited on the curb for the light to change. The young man rocked impatiently, shifting his weight from one dirty, bare foot to the other, as if walking in place. Jerry could see monkey-man's eyes jittering as if their control were periodically disrupted by an errant electrical discharge. He noticed Jerry watching him. Their eyes met briefly, giving Jerry a glimpse of the fire that burned under all that red hair. An apparent electrical discharge disrupted their connection. Monkey-man returned to watching the light. Jerry wondered how this noisy, tight-roping annoyance had been transformed from a cuddly, red-haired baby. Had his wires been loosened somehow, or were his synapses chemically fried?

When the light changed, monkey-man leapt off the curb as if galvanized by a cattle prod. He landed on the white stripe of the crosswalk, and tight-roped to the other curb. Jerry slowed, letting the red hair and flailing arms get ahead in the crowd. He watched the man manage another intersection and make it the full length of the next block without yelling. Jerry let him go to ground, like a weasel into its burrow. At last sighting, monkey-man was following the curve of the curb around a corner.

Jerry's newfound tolerance allowed him to be at peace with monkey-man's visitation, amused that he would once have been shocked by the spectacle. But, it was still concerning that people in such obvious need for help were left to run loose.

- - -

As so often happened when he wandered, he found himself in an unfamiliar part of Seattle. Momentarily without someone interesting to follow, Jerry reoriented by means of the distant downtown towers and headed that way, deciding as he walked that when his new path intersected familiar territory, he would navigate to the library; he hadn't been there in days.

Jerry loved Seattle's beautiful library. It was warm, dry, quiet, and filled with thousands of books that weren't in the Clark County Library System. He didn't have a home address to get a library card, but he could check his duffel at the entrance, hang his coat on a hook, clean himself up in the restroom, choose a book, and settle into an upholstered reading chair. It was a great luxury. Security never hassled anyone who was reading, so he was left alone, lost in the revelations of the written word until hunger interrupted.

However, on this day, the agent of the weasel had led him to a part of town nowhere near the library. When he first saw something recognizable, he realized he was quite near the Unemployment Office. OK, that was somewhere he hadn't been for quite a while. So, that's where he headed.

- - -

SERENDIPITY

Darren

Old Man Stamper maintained his routine, convinced every part of it was critical to keep him alive. His morning walk to the Unemployment Office gave him a manageable amount of fresh air and exercise. Then, when he'd taxi back to the shop to relieve Marilyn for her noon lunch-hour, he was reminded by those few minutes with her why he still wanted to stay alive. After that, it was up the stairs to his apartment to settle in the recliner among the bird cages for a long daily nap. When hunger woke him, he'd feed himself and the birds and go down the stairs once more to count the till at closing time. He liked to count the till himself. Old habit. But, it also gave him one more brief conversation with Marilyn to end the day.

He'd began to enjoy his mornings at the Unemployment Office too, watching all the young people waiting in line with their eager faces, their youthful energy and hopefulness. It helped him remember times when he'd been like that.

He sat in his lucky chair when he could, the one from which he'd first seen Emma/Marilyn. Sometimes he took a brief, inadvertent nap in the chair, but he tried to save that for the afternoon. He liked that chair also because he could see out the big windows in front to watch the strange people loitering around the bulletin boards, jostling for a view of the jobs on offer. He'd seen all types out there, hustlers, druggies, winos, pimps, and preachers. He was too old to be shocked by anything he saw any more.

Or, so he thought.

Among the people milling about outside, he saw Darren.

The shuddering astonishment of seeing his long-dead son threatened to stop his heart.

- - -

Jerry's claustrophobia had always kept him from going inside the Unemployment Office to wait out the long lines. He'd tried going in once months ago, but the low-ceilinged building was always packed with desperate, grim-faced people waiting under fluorescent lighting that made them look nauseous. Jerry just couldn't take it. Instead, he was limited to the job listings posted on bulletin boards outside the main entrance. He'd only found a few short-term day jobs so far, but they gave him some pocket change. He'd stacked produce for a few hours during a farmer's market. He'd helped to unload big rolls of carpeting from a truck. He'd painted a long white fence. That was a good one; it lasted two days, but he still had some white paint on his coat. He'd washed cars at a dealership and once spent a morning sweeping out an empty warehouse.

It was never easy to find even temporary jobs because of the logistical problems of applying for them. He might not have any way to call the number in time, or have bus fare to get to an address. Something at the limits of his bussing-and-walking range could take a whole day just to get to a job site and back. (He didn't want to get stuck overnight somewhere in suburbia, beyond his familiar nesting sites.)

That illusive "steady" job seemed impossible, but he kept trying, feathered hope perched in his stubborn soul.

Today all that caught his eye was 'Lawn Care – Must provide equipment.' He'd done lawn care for Mrs. Tipton back in Kilgore in exchange for lowered rent, but he had no equipment. 'Roofer – Two-year's experience.' He'd done that just one summer in Kilgore. 'Dish Washer,' no mention of experience. That was a maybe. He didn't recognize the name of the restaurant, so he'd have to look it up in the library's phonebook to see how far it was from downtown. He wrote down the number, shouldered his duffel, and turned away, eager to get out of the crowd and on to the library.

He was already anticipating what he wanted to read there, if it was still on the shelves. He would continue with *Gödel Escher and Bach* by Douglas Hofstadter. It was a wonderful exploration of ideas at the heart of cognitive science and a challenge to read, unlike anything Jerry had tackled before. He was about halfway through it and had learned a lot about the many connections between math, art, and music.

- - -

As soon as Old Man Stamper realized he was going to survive the shock of seeing Darren, he was desperate talk to him. He wanted to say all the things he'd discovered in the intervening years he should have said to his only son. There was a lot. He collected himself on wobbly legs and worked his way through the job-seekers and then out the big front doors, fearful his old mind had found another cruel way to trick him.

- - -

A wrinkled, old man came bursting out of the building, obstructing Jerry's departure. He came to a wobbly stop at the sight of Jerry's face. For a moment, neither of them moved, they simply stared wide-eyed at one another.

"What… where…?" the old man said, needing a full breath for each word. A liquid coughing jag consumed him, wracking his frail body. He began fumbling in his pocket for a handkerchief, while stumbling backward for support against the bulletin board.

- - -

Jerry was torn between concern for the old man and his desire to move on to the library, to *not* get involved.

- - -

Old Man Stamper was in a panic. Too wobbly to walk, too flustered to speak, he could only blink away the tears to study his son's face. He needed to gather enough composure to retrieve his voice. As he struggled to reconstitute, he also tried to recall all the things he'd never found a way to say to Darren, that he loved him, that he wished him only happiness.

But, something wasn't right. Doubt edged into his thinking. The resemblance to Darren was amazing, the same tall, skinny frame, the same green eyes, the same big, narrow nose like his own prow, as someone had once called it. Every feature matched his son, but there was something about the assembly of those features that wasn't right.

He needed a cigarette. Functioning on automatic, Old Man Stamper pulled out his lighter and a fresh cigarette. The smoke cleared his head. Logic returned.

It wasn't Darren. His son was dead. The familiar grief refilled his mind, flowing back dark and thick as old crankcase oil. He *hadn't* been thinking clearly; even if Darren hadn't been killed in Vietnam, he would be much older than this.

So, who was this young man? Sorting through dozens of questions that stormed his mind, Stamper decided which one to ask. He shuffled up close to the young man, took a deep breath, and growled his shrewd question.

"What's your daddy's name?"

- - -

The old man's coughing repulsed Jerry. He'd seen dozens of sickly old-timers like this one, living out their final drunken days on the street. He did his best to avoid them and their sad, bloodshot eyes. The asylum doors were open. Inmates were everywhere. The most tolerable of the mentally unstable kept to themselves, babbling away their days, but some lived on the edge of violence. Now, here was another inmate hanging around the unemployment building, providing yet another obstacle to job-seeking. This one had an unkempt fringe of Mark Twain hair and a lopsided, cigarette-stained moustache wedged under a big, narrow beak of a nose. For a moment, Jerry had been afraid the old guy was going to die right there on the sidewalk.

Pissed at the interruption, he shouldered his duffel and turned to leave. He couldn't think of a question he was less likely to answer than 'What's your daddy's name?'

- - -

"Wait! Don't go," Old Man Stamper yelled. The yelling brought on another coughing jag. He couldn't catch his breath. He dropped his Zippo. It bounced off his shoe and skittered across the cement past the retreating 'Darren.' His cigarette dropped too, sparking against the concrete. He slumped, sliding down the bulletin board wall, his world turning gray.

"Darren," he said, with less than a whisper.

He'd lost his son again.

The gray world turned darker.

"So, this is dying."

- - -

Jerry stopped to pick up the lighter and turned to see the old man in a sitting position against the wall, his chin resting against his chest, looking like any other lost soul sleeping off a morning's excess. Jerry wondered if the old man was alive, so he stepped closer. Hesitantly, he reached out to gently shake the old man's bony shoulder. There was no response. He put two fingers against the old man's jugular. His heart was still pumping.

The crowd that had been watching this street drama went about their business, evidently reassured Jerry must have felt a pulse.

Something about the quirky nature of this happenstance made Jerry retreat to a nearby bench to watch the old man. What was going on here. Was the weasel trying to get his attention? He studied the old Zippo. On one side of it, an emblem was almost worn away; only a bit of red and white enamel remained. Through the scratches on the other side, Jerry could make out a few of the words engraved there, '… Cavalry - Phu Loi.'

Maybe he'd wait to give the old man back his lighter. The library was open late; there was still plenty of time for that.

- - -

Old Man Stamper awoke from his blackout in a daze. Why was he sitting on a crowded sidewalk? Embarrassed, he struggled to his feet, grunting and straining against gravity. He brushed off his pants and straightened himself, trying to regain some dignity. He shook out a cigarette before he remembered dropping his lighter. He was saddened by the loss of it, the only present he could remember getting from his son. Darren had mailed it home from Vietnam along with a garish pink and blue Zircon cocktail ring for his mother.

He didn't notice he was being watched until Jerry stepped up to flick the Zippo under his cigarette. He contained his shock at seeing this tall Darren-like young man standing so close and gratefully accepted the light.

"I never knew my daddy," Jerry said. He handed Old Man Stamper the lighter and turned to leave.

"Wait! I may have… a job for you."

Old Man Stamper fumbled out his wallet and offered Jerry a business card.

"It doesn't… pay much," the old man said, taking deep breaths before every few words, "but it comes… with an apartment."

Wanting to believe this might be real and not just a sick old fart passing out stolen business cards, Jerry studied the card and then the man's face. Gravity had pulled the old stubbled cheeks down to expose colorful eyes. They were a bright, bloodshot green accented by the pink of the lower lids, but the look they gave Jerry was steady and defiant, challenging him to walk away from a job offer.

Both doubt and hope were evident in Jerry's expression.

"Come at noon... tomorrow."

Jerry took the card.

Before he could ask any questions, the old man checked his watch and shuffled away. Jerry watched him hail a taxi and disappear into traffic. He slipped the card into his coat pocket.

A copy shop?

And... why him?

Talking to the birds

"Hello my babies," he greeted the birds. "Come on out here and talk to Old Man Stamper." The finches packed their wicker nest, their shiny black eyes watching the wrinkled giant outside. "Come on out here where it's not so crowded. Look, I have some bread for you."

He'd pulled his chair up close, as he so often did, opening the cage door to tempt them out with a morsel of bread. He leaned his stubbled face in close; his tobacco-stained hands filling the opening.

Though most of the birds remained stuffed into the security of their basket nest at the rear of the cage, or huddled as close as they could to the basket on nearby perches, a few were conditioned to Stamper's frequent conversations and brave enough to begin hopping toward the tempting bread, watching Stamper with one eye and then the other.

"Here's the big news babies: I *think* I saw Darren today. Maybe. Maybe I should say I *thought* I saw Darren today. Maybe I'm losing it faster than I thought."

The bravest of the birds tried a quick peck at the bread before retreating.

"I know, I know. It couldn't have been him. But it sure looked like him, just like he looked on that last day home on leave, except for the long hair and beard of course."

Several birds began taking quick pecks at the bread now, seeing the success of their nest mates and not wanting to be left out. Excited peeps filled the air.

"Yeah, I know, stupid. What am I gonna do, offer him a job? Ha! Well... that's what I did. He might not show up, but..." Old Man Stamper watched the birds jostle for crumbs, his thoughts far away and long ago. "That would be something, putting Darren to work; he never had a job his whole life, just that paper route, and then the Army."

"Crazy," he said at last, tossing the remaining bread on the floor of the cage, and latching the door. "Maybe I should just invite him home, show him how far his old man has fallen."

He leaned back in his chair, lit a cigarette, and sat for a long time, his sad, red eyes watching the perky energy of the finches, his mind a jumble of then and now.

COPY/COPY

Jerry stewed about the card in his coat pocket for most of the night. Why would an old man offer a job to a stranger on the sidewalk? Something wasn't right. It had to be a come-on of some kind. "It comes with an apartment," the old man had said. That was hard to believe. And in a copy shop!? He didn't want to be disappointed, but hope, that thing with feathers, was singing to him all night long. In the morning, he began his breakfast-gathering walk in the general direction of the address on the card.

"Come at noon," the old man had said, but Jerry was lurking on the sidewalk across the street from the copy shop hours before that.

It was an old, two-story, tan-brick building... not very impressive. It appeared half empty, its street-level windows on one side were painted dark. Lights were on behind a collection of posters on the windows of the brighter side, clearly identified as COPY/COPY by a large sign mounted over the awning. A central alcove under the awning sheltered two doors, entrances to the two ground-floor shops. An OPEN sign hung inside the front door of the copy shop, but the dark door on the other side was padlocked. He ventured closer to peer between the posters. A large copy machine took up most of the narrow shop floor. There was someone moving around among the shelves behind the copier, but Jerry couldn't tell if it was the old man.

He still wrestled with misgivings. It appeared to be a legitimate business, but he was fearful of a cruel scam he couldn't yet imagine. He wandered away, walking off his anxiety. What did he know about working in a copy shop? The only copier he knew was the little desktop at the Kilgore Library. Maybe the job was something else. Maybe it was maintenance work of some kind. Maybe the old man wanted painting done and had chosen Jerry off the sidewalk because he was tall.

But it came with an apartment! That just didn't make sense.

He spent the hours before noon trying not to think about it, but his wanderings transcribed circles around it.

Not What He Thought

Old Man Stamper had just relieved Marilyn for her lunch break when the sound of the brass bell over the door penetrated the chunking of the big copier at exactly noon. He eyed 'Darren's' arrival over his reading glasses.

"Good afternoon," the nervous young man said.

It wasn't Darren, of course, Stamper knew that now, but he marveled again at the resemblance; he even sounded a little like Darren.

Stamper laid his glasses down and punched a few buttons. Layers of the copier's complex rhythm dropped away until it came to a halt.

"My name is Stamper," he said into the quiet, "Old Man Stamper." He pointed to his nametag as if to prove it and waited for the young man to reciprocate.

"Jerry... Jerry Gustafson."

"Gustafson," Stamper said, trying to recall knowing anyone with that name. "Where you from Jerry?"

"Idaho. You mentioned a job?"

"I did. But..."

- - -

"Here it comes," Jerry was thinking, "the alternative reality, bait-and-switch."

"But what?" he asked.

Stamper heard the skepticism. "It's probably best if I show you." He proceeded toward the back wall of the shop, past racks of supplies. "Turn that OPEN sign around and follow me," he said over his shoulder. When Stamper got to the back wall and saw Jerry wasn't following, he realized the cause of the young man's hesitation. With a magician's flourish, he opened the invisible door to a hidden passageway, with a narrow set of stairs leading upward. Stamper tilted his head toward the stairs and started up, clanking and scratching his old Zippo to fire up a cigarette. Stamper huffed and puffed a noxious nicotine trail, as if that might be powering his slow, painful progress.

Jerry lowered his duffel to the floor, flipped the OPEN sign, and walked around the big copier to look upward through the magic doorway. When Old Man Stamper reached the top of the stairs, Jerry steadied himself with a few deep, fortifying breaths to begin that claustrophobic climb.

Stamper was not waiting for him on the second-floor landing to brain him with an axe handle as Jerry feared might happen. Instead, he was simply waiting there to indicate, with open palms, a neighboring, mirror-image set of stairs going down.

While Stamper led the way, Jerry waited on the landing, using the time to look around. There were three doors on the landing, and three stairways leading down, the one they'd come up, the one Stamper was going down, and wider ones leading to double doors at the bottom that Jerry assumed opened to the alley behind the building. When he heard Stamper open a door and saw the lights come on at the bottom of the narrow stairs, Jerry took another deep breath, this time as much to avoid breathing the rising cloud of cigarette smoke as to steady his claustrophobic descent. At the bottom, he stepped into a large, musty, pale-green room filled with stacks of cardboard moving boxes and empty shelving units. They were in the empty store next door to COPY/COPY, the one whose windows were painted dark green. Jerry couldn't imagine why Mr. Stamper had led him up and then down stairs when they might have simply gone out COPY/COPY's front door to unlock the other front door in the alcove.

Mr. Stamper sat on the nearest cardboard storage box, breathing heavily, as if he had just finished a marathon. He indicated a box where Jerry might sit and said, "Let me give you... a little background."

"Please do," Jerry said, taking a seat. The shop air was stale and already filling with cigarette smoke. The stacks of packing boxes loomed all around, bringing Jerry's anxiety into the red zone as he readied himself for some sort of pitch from the old man, an offer laden with conditions, perhaps something illegal.

- - -

"When my twin brother died... a few years back, I... inherited all of this from him." Stamper swept his cigarette through the musty air to indicate the contents of the shop, tossing ash in the process.

"This is the inventory... from his last business venture. He was always involved... in some new..., marginal business... right up to the end." Stamper labored for each breath. "I guess he was... the black sheep of the family. Maybe every family has one..., maybe every generation does. I don't know. Anyway... unfortunately... he had no business sense at all." Mr. Stamper went quiet. Whatever thoughts passed behind his sad eyes didn't reach his voice. When he started up again, there was a raspy softness to his words. "I don't particularly care... for the merchandize he was selling..., but it came to me... with no encumbrances... and has some market value, so I kept it in storage... until I bought this building... and had it delivered here."

Taking a deep drag, Stamper looked around the shop. The only sound was of burning tobacco and his labored lungs sucking smoke. "I guess I was waiting for... the right time to deal with it. I'm thinking... it might be now or never." He turned his red eyes on Jerry. "When's your birthday?"

Jerry was taken aback by the sudden topic shift, but answered with his birth date. Stamper appeared to think about Jerry's birthday for a long time.

"You want to... set up this shop for me... and then manage it?"

Jerry was too stunned to respond.

"Don't answer yet," Stamper said, reaching into a nearby box. "You need to understand... what you'd be dealing with." Mr. Stamper held up a stack of magazines and fanned them out for Jerry to see their covers.

It was porn.

The women were flaunting well-lighted parts Jerry had only seen in the dimmest circumstances.

Stamper put the magazines back in the box, took another drag on his cigarette, and waited for Jerry to recover.

"These boxes are… full of magazines like those… along with sex toys… a few books and videos… some novelty items… and quite a bit of… lingerie."

Jerry looked around the shop with new eyes. "There's a lot," he said.

"Never seen anything… like this before, have you?"

"No, Sir."

"Is that going… to be a problem?"

Jerry hesitated. "You mentioned an apartment?"

Mr. Stamper nodded and pointed to the ceiling. "It's upstairs. I can only… offer you minimum wage… but you'd pay no rent… for the apartment… utilities included."

Jerry swallowed a big lump of doubt and said, "Then I'm your man."

For a job and a place to live, Jerry would have taken whatever this strange old man offered; he would have danced in the street wearing a pink tutu if that's what the job required, anything short of illegal. He couldn't imagine selling porn would be a problem.

"OK." Old Man Stamper trembled with the effort of pressing himself upright. "Then let's have a look at the apartment."

- - -

They returned to the second-floor landing. While Stamper fumbled with a huge ring of keys, Jerry's mind welled with excitement. He couldn't stand still; he had to move! "I'll just get my duffel." He plunged down the first set of stairs to retrieve it from COPY/COPY and came back up three steps at a time. Mr. Stamper was still sorting through keys.

"I haven't been in here since I bought the building." Stamper said as if to himself, then turned to Jerry, "I know this isn't as nice as your old room, but…" He shook his head as if telling himself 'no.' "But… it is what it is."

He opened the door to a two-room apartment stacked everywhere with expensive-looking, dark wooden furniture. "I'll get most of this extra stuff moved out of here."

The room was dark and musty, covered with a layer of neglect. Old Man Stamper flicked on the overhead light. "I think there's a bed in the other room... I'll find one for you if there isn't... I'll have to leave some furniture in here... whatever won't be in your way... cause I'm running out of storage space... in my place."

Beyond the astonishing stacks of elaborate, dusty furniture, the walls were painted the same pale-green Jerry had seen in the shop below. The brown linoleum floor, a half-hearted imitation of wood, was scarred and worn. It was the furniture that seemed out of place, much too grand for this space. There was just enough room down the middle for Jerry to take a few steps forward. From there he could see the adjoining bedroom was even more closely stacked.

There was a small, avocado-green refrigerator and matching stove. The bathroom had a tub, a sink, and a toilet, all white.

Compared to the damp rhododendron roof Jerry had over his bed the night before, the green apartment was paradise. Trying to reign in his bounding hope this might be his new home, Jerry said only, "It looks fine."

Mr. Stamper twisted a key off his collection and handed it to Jerry. "OK," he said.

Jerry was hired!

He swung his duffel to the floor and was, effectively, moved in. He gave Mr. Stamper a smile he hoped conveyed his acceptance and his gratitude, but probably looked more like astonishment.

Why had Stamper appeared to choose him out of hundreds of unemployed? What was he missing? Had his fortunes turned? What was the downside he couldn't see?

Jerry was compelled to ask. "Why me?"

Old Man Stamper's rheumy, red-rimmed eyes may have had tears forming in their margins, but it was hard to tell. "You remind me of someone." He nodded once and turned to leave, but hesitated at the door. With an unsteady voice and without turning to face Jerry he asked, "How about we meet downstairs around the boxes tomorrow morning at 9:00?" Old Man Stamper left without waiting for an answer.

Jerry listened to the sound of footsteps fading away as the old man puffed back down the stairwell to COPY/COPY. In an attempt to absorb what appeared to be the end of his homelessness, Jerry stood still, taking a good look around the space. It was glorious. His stomach growled in the quiet, making him realize how long he'd been without a place quiet enough to hear his stomach growl. There had always been noise around him on the street. He heard the distant sound of the big copier starting up. A car rumbled by on the street. Then, a door opened close by, onto the landing. Another, lighter, quicker set of footsteps faded away down the stairwell.

He must have a neighbor. His last neighbor had been old Mrs. Tipton back in Kilgore.

Jerry sat on the nearest chair, folded his arms on a beautiful credenza, laid his head on his arms and cried.

- - -

GOING TO WORK

Shelving

Jerry didn't want to leave the wonder of his new home to scavenge dinner for fear that, in his absence, it might all vanish like a dream. His new refrigerator was empty, so he ate a smashed packet of saltines from his duffle.

The bathtub proved to be ridiculously small, preventing Jerry from submerging more than half his length in any one position, but the water was warm and plentiful. A bottle of lemon-scented dish soap found under the kitchen sink provided a froth of bubbles. He dried himself with a patchwork quilt from the top shelf of the apartment's only, and otherwise empty, closet.

Jerry settled into the quiet. His stomach growled all night and his feet extended beyond the end of his new bed, but he was soon overcome by a deep and unbroken sleep.

- - -

Anxious but refreshed, Jerry descended the dreaded stairwell to meet Mr. Stamper the next morning. He wore the cleaner of his two plaid shirts, though it was as wrinkled and worn as everything he owned. He had not shaved, but his hair was clean, tied back in a ponytail that smelled of lemons.

Mr. Stamper was already there, sitting on the same box as before, a cigarette dangling from his lips and trailing smoke up the side of his face.

"Good Morning," Jerry said.

"Was that bed too small for you?"

"No, Sir," he lied.

Mr. Stamper nodded and studied Jerry's face, making Jerry wonder if he should have told the truth about the bed, or if something else was wrong.

"I'll shave the beard as soon as I get a razor," Jerry offered, in case that was an issue.

Stamper waved a hand, dismissing the topic as if an annoying fly. He studied Jerry a moment more, then stood up, gesturing Jerry to follow. They navigated the stacks of boxes to a glass-topped counter near the store entrance, upon which sat a green cash register. Stamper pulled an ashtray from a shelf below the counter, sucked in one last lungful of smoke, and balanced his cigarette on the lip of the ashtray. He blew smoke at the ceiling. "Have you used this kind of register before?"

"No, Sir," Jerry said in all honesty. When library fines were collected at the Kilgore Library, they were stored in a cashbox in Ms. Nervan's desk.

Stamper proved to be a good teacher, even if always short of breath, and Jerry was an eager student. When they finished discussing the cash register and the credit card reader, and when Jerry asked no questions, they reviewed a list of emergency phone numbers, including one to Stamper's apartment. Stamper gave Jerry more keys, one for the shop door, one for the padlock on the outside of the shop door, and another for the double doors at the bottom of the third stairwell, the wide one Jerry had seen from the landing and rightly assumed led to the alley.

Stamper checked the counter and the shelves underneath, as if searching for anything else Jerry might need to know. "I'll apply for a business license…, insurance, etc. My lawyer can help with that. I'll call a sign painter… and have him work something up… for the front of the shop. Meanwhile… you can start by moving the shelving into… some kind of logical arrangement. You'll have to shift… the boxes around to do it…, so save yourself some labor… by trying to keep the boxes next to… their appropriate shelves and racks. It'll be a kind of Chinese puzzle…, but the idea is to arrange things… before we start stocking the shelves. When you get them arranged…, call my apartment and… I'll come have a look. OK?"

"Yes, Sir."

Stamper nodded, lit a cigarette for the long trek back up the stairs and left Jerry to his assignment, which he attacked with an eager fury.

A few hours later, Old Man Stamper was nodding approval of Jerry's arrangement of the boxes and shelves when Jerry's stomach growled loudly. Stamper realized Jerry had worked through lunch. He fished two twenties out of his overstuffed wallet. "Here's an advance on your pay. Take the rest of the afternoon off to get some lunch and stock your kitchen. You can start loading these shelves tomorrow."

Louie's

Jerry found a little neighborhood store two blocks away called Louie's Market. It was unkempt, sparsely stocked, and empty of customers, but he only needed basic items and was glad to avoid the claustrophobia-inducing crowds and inane pleasantries of supermarkets.

An unshaven, cigar-smoker, likely Louie himself, slouched in a recliner behind the counter, scowling at a black and white television. Louie celebrated Jerry's entrance by ignoring him and by puffing another noxious cloud into the stale air. His expression suggested he would like nothing better than to get his hands on the daffy newscaster, show him something by-God newsworthy.

Jerry paced the narrow aisles, sifting through the possibilities, contemplating things he'd once thought he might never afford again, fresh eggs, meat, and cheese. Pastries! Everything tempted him, even the pictures of food on boxes and cans. But, since he didn't know if his kitchen had anything besides and oven in which to cook, he settled on a stack of frozen TV dinners. He chose one each of roast turkey, Salisbury steak, and fried chicken, enough to fill the little freezer in the top of his new avocado-green refrigerator. Jerry carried the dinners to the front counter and unnecessarily held up one index finger to Louie, indicating he would be back with more in a minute. Louie ignored him. Jerry began searching the narrow aisles for the next item on his list, bar soap. Louie continued to ignore Jerry's comings and goings until the pile on the counter reached a certain subjective size, at which point he abandoned the newscast, squared his recliner, and stood up to slowly punch Jerry's purchases into an ancient cash register. He lifted each item up where he could see it better, as if divining its price. When Jerry sensed he'd selected enough to exhaust his cash advance, he returned to the counter to begin bagging his treasures the moment Louie put them down.

Louie finished ringing it up, fortified himself with another noxious puff on his cigar and waited, staring at the total on the register to indicate it was time for the cash. Jerry held out the twenties Mr. Stamper had given him. Louie turned to look down his nose at Jerry, snatched the money, smacked the change onto the counter, and returned to his recliner.

No Sir, no inane pleasantries at Louie's.

Stocking the Shelves

Three days later, Jerry emptied the last of the boxes, sorting the merchandise onto the shelves according to his own system. Since it did not lend itself to organization by anything like the Dewey Decimal System, he shelved it according to whether it involved women only, men only, or men and women. He could think of ways he might organize it according to finer distinctions, hard or soft, indoors or out, etc., but the more he handled it, the less a system seemed important. By the third day, he was arranging things by type in whatever order they came out of the boxes.

- - -

Except for the men-only stuff, he was not seeing anything he had not seen before, though always previously in airbrushed, Playboy form, or "through a glass, darkly" during his episodes with Karen, his erstwhile, one-time Kilgorian girlfriend turned WAF. Their unabashed, enthusiastic romps had always been conducted in a dark room, more about touching than looking. The women (and men!) in the magazines appeared inordinately proud of everything they had and eager to display it in the best possible light for the cameras.

Jerry felt flushed throughout the process, both from the labor and from his embarrassment on behalf of all those well-lighted people who seemed not to have embarrassment in their emotional makeup.

And, well yes, he was a little aroused too, but not in a pleasant way.

Jerry kept thinking of his Grandma. While the women in the magazines appeared to be proud of how much skin they had available to expose, Jerry's Grandma had always covered as much of her skin as possible. She kept her "mad money" folded and safety-pinned inside the several layers of clothing she maintained as a proper, ecclesiastical bulwark against nakedness. Whenever she needed to access her mad money, she always turned her back to unpin it, not wanting to expose any more of its secret location, or her skin, than was necessary.

- - -

On the third day, while unpacking and hanging lingerie, some of which Jerry didn't recognize enough to know if he was hanging correctly, unfamiliar footsteps clumped down the stairwell. A sign painter emerged from the hidden door, catching Jerry with hands full of taffeta. The man ignored both Jerry and his merchandise, all business.

He went to the front windows, scraped away a small rectangular strip of the dark green paint well above pedestrian eye level, and began painting letters backwards in the cleared space. A shaft of natural sunlight shone through the cleared rectangle, shaming the fluorescents. Jerry continued with the lingerie, watching shadow words form where the sunlight hit the floor. "The Planet of Love."

Jerry was stunned by the synchronicity of the name; he was writing about a planet! He wondered how Mr. Stamper had come up with the store name. Was this merely a coincidence, or an auspicious clue from the weasel, telling him he was on track for The Right Place?

After work, on his way back to the apartment with another bag of TV dinners from Louie's to replace those he'd eaten, Jerry saw more of the sign painter's handiwork. Above the awning, bolted on the outside of the building was a hot-pink half-circle, eight feet across. It was roughly the size of the COPY/COPY sign, but it seemed to dominate the building, depicting the top half of a hot-pink, heavily cratered sphere, dawning above the awning. The words "The Planet of Love" arched along the planet's horizon.

Drifting Away

"Don't take shit off anybody," Mr. Stamper advised Jerry when The Planet of Love was ready for the public. "Watch out for shoplifters and call me if you have any problem."

"Yes, Sir."

Mr. Stamper glanced up at the clock over the front door. 10 o'clock.

"You ready?" Mr. Stamper asked.

"Yes, Sir."

Mr. Stamper nodded, zipped a fresh cigarette and unlocked the front door. He turned the OPEN/CLOSED sign around and puffed his way to the hidden door. Without a backward glance, he left Jerry alone in The Planet of Love to wonder what he had gotten himself into.

Jerry sat on the stool beside the register in an agitated state of nonspecific dread. His only cover against the horny hoards he imagined to be on their way was a glass counter full of dildos, vibrators, and other devices too expensive to be left unattended on an open shelf. At any moment, the Fates would choose his first customer from that vast, unstable menagerie of quasi-hominids he knew from first-hand experience to be out there. Furthermore, he imagined that only the sorriest specimens from that population were likely to interrupt the marking of their territory to venture into a store like The Planet of Love. His worst fear was that a large number of them might come into the store at the same time, at a minimum taxing his overblown need for personal space, but what if they got rowdy? How would he handle that?

Regardless, he needed to deal with it. He needed the job. He needed to stay put. There was no easy exit, so he sat and stared thankfully at the store's high ceilings.

The fluorescents buzzed and the clock over the entry door hummed away the passage of time. His ass numbed. He shifted on the stool. This was not a booming business.

His mind drifted to Mowdabb, a more interesting venue. He'd not thought about Mowdabb since Mr. Stamper handed him that business card. So, in his anxious state, he found peace in reviewing his most recent scribblings:

It covered a time when Lurk and the women were exploring their new Mowdabb home. Lurk explored the neighborhood on several extended solo expeditions, but learned nothing new; the architecture and the mosses were consistent wherever he went. He began clearing the moss from one nearby pyramid to reveal the extent of its mysterious carvings and make it serve as a beacon for their possible rescue. He and the women speculated that Mowdabb's original stone-carving inhabitants might have used the planet as a retreat from their home planet, or maybe as their emergency evacuation area in the event their home planet came under threat. If either of those was true, it was conceivable the Mowdabbians might return one day to take the place back.

Jerry was pleased with how he'd ended that part of it:

"Lurk's expeditions convince him that he and the women are the only higher life forms currently occupying Mowdabb. Until they are rescued (or dispatched by the returning Mowdabbians), Lurk and his clan are, in effect, the New Mowdabbians."

How do you turn it on?

The clanging of the brass bell over the entrance to The Planet of Love slapped Jerry back to earth, restoring his forgotten anxieties.

The man ignored Jerry behind the counter; his eyes were occupied by the merchandise. Jerry was relieved to be part of the furniture; it left him free to study the man. He entered tentatively, lingering at the doorway. He then took furtive sideways steps with his back to the wall as if wary of an attack, behaving like a chimpanzee entering a new cage.

He was about Jerry's age, but short and stocky, with an abundance of dark, body hair. Jerry's prejudiced state-of-mind suggested the man must have hit puberty early, begun shaving daily at fifteen, and hadn't changed much since. His knuckles did not reach the floor and he *did* have a forehead, but otherwise Jerry was pleased with the chimpanzee imagery. The man moved down the rows of magazines, panning his head side-to-side, as if smelling for something in the merchandise. His eyes passed briefly over the skin on the magazine covers, but moved on. He ignored the massage oils, personal lubricants, silly joke card decks, crass coffee mugs, and other tacky items Jerry had so painstakingly arranged by type and price. It was the lingerie that gave the man pause. He circled the racks as if something dangerous might be hiding in their diaphanous folds.

Jerry stayed alert for any shoplifting, dreading the need to confront him/it with accusations, dismayed even at the prospect of any sort of commerce with this creature. He entertained himself by mentally devolving this man's ancestors, convinced they must have swum in the backwaters of the human gene pool. This new-age troglodyte wore a cross-sports outfit comprising an oversized Seahawks jersey and baggy shorts that hung to his high-top basketball shoes, exposing only an inch or two of stumpy, black-haired legs. Jerry thought he might have done better with a one-piece jumpsuit, something that did not involve making as many aesthetic decisions. The unlaced shoes were loose around his ankles, slack laces ticking against the linoleum as he circled the lingerie, shoe tongues lolling licentiously.

The man became bolder, reaching out a curious paw to touch the fragile garments, then lifting individual pieces from the racks and holding them up to the fluorescent lights, looking through the material, jiggling it side-to-side, as if to imagine how much of his mate he would be able to see through the fabric.

Abruptly, he gave up on lingerie and strode directly to the glass counter separating them. Jerry was mortified, as his grandma might have said. There were a great many social situations he found uncomfortable, but being separated from this man by nothing more than an array of prosthetic penises was uncomfortable beyond anything he had known.

"Can I see that one?" the man wanted to know, still not looking directly at Jerry. He was pointing to a $39.95 chrome vibrator on the top shelf.

In the stress of the moment, Jerry was having a hard time applying his newly formed tolerance for human variety, instead he backslid into wise-ass mode, resorting to his innate, cheeky manner, the one that had so often gotten him in trouble in Kilgore.

"I'm not sure," Jerry told him. "Looks like you should be able to."

That sailed over the man's head, leaving him waiting patiently, studying the display of dildos, his cologne overpowering the store's moldy aromas. When Jerry did not move to show him the dildo, he attempted to clarify his request, not at all upset. "Could you pull it out for me to have a look?"

Even though the man's second question was even better than the first for purposes of wisecracking, Jerry restrained himself. It was too easy and he already regretted his first wisecrack. He opened the back of the case and brought out the chrome dildo, tensely fighting his manic temptation to mime whipping out a real one so the man could "have a look."

The man turned the dildo in his hairy hands, as if searching for a hidden engraving. Jerry thought of what Grandma would have done at news of his new job. She would have wailed her usual lamentations over the moral decline of civilization, and of Jerry in particular, and huffed off to the church to pray. She had done it many times, most recently after Jerry had told Kilgore's mayor he was a narrow-minded hick who needed to read something other than the Idaho Falls Post Register.

"How do you turn it on?" the man asked.

Jerry was too stunned by the question to contemplate a wiseass answer. Instead, he pointed to the switch at the base and raised one eyebrow in what he imagined might convey his sympathies that the man would have to endure the embarrassment of asking such a stupid question, but the man was too intent on the puzzling dildo to notice Jerry's complex expression.

Incredible! Standing across the glass counter was the latest winner in a long, unbroken winner-take all tournament of successive human sperm-races. In each race, only the fittest macho wriggler out of millions of contestants was awarded with a chance to enter the next generation's race. That natural, culling process, conducted over countless competitions all the way back to a time when the participants weren't human anymore, had resulted in a man puzzled by a dildo.

Finally, he just handed it back to Jerry, still not meeting his eyes, and shook his head as if amazed by its complexity.

He left, doomed to act out the remainder of his unimaginable love life without mechanical aids.

Except for the fluorescent hum, the store was quiet again, leaving Jerry to wonder first how such a man came to have a woman for whom to imagine buying lingerie, and then to wonder why he himself didn't have someone for whom to buy lingerie. He'd read of marriages between hospital patients with incurable diseases and between inmates serving life sentences for having killed their former mates. If such people could find a partner to prop them up and vow fealty, surely, he could, though probably not while perched on a stool in a porn shop.

Why did women bother with the problematic male? Unless they wanted to get pregnant, they would be better off with a couple of reliable girlfriends and a warm blanket. Even though Jerry had been raised by women, even though he had dabbled in the carnal arts with heroic enthusiasm on a few occasions, and even though The Planet of Love was stocked with magazines revealing their every nook and cranny, women remained a total mystery to him.

Counting the Till

As Jerry's anxiety abated, his customers began looking more like people he might see anywhere else. He sold some massage oil and several magazines. At 6:00 p.m., Mr. Stamper came wheezing down the inside stairwell, sounding like a tired monster descending from the attic, lungs wheezing with every step. It was difficult to watch. Jerry stepped off the stool and moved out of the way. By the time Mr. Stamper rounded the corner of the counter, as if in the last turn of a long race, he was too breathless to say anything to Jerry; his focus was the register drawer. He braced himself against the glass counter and mounted the stool. He pulled an ashtray from under the counter and shook a Kool to his lips. A quick sleight of hand, a clank and scratch from his Zippo, and the end of the cigarette was burning, a habitual efficiency. With the cigarette dangling from his lips and the Zippo back in his baggy pants, he counted the till. As he counted, he began to reconstitute. His noisy breathing gradually slowed.

"Any… problems?"

"No, Sir."

Jerry wondered why Mr. Stamper made that daunting stairwell journey from one store to the next when he could go more easily in and out the front doors. (Jerry still thought Mr. Stamper spent the day in COPY/COPY.) Maybe he didn't want it to appear that the clientele of COPY/COPY also frequented The Planet of Love. Or, maybe Mr. Stamper was just a peculiar old codger who liked to do peculiar things.

Jerry locked the front door, flipped the OPEN/CLOSED sign, and began edging toward the stairs, eager to get back to his apartment, anticipating a nice TV dinner, maybe a walk to Louie's Market for a replacement, then a hot bath, and a session with Lurk's exploits.

"Goodnight, Mr. Stamper."

"Night."

Jerry left Mr. Stamper sitting under the fluorescent lights, behind the glass counter full of dildos, smoke curling up his wrinkled face and filtering through his disheveled fringe of hair, as if his head was steaming. This became the image of the old man that Jerry would always recall.

The General Trend was Encouraging

Tuesday through Saturday, Jerry manned the store. He kept the place stocked and orderly. He spent a lot of mindless time re-pricing the more heavily fondled magazines. He did this by putting round, fluorescent-orange, $1 price stickers in strategic places on their lurid covers in a feeble attempt to return a small measure of propriety to his work. He swept the floor as closing time approached, just as he had vacuumed the floors at the library in Kilgore. Some days there were no sales, just lookers. Jerry made his minimum wage by keeping his bony butt perched on the stool, guarding the register, and waiting on the clock.

As bleak as it was, Jerry was thrilled to have the job and ever thankful for his good fortune (though ever-fearful of a reversal). He believed his life might have turned a corner, that maybe he was getting closer to The Right Place. At least the general trend was encouraging.

He was no longer living at the mercy of the city. Instead, it had become a city of possibilities.

Jerry settled into a comfortable routine, which he maintained with care, as though any deviation might end his good fortune. He managed his money, gradually accumulating accessories of the good life, towels, shampoo, a razor, and new shoes. His time on the street had made him attentive to nutrition and cleanliness. He took a bath every night and occasionally indulged in fresh edibles to accompany his cache of TV dinners. The new Jerry Garcia Gustafson was well-fed, beardless, and squeaky clean.

With no expenses for shelter, he even began to save a little from each paycheck, money he hoped to use for flight lessons and for his eventual move to Alaska.

While perched on the stool, Jerry's mind was free to soar. He either fantasized about future adventures his savings would make possible, or was lost in his novel. Even when his nest-egg was still too small to actually get him anywhere, Mowdabb was always accessible. Each evening, after his stint on the stool, he would hurry to his apartment to write in his notepads whatever he'd worked out for Lurk. Then it dawned on him that, with so few customers, he didn't have to write like he had on the street, reconstructing the day's thinking. He could bring his notebooks to work, spread them out on the glass counter full of dildos, and write in them directly. This change of venue profoundly accelerated the novel's progress and had a subtle effect on events in Lurk's life.

When did this happen?

Lurk awakes in a delightful tangle of legs and arms, surrounded by womanhood.

At first, he thinks that he must have moved during the night to the opposite corner of the cave, where the women made their bed, but all three women had moved to join him!

He adjusts his position to maximize skin contact and to place each of his hands over a favorite female body part. The whole, warm, breathing collection of sleeping feminine flesh adjusts to accommodate the new position, settling once again into slumber. In darkness, Lurk is not certain which parts belong to which woman, but doesn't care.

Normally, after long abstinence, Lurk would have been quivering with sexual anticipation, unable to endure such an intimate tangle without probing the various possibilities it presented, but something is different this time that he cannot identify. The desire is certainly there, the familiar engorgement has him at the ready, but he doesn't feel any sense of urgency and is willing to wait for sex to happen in its own good time, confident it will. He is at peace, content to savor the sensual moment, imagining it to be like immersion in a milky, estrogen bath.

Eve stirs. He gives her breast a gentle squeeze to say good morning.

She looks down at his hand and then up to his face, bewildered by the situation. She registers their relative position in the cave and then the way the sleeping twins are also comfortably involved in their tangle.

"When did this happen?" she whispers.

"I don't know," Lurk admits, "but I like it."

Lurk's rumbling murmur rouses one of the twins. She looks uncertainly from Lurk's hand on Eve's breast to Eve's face, and then to Lurk's other hand on her twin's butt cheek. She obviously has no memory of moving into Lurk's corner and is uncertain whether she should like the change.

It was a tense moment that might have gone either way if Lurk's response had not diffused the situation.

"What's for breakfast?"

A Trembling Excitement

Later that morning in Mowdabb's rising sunshine, Lurk and Eve peacefully recline on moss cushions. The moss is wet, but warm and soothing against their skin. They are in no hurry, have nowhere to go, and nothing to do. Eve asks, "What do you think is happening?"

"You mean the change in sleeping arrangements?"

"Yes, that, but it's more than that too, don't you think?"

"Yes, it's more than that," Lurk admits. "I feel different, about you and about sex. A month ago, hell even a few weeks ago, I was horny enough to jump your beautiful bones in a second if I'd thought I could have done it without a pitched battle."

"I feel different too," Eve confirms. "When we met, I was wound up tight, too preoccupied with business to think of sex, but now I've wound down enough to think about it, yet all the urgency is gone. And yes, a few weeks ago, you would have had a pitched battle."

"I figured." Lurk shows her the pearly-whites.

"Maybe there's a 'Mowdabb Effect,' of some kind," Lurk says. "Maybe we're being irradiated by something in the sunlight. Maybe there's something in the soil, some plant hormone in our diet acting like an aphrodisiac, or a soporific."

"Wow!" Eve interrupts. "Those are big words for a bush pilot."

"Maybe it's just that I can see you easing up and I know you can't get away from me, that time is on my side."

"Let's not be counting any chickens here big boy."

Lurk smiles at her. "Maybe you're such a hard case it has taken this long for my natural charm to have its inevitable effect."

"Yeah, right Tarzan." She says this without the usual sarcasm. "But your natural charm doesn't explain why none of us has menstruated."

"No, it doesn't," Lurk agrees. "My money is on the diet."

"Do you suppose we're missing something, some nutrient?"

"I don't know. Do you feel well?" he asks.

"I've never felt better in my life. But I also have this growing sense of..." she hesitates, "I don't know what. It's not tension, not really. And not really a sense of disquiet." She shakes her head. "I don't know, 'frisson' maybe. It's the closest I can come to what I'm feeling."

"What the hell's that?"

"It's French. It means, I think, 'A trembling excitement'."

Little Old Lady

Jerry would always remember exactly when he'd written that part. While perched on the stool in The Planet of Love, he was mentally engrossed in the dynamics of Lurk's little clan and sifting through infinite possibilities for their future. His notepads were spread across the glass countertop, competing for space with stacks of recently repriced magazines and helping to hide the dildos below. In that circumstance, thinking he was alone, he had wondered aloud, "How the hell do you spell 'frisson?'" The answer came with a sweet voice, as if by magic, apparently out of the dank air of the fluorescent-lit shop.

"F-R-I-S-S-O-N."

The voice continued from behind the countertop stacks of porn, "I'd like five copies of this please."

He discovered a gray-haired lady, just tall enough to see over the counter, looking up at him over her half-glasses, offering him a single sheet of paper. Where had she come from?

The sudden transition from Mowdabb rendered Jerry incapable of normal response. He stared at the developing scowl around her little blue eyes, expecting her to voice outrage such a store should exist. (His grandma would have been outraged in her place.)

"Young man," her voice insisted (this time a little less sweetly), "I'd like five copies of this please."

Jerry took the sheet of paper she offered. It made no sense. A hand-drawn organizational chart entitled "Daughters of the American Revolution." It didn't seem likely she was passing out flyers.

He said, "Sorry," and tried to give it back.

The Little Old Lady held up five fingers and said loudly and carefully, evidently guessing Jerry was a little slow, or did not speak English well, or was partially deaf, "Five copies."

Ahhh... She thought she was in COPY/COPY.

He asked her, "You just want five copies?"

She was still scowling at him over her half-glasses. She said quite firmly, "Yes, please. Just five."

"Well, OK," he said, "but this could take a while."

Jerry pulled a blank sheet of paper from under the counter, wet his pencil with his tongue, and made a show of adjusting himself to copy the page by hand. The wrinkles on her forehead bunched in puzzlement and she began looking around the store, noticing first the rack of new magazines near the counter, Penthouse, Hustler, and Playboy. She noticed the display of flesh-colored appendages under the glass counter top. "Oh my," she said quietly.

She reached up to retrieve her original and started for the door.

"Don't you want this?" Jerry asked, holding up the "copy" he'd started.

She looked back at him over her glasses with the same "don't-push-it-young-man" expression he had seen so often from his grandma. It warmed his ornery heart.

"I could finish it in fifteen or twenty minutes," he yelled as the door closed behind her.

It was a little mean, but it made him smile. He didn't get many opportunities to play with Little Old Ladies anymore.

For the first time in a long time, he missed his Grandma.

With the Little Old Lady gone, Jerry was alone again, surrounded by naked women and struggling back to Mowdabb.

Sex Storm

The next morning at dawn's first light, they awake as if from a shared erotic dream into a feverish tangle of insatiable sexual need, overcome by a storm surge of pressing urgency. Each responds without question, returning stroke for stroke with eager passion.

They are changed creatures, in rut. A steamy gaze reflects their ever-readiness. They come back strong again and again, as never before, seeking the next connection.

It is nearly mid-day when the urgency fades. They move away from one another without conversation, physically exhausted, looking for food and drink. Lurk and the women lounge away the afternoon, napping, gathering fruit, and cleaning. No one bothers to get fully dressed; they wear only the loosest of their outer garments if anything at all; clothes no longer seem to have a purpose.

When dark approaches, they return to bed, which now, by unspoken agreement, is in Lurk's corner.

Eve does not hesitate to curl up with Lurk on the giant nest of moss he has collected for the night. The twins hold back, hesitating for complex reasons Lurk can only guess involve deference to Eve. Her gesture in the last of the day's light waves them over and the four New Mowdabbians merge once again into a sensuous mass, relying on touch exclusively in the profound darkness, each powered by the same unrelenting need.

By morning, they are all, but particularly Lurk, limp and lazy. No one slept, but no one complains. Exhausted, they gradually untangle and leave the cave to sprawl about like shipwreck survivors on a mossy shore.

After the fourth such night, it is over. The frisson is gone. They are happy survivors, of what Eve calls their sex storm. Without sexual tension, they are left languid, loving, and playful, but in need of time apart for a good night's sleep and to recover from the rigors of their glandular upheaval.

Lurk is subtly changed by their intimacies, made even more protective of the women, even though he knows of nothing from which they need protection.

The changes in the women are less subtle; they are changed in the ancient way women change when they are pregnant. They have no doubt, and welcome their pregnancies, but Lurk is concerned with having to midwife three women at the same time nine months down the road.

One Shot at Life

Weeks went by unmarked, each day much the same, with Jerry lost in his notebooks behind the counter in The Planet of Love, and with Mr. Stamper (Jerry assumed) working in COPY/COPY. Jerry's only interaction with Mr. Stamper was when he came to count the till at 6 o'clock and free Jerry to bask in the security of his apartment.

Then, during a rare break in Jerry's routine, he encountered another side of Mr. Stamper. It happened late one weekend night when Jerry decided to walk downtown. He bought socks and underwear and indulged in a late-night Whopper. He walked awhile, enjoying how different the city felt now that he had a job and a home.

He entered the alley door and took the stairs three at a time. On the dimly lit second floor landing, as Jerry struggled to dig keys from his pocket while holding his purchases under one arm, Mr. Stamper came out of his apartment. He didn't notice Jerry. Mr. Stamper was searching through a ring of keys to lock his door, mumbling quietly, and moving slowly, perhaps not wanting to disturb his tenants so late in the evening.

Jerry couldn't understand Mr. Stamper's words, but the old man's hands fluttered away from their work with the keys to animate the air around his head. Jerry kept quiet, hoping not to startle the old man or embarrass him for being seen talking to himself, thinking it possible Mr. Stamper wouldn't even notice him.

Mr. Stamper pocketed his keys and turned toward the stairs, still mumbling. When he saw Jerry at the other end of the landing, he continued his dialogue, though now in a more normal voice and directed to Jerry, as if to include him, or perhaps as if he had been talking to him all along.

"… wasted so much time… I know it hasn't been easy… Well, you know that too," he said, his rheumy eyes bright in the landing's overhead bulb. "It's just been me, now, for a long time." He jiggled the keys in his pocket. "My family… everyone I loved is gone. I outlived them all, my wife, my twin brother, even… my son."

He paused, either studying Jerry or waiting for him to join the conversation. Jerry remained still, with no idea what to say except, perhaps, to share that he had no family either, but Mr. Stamper continued, apparently on another subject.

"I wouldn't expect you to live my way; every generation has to make its own mistakes."

Jerry was reminded of his discomfort around crazy Uncle Harold when he wasn't making sense. Jerry thought he should do something, so he nodded. Mr. Stamper continued with the non-sequiturs.

"I never wanted to be a burden on anyone. I never asked anyone for help. I was always so proud of doing everything on my own." He looked down at the floor between them for a long time, jiggled his keys once more and added, "What a shame."

Mr. Stamper looked Jerry in the face, "It's been hard. But you can't go back and do something over; you just get one shot at life."

Then Mr. Stamper... disengaged. His eyes darted around the landing, as if looking for something misplaced. When he looked again at Jerry, he seemed surprised.

"Did I wake you?" he asked, sounding more like the Mr. Stamper Jerry thought he knew.

"No, sir."

Mr. Stamper nodded and headed down the stairs toward the alley. "You get your rest, now Son," he said before exiting into the dark alley, the heavy door closing behind him.

Senile dementia, Jerry decided.

- - -

DISCOVERING MARILYN

Burnt-Turkey Haze

More on Mowdabb than on earth, Jerry rarely left the building. At the end of a workday, he climbed the stairs to his apartment, tossed a TV dinner in the oven, and returned to his notebooks. He was too self-involved to investigate the domestic sounds from the neighboring apartment, the rattle of pots and pans, the scraping of a chair, or the opening and closing of the apartment door. Until that fateful evening he first saw her standing in his apartment's open doorway, he hadn't even known his neighbor's gender.

She appeared in his doorway because Jerry had, once again, filled the upper half of his apartment with a burnt-turkey haze, setting off the smoke alarm and contributing a little more to the smoky caramel odor that persisted no matter how long he left the window open.

The fire alarm had sounded often enough under such circumstances that it functioned almost like an oven timer. As a result, he'd developed a well-choreographed response: When the alarm sounded, he'd flee Mowdabb and run to the stove. There, he'd jerk open the oven door and snatch the aluminum tray using a kitchen towel. He'd toss his ruined dinner on the stovetop, open the apartment door, and race to lift the window. He then used the towel to fan the gray haze outside. After a couple of minutes of vigorous, towel-flapping at the open window, the air would clear and the alarm would stop. He'd found this technique to be easier than trying to see through the smoke to quiet the alarm.

He was most of the way through this choreography, kneeling in front of the open window and well-involved in the fanning process, when he heard someone yell, "Hello." Because of the haze, he saw her indistinctly. And, since he was keeping his head low to avoid the smoke layer, his view was sideways of a pair of quite obviously female legs standing in his doorway. Hot-pink leotards extended from a pair of white running shoes on one end, to a pair of silvery satin running shorts on the other. Though the burnt-turkey haze obscured anything above the running shorts, he could tell she had her hands to her ears against the noise.

- - -

Marilyn relaxed when she identified the source of the smoke, still steaming on the stovetop. Relieved the building wasn't on fire, she exercised her long-standing curiosity about her reclusive neighbor. She couldn't see much more than a tall man flapping a towel at the open window in an obvious effort to vent the room, so she moved her hands from her ears to her knees, leaning down to get a better look at him under the smoke. The tipping of her head matched that of the man looking back.

- - -

Jerry stared back, transfixed by the woman in his doorway. Though his arms continued the familiar fanning motion, they now moved without sufficient purpose to move the air. When he realized how foolish he must look, raising and lowering a towel, he stopped.

"Hi," she yelled above the noise of the fire alarm. "I'm Marilyn, your neighbor."

Jerry was stunned. He did not introduce himself, as he might have done, or even apologize for the noise; he was unable to find his voice at all. While he was astonished at the sight of his neighbor, it was more than that. Standing in his doorway was a Beautiful Young Woman, dressed for something athletic, wearing a baggy gray U.S. Marines t-shirt above the silvery satin shorts. A black headband with pink and white polka dots contained her curly blond hair. She was quite short, though beautifully proportioned, and obviously in great shape. But, it was her eyes that rendered him speechless. They were big and dark and... he struggled to find the right word... *warm*. Yes. Her eyes were warm, and... intelligent.

- - -

The fire alarm still blared, even though the smoke had cleared somewhat, so Marilyn thought it best to continue on her way. She stood upright and hollered, "I guess everything is all right." There was no response from the man at the window. *He must not be... right, a little slow perhaps.*

- - -

Jerry wondered if she was talking about the smoke, his speechlessness, or his shameless ogling. She gave him a look he interpreted as doubtful, yelled "OK," and left.

Instead of calming down when the alarm finally stopped, he became more agitated, pummeled by an anxious set of novel emotions. He was excited to discover a Beautiful Young Woman living next door, but embarrassed by his behavior upon their first meeting. Moreover, he resented the fact that he now couldn't think of anything else. He didn't want the distraction; he wanted to write.

Hunger exacerbated his distress. His dinner was, once again, caramelized in its own sauce, dried beyond consumption. It was a shoe-sole of turkey and plasticized Monopoly pieces of peas and carrot all spot-welded to the aluminum tray. Worse yet, with his obsessive writing, he had failed to replenish his stockpile of TV dinners. He had nothing else to burn. The refrigerator contained only a plastic container of leftover Chef Boy-Ar-Dee spaghetti, a remnant of an earlier culinary venture. In desperation, he tipped the solidified block onto the counter, sliced off the discolored top section with a kitchen knife and cut the remaining slab into cubes. He speared one, examined the interesting cross-section patterns of spaghetti and congealed red sauce, and chewed it experimentally, hoping it might fill the void, but it tasted as bad as it looked.

His growling stomach insisted he walk six blocks to an all-night AM-PM for some greasy, animal protein, which he consumed on the way back to his apartment. But, he couldn't get back to the writing; those big, beautiful eyes were an unprecedented disruption to the status quo. He wasn't able to restore his full Mowdabb momentum for days afterward.

Curiosity

Marilyn learned a surprising amount about her next-door neighbor in their brief encounter. He was tall, had no apparent interest in cooking or fine food, lived in a minimalist fashion she found incomprehensible, and appeared to be somewhat... socially challenged. None of that made her want to learn more. Though she felt one ought to be neighborly, her ordeal with Coby and the other permanently horny macho types she had come to know all too well was still too fresh to welcome the company of any man, especially one that managed a porn shop.

Marilyn was always curious about men in general and then tempted to adopt the flawed ones as "projects." She considered both these traits to be weaknesses. Consequently, she thought it prudent to avoid interaction with her neighbor. Nevertheless, while the big copier chunked and whirred over the next few days, she could feel her curiosity rising. What sort of man manages a porn shop? Why did he live such a Spartan life? When she could contain it no longer, Marilyn asked Mr. Stamper while he counted the till, as if merely to make casual conversation, "What's my neighbor like?"

Mr. Stamper stopped his counting and got a far-away look in his eyes, as if reliving an ancient memory or some more recent amazement. Then he resumed counting and said, "Jerry seems an earnest young man."

Marilyn's curiosity flared. She had never heard "earnest" used to describe anyone she'd ever known. What did "earnest" look like, and why the far-away look from Mr. Stamper?

At least she had learned Jerry's name.

Marilyn began to think about how she might learn more about her earnest neighbor. She obviously could not wait for Jerry to initiate contact; he'd been next door for weeks. Maybe he was gay; Seattle was famous for its gay community. But, didn't gay men love to cook? And decorate? Marilyn wasn't sure. She had no experience around gay men; they tended to keep a low profile around Marine bases.

She'd need to initiate something herself, but she would need to be careful. Contact would have to be an innocent, neighborly gesture of some kind, because, assuming he was not gay, she didn't want to give the impression she was, in any way, sexually interested.

It took her days to find the right approach, and to work up her courage.

Hazelnuts

The Planet of Love was closed on Sundays, so Jerry spent the whole day typing Lurk's latest adventures directly into his first major purchase, a used computer. Late in the day, he celebrated the restoration of his writing groove by opening a can of cold Japanese beer. It was something he'd never had before and a rare indulgence. Before arriving in Seattle, it had never occurred to him that Japan might make its own beer. It wasn't bad.

As he returned with his beer to his typing, there was a knock at the door. "Who is it?" he responded without thinking how unprecedented it was to have someone knock on his door.

"It's me, Marilyn."

Marilyn?

Jerry opened the door to the limit of the chain. He saw no one until he looked down. She was smiling up at him, holding a plate of cookies. "I made too many," she said, as though it was a foolish thing.

"Too many what?" Jerry was curt, unable to avoid resenting her warm, up-close eyes threatening to disrupt his reestablished groove.

"Cookies, silly," she giggled. "Do you like hazelnuts?"

She had him reeling. "I don't think so," he said, clinging to his negativity. He had no idea whether he liked hazelnuts.

He wanted to do the right thing, but didn't know what it was. He couldn't let her in; the novel-in-progress spread out behind him would reveal his nascent ambition. His instinct was to end this anxious-making conversation and get back to the safe-haven of Mowdabb, as if fearful Lurk's clan might founder left unattended too long.

Part of him wanted this Siren to go away; her eyes were sweet traps. But, he missed having someone to talk to and this little woman was very attractive. He had no idea what to say. Their inane conversation to this point (largely from his lack of contribution to it) wasn't something he relished prolonging. He felt cornered. All he could do was look back into those eyes.

He wondered if her arms were getting tired. Was she offering a cookie or a plate of cookies? Should he take one cookie now to render a verdict on hazelnuts, or accept the whole plate and get back to her with the answer? In a mild panic, he mumbled, "Uh... thanks," and reached out to take the plate. But, it wouldn't fit through the opening limited by the chain. With the plate in his hand, he closed the door on his wrist enough to release the chain. When the door was opened enough to admit the plate, it also admitted Marilyn.

She was inside!

With Jerry still holding the cookies and the doorknob, Marilyn occupied the center of his sanctuary, absorbing every sordid detail, in full view of his manuscript and of a pair of dirty socks on the floor.

She seemed a bit anxious too, filling the air with innocuous banter. "I don't know if you like to have things around to nibble on like I do," she began. "I like to bake things. Mostly I like the way they smell when they're cooking. It just makes me feel all warm and safe when the apartment smells like something good to eat. I know Mr. Stamper likes a cookie now and then and he is partial to hazelnuts. You know, even with that wonderful kitchen he has over there, he never seems to cook for himself, so I try to bring him something now and then. Last week it was peach cobbler and he loved it. I thought about giving you some too, since maybe..." Here she hesitated slightly, remembering the turkey dinner, "... you don't seem too interested in baking. But, we haven't really introduced ourselves, I guess, at least not in any formal way. So, I thought I'd welcome you to the neighborhood, so to speak..." etc. etc.

Having this exotic creature violating the heart of his sanctuary, prattling uncontrollably down her stream of consciousness, made Jerry rude enough to interrupt.

"What can I do for you?"

"Oh, nothing really," she said, casting off again. "It just seems like we've lived so close, as neighbors I mean, and we've never really gotten acquainted, you know? So, I thought; what better way to get to know a neighbor than to share some baked goods. I hope you do like hazelnuts. My friend gets them for me from her aerobics class. Oh, that's not right, of course." She giggled and corrected herself. "She doesn't get them from her aerobics class. I mean a friend from my aerobics class gets the hazelnuts for me. She's got a sister who has trees in her back yard so they have more than they can use." She paused here a moment to sneak a quick look his way, as if expecting he might speak.

"More what?" he asked, quite lost.

"Hazelnuts, silly. Oh look! You have a computer. I don't know beans about computers except for the reservations program I used when I worked at a travel agency but that was just a dumb terminal. What do you use yours for? No, that's not right either, of course." Again, the giggle. "I don't mean to say yours is a dumb terminal because it's obviously not, but, I mean what do you use your computer for? Do you write letters? I've always wanted to get better at word processing. I sometimes write little poems, they're nothing much really, but it would be so much easier to write them with a word processor, not that it would save much time, of course, it's just that I like to learn new things."

She stopped, shutting off the flow, and stood there looking at him. Jerry realized that somewhere back there she must have asked him a question and was now awaiting an answer.

"What was the question?"

"Do you write letters with it?" she asked again.

"Ahh... sort of, yeah," he said, impatient with her curiosity. "As a matter of fact, I was kind of in the middle of something..."

"Well, I won't keep you," she said, jolly-like, and resumed blathering, turning toward the door. "I have another plate of cookies for Mr. Stamper, but he wasn't answering his door earlier. I'll need to try him again. That would be something, huh, if Mr. Stamper went out. When was the last time you saw him go anywhere? Except to the bank, of course. He's a nice man though. He really loves his birds. He has promised me some finches from their latest batch of eggs. I think they're beautiful, not the eggs of course, but the finches. Well, not Society finches so much, which is all Mr. Stamper has, they're not so beautiful. They're actually rather plain compared to other finches, but they have the most wonderful song and I love the way they pile up together in their nests. I think they're charming and cannot wait to get some. It's funny he didn't answer his door. I didn't hear him go out. I can usually hear him leaving his apartment because he always rattles the door to make certain it's locked and then he breathes so heavy, poor thing. I wish he wouldn't smoke so much. I don't think he's healthy, do you?"

"No, I don't," Jerry said, jumping on the merry-go-round. "And thanks for the cookies," he said, raising his arms and inclining his head toward the door, screaming in body language for her to make an exit.

"Well, I won't keep you." she said again, taking tiny steps toward the door, but still talking up a froth. "We'll probably see each other off and on. Your apartment is exactly like mine except it's reversed. The floor plan I mean. Well, of course, there are many other differences. I just mean the floor plans are identical, except for the fact they are exact opposites, flipped like, you know, like in a mirror. Of course, mine is painted a sort of an "off-pink", so it has more of a feminine feel about it I guess..." She looked around Jerry's barren, green apartment, and the topic of decoration ground to a stop.

"Stop by anytime." he said in order to say something, then wished he'd thought of something else.

"Really, yeah, great!" she said. "You don't know how much better I feel knowing I can visit with my neighbors. The only one I know around here, outside of a few regular customers at the shop, is Mr. Stamper and I don't think he'd be much help in an emergency, if I ever had an emergency. Just knowing someone else in the building makes me feel safer somehow. You know what I mean. This neighborhood is a little grungy sometimes."

"Sometimes?" Jerry asked, wondering what she meant; it always looked grungy to him.

"Yeah, you know, after dark. I don't feel safe going anywhere after dark. I don't have a car; I always call a cab whenever I need to go anywhere, cause I don't feel safe."

"Well, I plan to get a car..." he caught himself before offering to drive her around in a car he didn't have yet, "... but I doubt it will make me feel any safer," he said, attempting to recover with a joke.

Marilyn tilting her head to one side as dogs do when trying to understand humans. Then... she laughed! Not just a giggle, like before, but an honest, throaty laugh, so natural and *female* Jerry was momentarily disarmed and almost sorry he was rushing her out.

"Well, I'd better go," she said near the door. "I hope you enjoy the cookies."

"Yeah, me too."

She laughed again from the hallway.

Before closing the door, he said through the opening, "I'll return the plate." Then, when he realized that sounded like a promise to call on her, he added, "I'll leave it outside your door."

Staying on Mowdabb was difficult. He kept seeing Marilyn's big, brown eyes and hearing all the rude things he'd said to her and imagining what might have happened if he had been more gracious. While he struggled to get his mind on writing, he wolfed down the cookies, discovering he did like hazelnuts even though the flavor proved an odd combination with beer.

Rescue

Lurk learns the twins are Kim and Lin, but he struggles to tell them apart. He settles on calling them both Babe. In Lurk's eyes, they are magically identical and exotic. Their olive complexions have darkened under Mowdabb's sun since that time so long ago when he first checked their seatbelts. He loves when their dark eyes follow him while they conspire some new playfulness.

Eve's relationship with the twins has changed too. She is no longer their business manager, but more like an older sister, amused by their flirting games with Lurk. She addresses either one of them as Sister.

The women are the center of Lurk's world, all the more so when he learns they are to bear his children, the *real* New Mowdabbians.

The strengthening inward focus of Lurk's clan is shattered when they hear a familiar, distinctive droning in the distance. They have heard nothing like it for months, but they all know the humming buzz of a hovercraft. The stone cleared of moss around them ricochets the sound so that it might be coming from any direction. They climb to the top of the nearest pyramid and stand together, trying to see it, but the usual haze makes visibility poor and they don't know where to look. The sound fades in and out, and then away, leaving only the accustomed silence of Mowdabb.

"They'll be around again tomorrow," Lurk says.

Together, they make the somber climb down the pyramid, knowing they will likely be rescued, but there is no celebration, no relief at surviving their ordeal. The women welcome rescue for the hot baths and hamburgers they miss, but they also mourn the end of their idyll.

The distant hum returns for brief periods over the next two days, each time causing them to reassemble on the pyramid. They spot the hovercraft once at the limits of visibility. Then, for almost a week, there is nothing. Still, they know it is only a matter of time. They use the time to prepare themselves mentally for rescue. They are in no hurry. Apart from Eve's camera gear, there is nothing to salvage.

Eve spends more time with Lurk than usual, at peace when he is beside her, resting his hand on her swelling belly, waiting to feel the baby move. She has undergone changes she would not have thought herself capable in such a short time. The tense world of advertising photography she had once found so satisfying seems alien compared to the peaceful, and now maternal, world she has come to know on Mowdabb. She imagines cuddling and nursing her child-to-be, of fashioning moss bassinets.

Lurk is surprised to find thought of rescue depressing him. Not long ago, it had been the only thing he wanted. A return to the edgy, competitive life of civilization would mean the loss of their simple life on Mowdabb and the end of having three beautiful women to take care of. It would also mean missing the birth of his children.

The next time they hear the hum of the hovercraft, it flies straight to them, as if finally noticing the cleared stonework around their Mowdabbian home. It circles the area once and settles not far from their now-overgrown crash site. It is a brand-new ship, a Toshiba Skipper 400, a model Lurk has only read about. He'd been scavenging parts for the old Skipper 250 for years and had seen a few of the 300s before coming to Mowdabb, but, as far as he had known, the 400 only existed on drawing boards. Seeing it appear out of the haze like a vision of the future made him realize the competitive world had forged ahead while he languished. He wondered if he could catch up.

The women hold back. Lurk greets the pilot as he opens the door. It is no one he knows, but he recognizes the type, an independent hotshot, a wildcat entrepreneur, hoping to get rich off new-world exploration, exactly like Lurk had been a few months earlier.

"Everybody thought you folks were dead," the pilot says with a wide, toothy grin. "We figured you had crashed and burned somewhere or maybe made a landing and starved to death." The grin is relentless.

"Engine failure," Lurk explains.

"Figured as much," the pilot says. "Or run out of fuel, or got lost, or hit a pyramid. It's all the same in the end isn't it? 'Pilot Error.' It's always 'Pilot Error.' No matter what the hell happens, if it ain't good, it's 'Pilot Error.'"

Lurk nods.

"Hey, looks like you've had it pretty good here," the pilot says, eyeing the nearly naked women. "Not such bad duty stuck here with these three, huh?" The grin has twisted into a leer.

Lurk finds the randy pilot's prurience offensive and turns it back on the man to cut off the topic. "You've been living without a woman for quite a while, I'd guess."

It works; the leer subsides.

"Well, get your shit together." The pilot is all business now, impatient to get this detour over. "We need to get back before the fucking fog rolls in."

- - -

LEARNING TO FLY

The Piece-of-Shit Car

The awkward transfers required by Seattle's bus system between The Planet of Love and Boeing Field made Jerry consider a car-for-sale notice on the bulletin board outside Louie's Market. It claimed someone named Wendell had a Ford Pinto for sale that ran well and could be had for only $400. Jerry could almost afford it if he didn't get insurance. He called Wendell's number and arranged a meeting in front of Louie's the next afternoon.

Wendell rolled up in a little yellow junker that had suffered hideous abuse. Despite Wendell's honest tour of the car's glaring shortcomings and eccentricities, Jerry figured it might do for a few round trips to Boeing Field. It had obviously driven to Louie's under its own power. He walked around it once to give the impression he was a discriminating buyer.

Wendell said, "Well?"

Jerry pull the rubber band from his roll of bills and counted out $360 on the faded yellow hood, exhausting the roll. He shrugged and gave the man an apologetic look.

Wendell scooped up the stack of bills and counted them himself.

When he finished, he raised one cynical eyebrow, expressing his doubt Jerry had only $360.

Jerry turned his pockets out and held Wendell's gaze.

Jerry drove it away from Louie's and parked it on a street not far from The Planet of Love that didn't have parking meters. There it remained until Jerry had saved enough for a first flight lesson.

Ground Instruction

The first words the instructor said were immediately puzzling: "Rain is forecast," as if this might be a variation on "hello."

Jerry had been forewarned to expect "ground instruction" for his first flight lesson. He surmised this meant they would not actually fly, so he could see no reason why the weather forecast mattered at all. He had no idea how to respond. Perhaps this greeting was his first lesson, that as a proto-pilot, he should care about the weather all the time, even inside a Quonset hut classroom on the flight line margins of Boeing Field.

While he puzzled over this, and even before he could pull his chair up to the table to join the instructor, the questions began.

"If you're outside controlled airspace and more than 1,200 feet above the surface but less than 10,000 feet MSL, what's your flight visibility requirement?"

Jerry draped his field jacket over the back of the chair, pulled it up to the table, settled his books beside him, and folded his hands carefully, all the while deconstructing the abbreviation MSL to Mean Sea Level and otherwise stalling for time to think. "One mile?" he guessed.

From the instructor's reaction, Jerry figured he must have gotten it right, but the man was still obviously, and rightly, suspicious Jerry's answer was anything more than a guess. The instructor leaned into the next question. "In the same situation, how close can you fly to clouds?"

Jerry knew enough to be certain any guess he made would only reveal his ignorance. So, to avoid giving the impression he hadn't the foggiest idea, he shrugged his shoulders and shook his head in such a way he hoped might convey that, no matter how hard he tried, he couldn't seem to recall.

"FAR Part 91, paragraph 105 requires five hundred feet below, 1000 feet above, and 2000 feet horizontally from any cloud."

Jerry nodded in a way he hoped might make the instructor think he could remember studying that regulation. He was embarrassed for having his ignorance uncovered so easily and upset with himself for not studying more. He was paying for these lessons, yet he had spent his spare time on his novel. While Jerry wrestled with this, he mouthed the numbers, as if setting them into memory. Instinctively, he tended to disparage whatever revealed his shortcomings, so was already convinced the entire first lesson was bullshit, with no other purpose than to make him feel stupid. Furthermore, in the specific case of FAR Part 91, paragraph 105, he was thinking any sensible pilot wouldn't pay the slightest attention to such a regulation. How the hell could anyone know how far it was to the next cloud? How do you measure that kind of thing? Where, exactly, is the edge of a cloud anyway? The regulation was nonsensical and unenforceable.

"Well, since you haven't studied VFR rules, let's try something else," the instructor said. "If your radio is not working and you are on approach to land at an airfield *with* a control tower, but you see a flashing red light from the operator *inside* the control tower, what message is he trying to send you?"

Jerry was adrift on this one too, but desperately wanted to show this arrogant sonofabitch he wasn't dealing with a dummy. Unfortunately, at least on this subject, that was exactly what he was dealing with.

While the instructor waited for an answer, Jerry wasted time considering a smartass answer, that a flashing red light meant 'Stop where you are.' But, he tried a more plausible guess, "Make a go-around?"

"Almost," the instructor conceded. "It means 'Airport unsafe—do not land.'"

Jerry nodded appreciatively, attempting to put a lid on his attitude. He had to admit it was a good question and a regulation worth knowing.

"Let's try one more," the instructor said. "What is the VFR minimum fuel requirement?"

"Enough to get there plus a little extra," Jerry responded without hesitation, though more from suppressed antagonism than from any real knowledge.

"Yes, but how much extra?"

"Ahh… five gallons," he guessed.

"If you were flying a 747, five gallons wouldn't last long," he pointed out.

"I'm never gonna fly a 747," Jerry countered, grasping for a clever comeback and falling far short.

"I've no doubt about that," the instructor agreed and gave Jerry the answer, "Enough extra for thirty minutes of flight."

Jerry willed himself to show no reaction whatsoever to being bested.

"You were told to study this material before your first lesson, weren't you?"

Jerry nodded solemnly.

"But you didn't study much at all, did you?"

Jerry's scowling silence admitted it.

"I'll give you one more classroom session. If you can demonstrate to me you have done some serious bookwork, we'll go up for our first flight. Otherwise, I'm going to discontinue these lessons. If you don't take the bookwork seriously, you're wasting my time and your money."

Jerry was thoroughly pissed because he had no defense, but he nodded his head in agreement.

"OK, so next time, I'll expect you to answer questions from *any* regulation in Part 91—General Operating and Flight Rules. Know all of it except the parts pertaining to instrument flight. If you do well, we'll be airborne."

- - -

Jerry avoided the freeway driving home after his "ground instruction," not wanting to push the yellow, uninsured piece-of-shit beyond its performance envelope. He was so busy being angry with himself for not studying that he became semi-lost somewhere south of downtown. When he decided the morning could not get worse, it did. The car sputtered, the engine quit, and he coasted to a stop in a No Parking zone.

Jerry knew it was probably out of gas; the previous owner had pointed out the broken gas gauge and explained his eccentric system of yellow sticky-notes on the dash to record the mileage at the last fueling. "But it gets good mileage," Wendell had said.

Jerry had been so anxious that morning about his lesson, and about driving the car without registration, without a driver's license, and without insurance, that he failed to check the mileage on the sticky-note. That, if he counted right, was four layers of stupid.

Jerry pounded the steering wheel and cussed a string of profanities until he had to pause for lack for breath. In that pause, he noticed a small gas station about a block away.

Arnie

Grease layered the once white oval of the station attendant's nametag.

"Arnie," Jerry addressed the man, "I would like to buy some gas."

Arnie looked past him to the empty pump islands. "Where's your car?"

"It's just down the street," Jerry said. "It's that yellow piece-of-shit down there in the No Parking zone." He leaned in closer so Arnie could look down his arm as he pointed it out for him.

Arnie smelled like gasoline.

Arnie sighted obligingly down Jerry's arm and then back to him, his greasy face perfectly blank. With a flat voice, he said, "The hose don't reach that far."

"No shit, Arnie," Jerry said.

There was no change of expression from Arnie, so Jerry continued; playing along with what he assumed was Arnie's sarcasm. "I was fully expecting to have to carry the gas to the car." Jerry was in no mood for verbal tomfoolery, but there was nothing to be gained by cracking-wise while he still needed Arnie's gas.

Arnie looked down at Jerry's empty hands. "Where's your gas can?"

Jerry stared at the eyes resting quietly in the middle of Arnie's vapid, grease-dulled countenance and realized Arnie was operating in his standard mode; there was no duplicity in Arnie's toolbox, no reason to believe his words carried more meaning or implication than they bore at face value. He was not trying to give Jerry shit on this issue as his crazy Uncle Harold might have said; it was self-evident Arnie simply needed to take baby-steps through the vagaries of normal communication.

Keeping it simple and speaking slowly, Jerry said, "I was hoping to borrow a gas can from you."

"Can't loan nothing," Arnie stated flatly and without hesitation, as if it was something he had been told many times, and had finally learned.

"That's my car right there, Arnie, that yellow piece-of-shit." He pointed it out again for him. "I'm not going to steal your gas can between here and there. You can watch me all the way."

Then, thinking maybe he had been reading Arnie wrong, Jerry extracted a lonesome five-dollar bill from his Levies. Maybe Arnie wanted a bribe. "Look, I'll give you five bucks cash for a gallon of gas if you loan me your can."

"Can't loan nothing," Arnie said in exactly the same way he had said it the first time.

"How the hell do you suggest I get gas in my car?" He was starting to lose it, but Arnie was unfazed by Jerry's rising anger and appeared to give the question some serious thought.

"You could buy a gas can."

"OK, goddamn it," Jerry was truly getting pissed, "Sell me a gas can."

Arnie reached up to a shelf of oil products behind the counter and pulled down one of several new, red, one-gallon gas cans.

"It's $4.98 plus tax." Arnie said. "Comes to..." he cranks it into the register, "$5.38."

Jerry stared in open-mouthed disbelief at Arnie. "You *are* giving me shit on this, aren't you Arnie."

Arnie's guileless deadpan denied the accusation.

"Look, Arnie," he began again, summoning the dregs of his patience and forcing himself to continue speaking slowly, "you can see I only have a five-dollar bill here. If I buy the can, I can't buy any gas."

A solution to this dilemma was clearly beyond Arnie. He leaned over to take another good look at the five in Jerry's hand as if a solution might be written there.

"Tell you what I'm gonna do," Jerry said, switching to a more proactive mode, "I'll make a trade with you." He reached inside the breast pocket of his jacket, looked both ways as if to guard against eavesdroppers, and pulled out the $39.95 chrome vibrator he'd put there that morning.

"I'll trade you this for a gas can full of gas."

Because Jerry had paid for flight manuals he'd been too stupid to read and for a piece-of-shit car he could not afford to register or insure, he had only $5 left. To compensate, he'd loaded his coat pockets with the dildo and a couple of packs of playing cards before leaving the store. There was plenty of room in his coat for such things and, if he had to trade them for something, he could simply reimburse The Planet of Love out of his next paycheck. Carrying things that might be bartered was a holdover from his time on the street, much like Grandma's "mad money," the five-dollar bill she kept pinned near her bra strap.

Jerry had never handled a dildo outside the store and was a little uncomfortable with it now, but he had nothing else to offer and nothing else to lose.

"Now you gotta see this is a hell of a deal for you." Jerry said, switching to a sales pitch he hadn't realized he could do. "This puppy normally sells for $39.95."

"Puppy?" Arnie said.

"Damn straight, Arnie. This puppy will drive any pussy right up a tree." It was something he had overheard a customer say. He gave Arnie his best leer.

"Up a tree?" Arnie was struggling, either with the concept or the imagery.

"What do you say? Is it a deal?"

"What is it? Arnie asked.

Arnie's innocence was the last straw. The stress of Jerry' day became too much. He screeched at the man. "It's a dildo, Arnie, a goddamn, vibrating dildo! Where have you been living, man?"

Jerry was immediately sorry for his rude outburst, but Arnie was unfazed, as though he was used to having people yell at him.

Then, for the first time, Arnie's expression changed. A crooked grin wrinkled up the shiny, black smear of grease on one side of his face. "Are you tryin' to con me?" he asked.

"Con you?!" Jerry shrieked, startling Arnie, "Would I go to this much trouble to con you out of a five-dollar gas can? God*damn* it, Arnie! You been sniffing that gas? Look," he stuffed the dildo back in his coat and turned his pants pockets inside out, "I don't have any more goddamn money!"

Two quarters fell out of his pocket and rolled in innocent circles on the cement between them.

- - -

Arnie had to resort to a calculator to figure that Jerry could afford a grand total of twelve cents worth of gasoline to fill his new gas can. Jerry hoped such a small fraction of a gallon might be enough to get him home, so he handed over the five and both quarters. Arnie unscrewed the gas can lid and inserted the nozzle. As soon as he squeezed the handle, the numbers jumped well beyond the twelve cents he had so painstakingly calculated Jerry could afford. Arnie released the handle, but the pump already read forty-eight cents.

"Oh oh," Arnie said.

"Never mind that, Arnie," Jerry said, trying to distract him before he might want to siphon off the extra, or begin another excruciating episode with the calculator. "I think you did the best you could," Jerry said, using the pathetic truth of it to ease Arnie's conscience over giving away thirty-six cents worth of gasoline.

Arnie pulled the nozzle out of the can and stood there with it dripping on his greasy boots. Jerry snatched the gas can and scuttled away, screwing on the lid as he went and smiling a good-bye over his shoulder at Arnie, who was simply watching him leave.

Jerry was so intent on getting away, and still so flabbergasted by Arnie in general, he'd gotten all the way to the No Parking zone before noticing his car was gone.

Jerry looked up and down the street, thinking first the yellow piece-of-shit might have somehow rolled down the gentle incline or that he might have returned to the wrong No Parking zone, but there was nothing resembling his car in either direction and no other No Parking zones. There was no one around to witness his latest problem, or who might have caused it. Even Arnie had gone back to work.

Jerry was numb, between emotions, holding a splash of gasoline for a missing car, stranded in one of the few places in a crowded city with no one around. Suddenly, all of the emotions of the day came slamming into his head. He executed a furious, teeth-clenched sidewalk dance involving a flurry of every obscene gesture he knew, setting down the gas can to involve both hands and then repeating the more satisfying ones. It left him winded and no better off.

This was not logical. Either a fast tow truck had swooped in to remove his illegally parked piece-of-shit, or an enterprising car thief (with a can of gas) had chosen his car as a worthwhile score. Maybe Wendell had been following him to steal the car back. Any explanation seemed well beyond remote.

Whatever had happened to his car, Jerry was, once again, afoot.

He attempted to get a refund on his gas can, so he would have cash to ride the bus, but Arnie was suspicious of another con, explaining to Jerry the can was now used and besides he was not supposed to buy anything, even if it was new.

Jerry gave up; it was like talking to a stump.

Arnie generously suggested Jerry could leave his used gas can at the station, so he wouldn't have to carry it as he walked home, saying Jerry could pick it up, after he found his car. He asked for Jerry's name to write on the can with a black felt marker.

Jerry said his name was Doofus. When Arnie had written that on the can, (Jerry had to spell it for him) Jerry shoved his hands into his coat pockets, hunched his shoulders against the gathering wind, and headed off in the general direction of The Planet of Love, pushing his thoughts to the more accommodating world of Mowdabb as he walked. He used the distant downtown buildings as navigational guides as he had done so often before.

Jerry never saw the car again, never owned another one, and, in fact, never drove again. There is a gas station in Seattle that may still have a gas can on its shelves labeled "Doofus."

I'm Staying

The front passenger door of the hovercraft stands open, waiting for Lurk to climb in beside the pilot. The engine is running. The twins and Eve are already belted in, beautifully filling the back seat. Eve has her arms around her camera case, centering it primly on her reduced lap. None of the women appears happy to be leaving, but especially Eve, who is looking directly at Lurk, sadness plain on her face. The pilot is ready for liftoff and now turns his sunglasses to Lurk. The twins turn their beautiful eyes his way too, apparently confused that Lurk is just standing there at the door.

Lurk wants desperately to stay on Mowdabb, but not alone. Without the women, without, especially, Eve, there would be no point to it. But returning to the thuggish gypsy life he had lived before, chasing the easy dollar and the next woman, also now seems pointless.

The pilot leans across the empty seat to yell above the turbine's whine. "What the hell's your problem?"

Lurk ignores him; he is looking at Eve, mirroring her sad face.

Lurk begins to shake his head, "No."

"I'm about to leave your ass behind," the pilot yells.

Lurk continues to look at Eve and shake his head as he answers the pilot. "I'm staying." He mouths the words deliberately so Eve can read his lips, imploring her with his eyes.

"You're out of your fucking mind, buddy," the pilot yells. "You been here too long. You need to get out while you can."

Lurk continues to shake his head.

"You get your ass under a seatbelt right now or I'm leaving it here."

Lurk mouths the words again to Eve, a whisper in the engine's whine. "I'm staying."

The pilot tries again. "Pal, they are severely restricting access to this planet because of its 'archeological significance' or some such bullshit. Bottom line: You pass up a ride now, you might be here a long damn time."

Lurk does not move. He watches Eve, desperately hoping she wants to join him, imagining her mind whirling like the big fans idling under the hovercraft, struggling with the choice of returning to the aggressive world of talent management or of delivering her child on Mowdabb without medical help.

The pilot is saying something, but Lurk doesn't hear it. Eve says something to the twins. There is a brief exchange. The twins appear distressed, but Eve seems sublimely peaceful when she turns to meet Lurk's eyes once again. She smiles at him and then unbuckles the seatbelt from around her growing belly, from around their child. She opens the door and steps out. She places the camera gear on the seat and gives it a tender pat before walking to Lurk's side. She puts her arm around his waist and smiles at the dumbfounded pilot. "I'm staying too."

The twins seem in a panic, perhaps struggling with visions of new clothes and hamburgers and of leaving the father of their children, and Eve. They are sobbing, on the edge of hysteria, but they too climb out of the back seat and run to wrap themselves around Lurk and Eve.

The four of them wave good-bye to the mystified pilot.

Adam

Lurk's clan has no real reason to keep track of time in a conventional sense. They have no clocks or calendars. There are no discernable seasons. Each shorter-than-earth day is much like any other, with heavy morning and evening fogs blurring the light and dark cycle from the rotation of the planet. They accept what their senses tell them. Anything more precise is unnecessary. They eat when they're hungry and sleep when they're tired.

The women can only assume they are pregnant for the usual nine earth months, but they don't really know.

Eve delivers first, a large baby, glowing with good health and normal in every way. Eve names him Adam. The twins are both so large with child during Eve's labor they cannot do much beyond encouragement and guidance for Lurk. Afterward, everyone is in a state of exhausted euphoria except Lurk, who buzzes with excess nervous energy, which he spends cleaning and organizing the cave, bringing in new moss beds, and searching for anything else he can do. The next day, true to their twinness, within hours of one another, both twins go into labor. Eve is still a little weak, but is able to help in their deliveries, which both prove to be long and difficult. The twins are young and relatively small and the father of their children is larger than average. But finally, within a few hours of one another, the twins each add a perfect little girl to the growing population of Mowdabb.

The babies are all extraordinarily healthy and peaceable. There is nothing else on the planet even half as fascinating and the adults have nothing to do but care for them, providing a bath, a cuddle, or a suckle as required. They do not give rescue another thought. Lost in the ancient wonderment of parenthood, they are proud of every sign of development and marvel at every little accomplishment, convinced, as every parent is convinced, that their progeny are super-normally precocious and the first of such miracles.

They have no way of knowing how right they are. Also, with no way to mark the passing of time, they don't realize how quickly the babies are growing.

After what seems like several months, the adults are consumed by another sex storm. Just as before, it lasts four nights. During that time, they are feverishly insatiable after dark and exhausted during the days. The latest sex storm is even more exhausting because there are interruptions to tend to the babies.

Again, each woman becomes pregnant.

The cause of their recurring season of desire remains a mystery. Normal menstrual cycles have been replaced by a brief time of estrus. No one understands the sex storms, but no one complains. It is the new natural.

Again, Eve has a boy and the twins each have girls. They are as healthy as the first three and join the new focus of life on the planet.

The adults begin to think of the passage of time as seasons of children. The regular sex storms and the following births direct their lives. By the fourth season of children, there are four boys and eight girls. Eve has had all boys, the twins, all girls, but the distinctions of motherhood are blurred because all the children are nursed and cuddled by the nearest available mom. The boys are all large and sturdy, like their father, but with their mother's dark hair. The girls have the faintly olive skin tone of their mothers and variously brown or rusty blond hair. Which twin bore which daughter is something they are never able to keep straight.

Lurk is fascinated by them, and by his own tolerance of their constant desire to play with him and on him; they climb his reclining torso like playground equipment.

Lurk's growing tribe spreads across the immediate terrain, living with what Mowdabb provides. The children spill out of the cave to greet the daylight, playing among the mosses outside, rain or shine. The older ones adventure the farthest, their world expanding with their confidence. Darkness returns them to the cave.

The children quickly learn what they need to know, how to behave, what to eat. The older ones teach the clutch of toddlers from each new season. They all seem to instinctively care for the moss.

Adam and the older children are soon intimately familiar with the terrain within a day's travel of their home cave. Their explorations result in a network of tunnels through the moss with dozens of elaborate "nests" at intervals throughout their range. Entrances to the tunnels are often hidden from view, beginning behind a stone outcrop or in a tangle of moss stems. The children have names for their favorite tunnels and nests, names the adults never learn because they are places the adults never go.

Coming Home

The sky darkened, the wind picked up, and it started to rain.

"Rain is forecast," the instructor had said.

Of course.

Jerry sloshed home with his arctic-weight, non-waterproof, fifty-pound, Army surplus field jacket soaked through once again.

It was all so familiar.

At least now he has a home toward which to slosh.

He was nearly there when he realized his only copy of the flight regulations he was supposed to study, in fact all of his lesson books, had been in the back seat of that yellow piece-of-shit car. He would have to figure out the bus routes or use an expensive taxi to go back to Boeing Field for another set of books before he could study for his next lesson. It would take several paydays before he could afford it, and several more to afford another flight lesson.

When Jerry finally reached his building, he squished up to the alley entrance, anticipating a hot bath. He forced his hand into the pocket of his waterlogged Levi's and found it empty. Of course. His door key was on the key chain with his car keys, which he'd reasonably left in the ignition.

Jerry was as near to tears as he was to kicking something. Then, he joyously remembered he had neighbors. There were other people in the building; he wasn't totally alone anymore. Surely, either Mr. Stamper or Marilyn would be home and could come down to let him in. There was no doorbell, so, with the rainstorm raging, Jerry knocked on the solid metal door as hard as he could. There was no response. He thought about throwing something against Mr. Stamper's second-floor windows, but in the darkness and downpour, he was unable to find anything in the alley to throw.

Jerry walked to the front of the building and shielded his eyes against the rain to look up at Marilyn's apartment window. Her light was on. He was reluctant to ask for Marilyn's help after his rude reception of her hazelnut cookies, but he searched the street for something to toss against her window. Within the circle of streetlight, he found a few pieces of detritus to heave one-by-one, toward her window. A bottle cap went sailing away with the wind, missing the whole building. So did a Popsicle stick. A piece of broken taillight plastic might have connected with the window, but it evidently made too little noise to be heard over the rain. Since everything blew away into the darkness, he couldn't throw it again. He picked up an empty Squirt can floating by in the gutter. He stood it on end, and stomped it into a solid aluminum hockey puck. His first throw nailed the window dead center, shattering it. Some of the glass fell onto the sidewalk at his feet.

Within seconds, Marilyn's silhouette appeared at the window, peeking through the curtains.

Jerry waved his arms in the light of the streetlamp, so she would see him through the rain.

She pulled the curtains wide and shouted down through the jagged glass. "Jerry! What are you doing?"

She was wearing nothing but a thin layer of something semi-translucent and was backlit by the room light. Her hair was stringy-wet, evidently from a bath, and her nipples stood proud against the cold air he'd caused to blow through her window.

"I lost my keys."

"Just a minute, I'll come down and let you in," she yelled back.

Jerry returned to hunker against the alley door and listen to his stomach growl while he waited, the chill settling deeply into his bones now that he was no longer moving.

When Marilyn finally opened the door, he was barely able to turn his head to look at her, but he liked the way she looked and smelled. Her hair was wrapped in a pink terrycloth turban and the rest of her wrapped in a baby-blue chenille robe just like one his Grandma used to wear. She also had tiny blue slippers on her feet.

She began talking the moment she opened the door. Jerry could tell she was asking him questions, but he was not registering any of them. He gave her a lame smile of apology and stepped inside to begin draining on the stairs. He shivered out of his waterlogged coat and hung it on a hook in the entryway. He followed Marilyn's firm, blue chenille butt up the stairs, his shoes squishing a trail of puddles.

At the top of the stairs, Marilyn stopped with a sudden realization. "You can't get in your apartment either can you?"

He shook his head from side to side in syncopation with the shaking that seemed to be taking him over.

"I guess you can come into my place to get warm," she said with obvious reluctance.

Once inside her apartment, Marilyn ordered him to strip down in her bathroom and gave him a large flowered sheet in which to wrap himself. Shaking uncontrollably, he managed to get the heavy, clinging clothes off and wrap his slightly blue frame. When he emerged from the bathroom, she installed him on her overstuffed, flowered loveseat, covered him with a down comforter (not flowered), and put his clothes in her dryer.

Jerry was impressed that she had a dryer.

After a few minutes of kitchen clatter, she brought him a big mug of hot chocolate and immediately returned to the kitchen on some mysterious mission he was too phlegmatic to track. After a few grateful gulps of chocolate, his shakes began to subside and he began to get drowsy.

A knock on the door roused him within seconds after he dozed off, or so it seemed. Jerry rose from a warm, flowery dream he could remember only vaguely as having to do with chocolate and chenille. When he opened his eyes, he found himself disoriented in Marilyn's apartment, and apparently alone. The second knock on the door did no more than the first to realign him or to tell him what to do. Where was Marilyn? Why didn't she answer the door? Would she want a man wearing only a flowered sheet to answer the door for her?

The third knock was much louder.

Still muzzy, he threw off the down blanket, stood up, wrapped the sheet around, and shuffled like a Geisha to the door.

"Who is it?" he asked.

"Open the door." The voice was insistent and female, but it didn't sound like Marilyn, and it didn't make sense that she would be outside wanting in.

He attached the chain as a precaution, placed his shoulder against the door, opened it about half an inch, and peeked out.

There was no one there, until he looked down.

"Open the door, Jerry!"

It *was* Marilyn!

He opened the door all the way to the end of the chain.

She shoved her face into the opening. "Jerry, Goddamn it, open this fucking door right now, and let me the hell in!"

He was so stunned by the vulgar assertiveness of this new Marilyn he could only comply.

She marched in, glaring at his gaily-flowered self as she passed. She stopped in the center of the room with her arms straight down at her sides, her hands balled into little fists, and her bottom lip sticking out in a perfect, angry pout. Her eyes snapped around the room as though selecting a target.

Even though still dopey from sleep and puzzled by her anger, Jerry was attracted to this blue-chenille pillar of fury. He shuffled toward her in his sheet.

"What's the matter?" he started to ask, but she interrupted with the answer.

"You locked me out!"

Jerry was perplexed by this curious accusation, but more than that, was astonished such a simple thing could have made her so angry. He didn't know whether to deny it directly or to explain why it had taken so long to let her in. His eventual response was a combination of the two that proved to be worse than either one alone. "No, you woke me up." he said stupidly, making her even angrier.

"What an ungrateful bastard!"

Jerry was again running well behind in their conversation.

"I was getting you an extra set of keys from Mr. Stamper," she declared indignantly.

"But..."

"You'd better get dressed." She used a tiny raised palm as a stop sign, making it clear she would have no more verbal intercourse from the likes of him. She began to impart only those necessary directives that would get him out of her apartment. "Your clothes are in the dryer. You can dress behind there." She pointed to the folding screen behind the door that normally hid her washer and dryer. "Here are your keys." She said with stiff righteousness, making certain her fingers did not touch his hand as she dropped them into his palm. Whereupon, she turned her back, strode to the kitchen, and began a noisy cleanup.

Jerry dressed quickly, all the while trying to think where he had gone wrong. When he was dressed, she was still in the kitchen, still with her back to him, still clattering something around in the sink that didn't stand a chance in hell of remaining dirty. He hesitated at the door. "Thanks for your help."

There was only her unresponsive back.

"Sorry about the window."

Jerry slunk to his apartment.

Map Pocket

Jerry persisted with his dream, saving until he could afford a new copy of FAR Part 91 and his second flight lesson. He arrived at the flight center early and sat in the coffee shop to study until lesson time. He did not have every answer, but enough of them to prove that he'd studied. They took to the air.

Jerry was far too nervous to enjoy his first flight in an airplane. Fortunately, in the beginning he was little more than a passenger. The instructor conducted the preflight, made the takeoff, and brought them to a cruising altitude of 2000 feet somewhere over the farmland outside Auburn, talking all the while, describing exactly what he was doing as he did it.

Then, while Jerry was still enthralled by the miniature world far below, by the layer of clouds slowly dragging across the peak of Mount Rainier, by the cloud-shrouded Olympic Mountains to the west, and by the skyline of downtown Seattle, the instructor said, "OK, you fly it for a while."

Just like that.

Jerry clutched the controls with a grip that would surely survive any crash. He focused his entire being on holding the controls in precisely the same position in which they had been when transferred to his custody. For a time, that was enough; the airplane flew straight and level behind the steady drone of the engine. Then the faintest of changes began to appear; the line of the horizon, as seen through the windshield, began gradually to move downward. Soon it had dropped out of sight below the nose of the airplane, leaving only blue sky and a few wispy clouds above. Jerry looked around for other changes that might explain the disappearing horizon. He noticed the needle of the airspeed indicator was creeping downward. They were slowing! In that moment, he could not figure why. It was definitely *not* something he had done; he had not forsaken his grip on the yoke or twitched a muscle. He couldn't even remember having breathed. Only his eyeballs were moving.

The instructor said, "You need to lower the nose a little." Jerry translated that information as best he could and (correctly) pushed forward infinitesimally on the yoke. Nothing much happened. "You need to lower the nose a little." The instructor said again, just as if Jerry had not already made what felt at the time like a brazen correction. This time, he pushed forward on the yoke a little more. After a few seconds of almost unbearable anxiety, the horizon slowly reappeared. However, it came back tilted a little to one side. "You're in a slight left turn." The instructor said. Jerry turned the yoke infinitesimally to the right. While he waited to see if the horizon would level, he noticed it continued climbing higher on the windshield. More and more of the green earth below became visible in their wrap-around view. Jerry had never been more anxious in his life. He pulled back on the yoke to compensate, this time a little more than infinitesimally. Responding to the still tilted horizon, mustering all of his physical coordination, he simultaneously managed to increase the right turn. By this time, the engine rpm was starting to whine because they were in a mild dive. "You need to reduce throttle," the instructor told him. Jerry managed to disengage one clawed hand from the yoke to reach for the throttle. His effort to push the throttle in while pulling back on the yoke required the complete dedication of every synapse in his upper body. The engine changed pitch slightly and the horizon returned to a more appropriate location, but they were now in a slight right turn. He turned the yoke a little to the left. "You'll need to increase throttle," the instructor said, so Jerry pulled the throttle a little, but, while he was watching the engine rpm and airspeed gauges, the horizon started to drop below the nose again.

And so it went.

In the middle of all that intense concentration, operating well into his personal red zone, Jerry realized he was not having any fun. His armpits were soaked with sweat and his hands ached from their death grip on the yoke.

Then things got worse.

The instructor said, "I have the controls."

Jerry gratefully relinquished his grip, peeling his now useless hands from the yoke and resting them on his thighs, where they lay like stunned animals. The instructor proceeded to demonstrate a few maneuvers. He demonstrated a standard turn, how to make a turn about a point, slow flight, and a few other things, talking all the while. Jerry was fine with all of that, basking in the relief of *not* flying, until the instructor decided to demonstrate a stall. Having little understanding of a stall beyond that it was to be avoided, Jerry was unprepared for the ensuing horror. The instructor began a climb and then reduced throttle to slow their airspeed. While he did this, he continued his narration, just as he had during the standard turn, the turn about a point, and all the other non-horrifying maneuvers.

"When the forward speed is insufficient," the instructor explained, "to maintain enough lift from the wings..." On cue, the left wing dropped, as if it had broken from the fuselage. The airplane flipped onto its nose, pointing straight toward the center of the earth in a spiraling dive toward a spot in a cornfield around which the whole world now appeared to be turning. "... one wing or the other will stall," the instructor finished his sentence.

Jerry was trying to merge with the upholstery of the passenger seat, shoving himself away from the obvious doom racing to meet them.

The instructor continued his casual narration. "You'll notice the controls no longer respond normally." This he happily demonstrated by vigorously pumping the yoke forward and back a few times.

Having unresponsive controls was nearly as terrifying to Jerry as having an insane instructor, still trying to teach while they plummeted to their deaths.

"A stall is a tight, turning descent," the instructor explained while they were in their tight, terrifying nosedive, "in which the wing on the outside of the turn travels farther than the inside wing, giving the outside wing sufficient forward speed to fly normally and provide a nominal amount of lift, while, simultaneously, the inside wing, traveling a shorter distance in the same amount of time, has insufficient forward speed for the air to flow normally over the airfoil. Thus, the inside wing provides no lift, or, as we say, it 'stalls' and is rendered completely worthless. Dead weight."

The instructor calmly looked over at Jerry and smiled while he said the words "dead weight," either with genuine wonderment over the miraculous quirks of aerodynamics, or with pointed delight at the sight of pure, baffled, terror on the face of the dead weight sitting next to him. Jerry suspected the latter.

When it appeared they would inevitably pop a patch of Auburn cornfield, the instructor began the next portion of the lesson. "In order to break out of a stall, you have to move the controls in just the opposite direction your instincts tell you should work in this circumstance."

Jerry's instincts were telling him he should begin inflicting pain on the pathological sonofabitch beside him. While there didn't appear to be much point in expeditiously killing the man outright just before they were about to die, Jerry reasoned that if he could inflict pain on the man right up until impact, he might still be able to squeeze some satisfaction out of his last moments of life.

"By pushing forward on the yoke and by pushing the pedal in the direction of the turn," the instructor continued, "the inside wing will begin to fly again and the plane will enter a normal dive." He did those things to the controls while he spoke and, miraculously, the spinning stopped and the nose began to come up. Still, there was nothing other than corn visible through the windshield. The instructor continued to pull back on the yoke and the g forces began shoving them down in their seats. The instructor kept pulling and the g's kept shoving until Jerry's cheeks weighed about ten pounds each, until all the blood in his head drained into his stomach, and the whole world started to get dark around the edges. When the horizon finally made it to the middle of the windshield, Jerry pulled open the elastic map pocket on the side door and vomited into it, soaking all the vomit bags in there with what little was left of his morning cup of coffee and the remnants of last night's Swanson's turkey dinner.

That seemed to end the lesson.

Post-flight

During their "post-flight debriefing," the instructor called it, in a condescending tone that immediately rankled his already irritated student, he explained that, "A pilot has to do more than one thing at a time, you know. And, it has to be done with great precision. To do this, you have to think ahead."

Jerry rudely interrupted his post-flight debriefing to demonstrate he could do more than one thing at a time, and with great precision. He might have done better with more time to plan ahead, but was pleased with his coordinated delivery. He told the instructor what he thought of his instruction technique *and* simultaneously punctuated it with appropriate gesticulations. He followed that (thinking ahead) with a suggestion for what the instructor might do with plans for their next lesson. When he finished, with as much dignity as he could feign, he turned away from his post-flight debriefing, leaving behind a stony-faced instructor and Jerry's dream of becoming a pilot.

His heart was pounding with anger, mostly at himself, when he left the flight line. He fumed while he waited for the bus, reviewing his tirade, reveling in the well-chosen turns of phrase that had come together as he needed them, but the satisfaction of exercising a long-dormant temper faded quickly. He threw his replacement copy of FAR Part 91 into a trashcan.

On the bus, he was well imbedded in a funk. Flying was nothing like he'd imagined. There was no time to enjoy a soaring sense of freedom or the grand, cloud-strewn vistas. It was stressful, disorienting, and of course, nauseating. His distaste for being airborne dashed any hope of living in Alaska as a bush pilot. That ambition was as soured as the odor he'd left behind in the cockpit. It was as if he'd upchucked his dream, leaving a huge hole in his grand life plan. The only possible upside he could pry from the experience was the hope that the instructor would be the one who had to clean out that map pocket. Later, as his funk faded, he realized another benefit from the experience: The horror of facing certain death had filled him with a fresh appreciation for life.

- - -

Halfway home from Boeing Field, Jerry made an impulsive move that had profound consequences: He got off the bus and went into a bar.

Drinking was something he rarely did, and never in the middle of the day. It wasn't logical to deal with an angry funk by drinking large quantities of a depressant, but he needed to come to a full stop somewhere dark and quiet, in order to think about where his life was headed. Once inside the bar, there was nothing else to do but drink.

- - -

The bartender was about Jerry's age but already balding.

"What'll it be?" he asked.

While Jerry deliberated (he was not a regular bar patron, so had no favorite drink), the bartender waited with an expression Jerry interpreted as disgust, perhaps that the bartender's own life had come down to this, to tending bar for a single, novice drinker. Beer would have been an easy choice, cheap and eventually effective, and it would probably be the bartender's choice, judging from the size of the man's gut, but Jerry's funk demanded something with more kick.

"Tequila," he said, "the good stuff," He added that last bit in a useless attempt to convince the bartender he knew what he was doing, drinking wise.

The bartender knew what he was doing too and waited to see some money.

Jerry cleaned out his wallet, slapping two one-dollar bills on the bar.

The bartender remained as he was, leaning on the bar with locked elbows, his shoulders around his ears as if to support the weight of his disparaging expression. Jerry sheepishly returned to his wallet, retrieving the maddest of his mad money from deep within a secret pocket. He laid the tightly folded twenty on the bar beside the two ones and worked the wrinkles out of it.

"Stop me when that's gone," he said, trying to recover his erstwhile bravado, drawing heavily on his notion of the hard-drinking cowboys and hollow-legged detectives about which he'd spent so many hours reading.

The bartender managed an eloquent combination of body language and facial expression to convey that his good nature was being imposed upon to an extraordinary degree for a lousy twenty-two bucks. Nonetheless, he took the money and turned away to exercise his craft, ringing the register, grabbing a glass, upending a tequila bottle, and snatching a lemon wedge and a bar napkin with impressive coordination. The drink was in front of Jerry before he had time to regret the disappearance of his last dollar.

The bartender stationed himself out of conversational range at the other end of the bar, leaving Jerry alone to contemplate his future. All of his money was gone, but the drink glistened in front of him and the bar was dark and quiet, so he downed the shot and bit into the lemon. When the initial alcoholic jolt reverberated back to his brain, he slid the shot glass toward the bartender and met his glare.

"Fill 'er up," he said.

The second shot went down more easily. Using his last vestige of good judgment, Jerry switched to beer. When his first draft arrived, he smiled grandly and bounced his eyebrows at the unamused bartender.

Maybe this could be fun.

The first sip of beer coincided with the second tequila slamming into his sense of balance, setting off a small alarm, making him glad he switched to beer when he did. He had to take this slowly; at some point he would have to walk home.

He became sullen and introspective, regretting the loss of his mad money. This wasn't the dire emergency he'd had in mind when he squirreled that twenty in his wallet. He could've bought a whole bottle of tequila and drunk it in the privacy of his apartment.

Short-term, all Jerry had was a plan to get drunk and stay that way, right where he was, for as long as he could, or until he came up with a better plan. So far, so good; he was already wobbly. Of course, spending the last of his money on a distillate in which to dissolve his funk was an ill-advised exercise in self-indulgence; one requiring a delicate balance of good judgment (all the while judgment is being impaired) and self-control (as inhibitions come tumbling down). But, if he stuck to beer, twenty-two dollars might be enough to maintain his planned state of uninhibited thinking until he had a long-term plan of substance, a new dream to replace being a bush pilot.

It had to be realistic; he had obviously set his sights too high. On the other hand, was it realistic to dream while drunk?

"What'll it be," indeed.

He could not remember a time when he had *not* wanted to be a pilot. The ambition had been with him so long he had no idea where it first came from. With the alcohol simmering inside him, it seemed a childish dream, something he had never truly understood.

He began to think of Karen, not because he missed her, but because of the tequila; it had been her favorite way to dissolve the last remnants of inhibition during their several sloppy, tequila-inspired nights together before she heard the Air Force calling and jettisoned Kilgore and him from her life. Jerry rarely thought of Karen any more, but when he did, it was in relation to drinking and her enthusiastic ministrations in bed. Her vigorous touch was as near to affection as anything he had known and was what he thought he needed as he sat on that barstool somewhere in Seattle, somewhere between his old dream and a new one.

- - -

"It's gone," the bartender said.

"What's gone?" Jerry asked, the bar reeling around him as he turned his head to face this new loss.

"The twenty-two dollars. You said to stop you when it's gone. It's gone."

"Tell ya what I'm gonna do," Jerry said with surprising difficulty, but with perfect, instinctual reaction to his poverty. "I'll make you a deal on this puppy right here." He pulled the chrome vibrator out of his coat pocket.

"Oh, yeah. This'll be good," the bartender said with only a little cynicism, as though anticipating an addition to his bartender stories:

"One day," Jerry imagined him saying to his bartender cronies, *"some clown tried to trade me a dildo for drinks."*

"Ha, ha, ha," all his cronies would chorus.

Fuck em, Jerry thought and forged ahead.

"This sells for $39.95 in stores, but it's yours for twenty bucks credit at the bar."

"Is it used?" the bartender asked.

"Hell no!" Jerry was shocked at the question.

"Too bad." the bartender said, trying to keep from smiling. "Be worth more if it was used."

Jerry realized the man was jerking his chain, so he played along. "Sorry. It's a virgin."

"All right, what the hell," the bartender said. "I'll give you ten bucks credit."

"In that case," Jerry said in a final lapse in judgment, "screw the beer. I'm going back to tequila."

Jerry slammed down the next shot as soon as it came and opened a pack of playing cards adorned by photos of naked fat women, more of his emergency bartering stash. He threw the cellophane wrapper over his shoulder and dealt a game of solitaire on the bar. When the bartender came to look at the fat women. Jerry gave him his best prickly glare.

"You wanna buy a deck?"

"No."

"You know the name of this game I'm playing?" Jerry asked, continuing to deal the fat women.

The bartender shook his head "no," absently scanning the cards.

"It's called *solitaire*," Jerry said, making big eyes at the man, simultaneously realizing how drunk he was. "You know why they call it that?"

The bartender got the message, showed Jerry his palms, and moved away, wiping up imaginary wet-rings on his way down the bar, leaving Jerry to become as sour as he pleased until his credit was gone.

A Stumble

Jerry made it all the way to the top of the stairs coming home. There he slipped and fell with a clumsy crash on the last step. He would have passed out on the spot, except that the pain from his shin kept him conscious. He managed to sit upright and raise his pants leg to examine the bloody mess he'd made. He was involved in what he thought was, considering his drunken state, a passable assembly of mumbled epithets, when Marilyn opened her apartment door to investigate the noise.

Jerry was too drunk to feel the embarrassment that normally would have consumed him at being discovered in such reduced circumstances by a Beautiful Young Woman.

Marilyn recognized Jerry's condition and took it all in without expression; she'd grown up in a household of hard-drinking men. It was the sight of his bleeding shin that kept her from closing the door on such a drunken, unreliable wretch, one who locked people out of their own apartments, and drank too much.

"Wait right there," she ordered unnecessarily, clearly over-estimating Jerry's mobility. She disappeared into her apartment and returned with a plastic first-aid kit.

"You have a fursade kit." Jerry observed.

"Let's get you inside," she said, offering Jerry a hand to help him to his feet. He assembled his limbs under him one by one and applied the necessary effort against gravity to regain the vertical, leaning, out of great necessity, on her proffered hand and then her shoulder, which conveniently aligned itself under his elbow. They waited to see if he could keep his balance.

"Where are your keys?" she asked.

He remembered having them in his hand as he fell and began to look around on the landing as it bucked and heaved like the deck of a ship at sea.

Marilyn took his behavior as a clue and located his keys on the landing where they had flown during his fall. She left his side long enough to retrieve the keys and unlock the door, then returned to support him inside. Once Jerry was seated, Marilyn scurried about at a pace he couldn't follow. When she came back into steady focus, she was kneeling on the floor at his shin, cleaning his red badge of clumsiness.

Jerry began to babble. "I puked on the vomit bags," he said.

She appeared to accept this as intelligible, or at least as something not unexpected from a reprobate in his condition, and continued her nursing without comment.

"The exstructor wanna me to do that," he explained. "He wanna me to hate flyin' and quit, so he gomme sick and I did jes what he wanna me to."

Marilyn folded a large gauze pad against his shin and said, "Hold that."

Jerry held it while she cut strips of tape.

"At's why I used a dildo to get drunk," he explained in watery-eyed sincerity.

She paused at that, but only for a heartbeat. She smoothed the last of the tape around his skinny leg and returned the remaining supplies to her fursade kit.

Marilyn stood in front of him, looking at him steadily. Jerry was embarrassed he could not meet her eyes. He still felt the need to explain how he had come to be so drunk. "I even sole my fat women," he said.

Marilyn left the apartment, without another word.

- - -

CONFESSION

Would you like a muffin?

There was unrelenting thunder in Jerry's tequila sunrise the next morning. It pounded his consciousness until he surrendered to it and flailed up out of sleep to realize there was someone pounding on his door.

"What?" he managed to say.

"Jerry, it's me," Marilyn said.

This sobered him somewhat.

"Just a minute," he said through gritted teeth, struggling to the vertical.

When he had pulled on his pants and got the door open a little, Marilyn pushed past him and strode to the center of the apartment; apparently, her usual method of entering a room. Once there, she turned to face him, as if to face a firing squad.

"I have a confession to make and an apology to give," she said.

"OK," he said, accepting her agenda, still far too fried to question her urgent need to confess and apologize.

She jingled her room keys nervously, looked around his dump, and came to a decision. "Would you like to join me for a cup of coffee?"

"Yes," he answered with great relief. Coffee was what his brain began demanding from the moment consciousness was forced upon it. But also, he really wanted to join this woman for a cup of coffee, or for most anything.

"First the apology," she began after they were sitting around her dining table with tiny cups of coffee in a sunny corner of her pink and frilly kitchen. "I'm sorry to have treated you so poorly the other night."

"Oh, I think you did a great job." He pulled up his pants leg to reveal the bandage, still gracing his pale shin. He gave her a goofy smile, hoping to lighten her up a bit.

"No, no," she said, all business, "I'm talking about the night you lost your keys."

"Oh."

"You see…" She hesitated. "After I bandaged your leg last night, I spent the next hour sitting on the hall stairs outside, where you fell."

"Why?" Jerry did not see how this was anything like a confession.

"I was locked out of my apartment!" She said this as though it explained something. Jerry pondered the possible implications, but came up with nothing.

Seeing his incomprehension, she explained. "My door was unlocked when I came out into the hall to bandage your leg. I know it was; I checked it. I always check it. Never-the-less," she shook her head sheepishly, "when the door closed behind me, it locked itself."

Still lost in a residual tequila fog, Jerry merely nodded.

"Don't you see? The night you lost your keys, the same thing must have happened. When I left to get a spare key for you from Mr. Stamper, the door locked me out. I assumed you did it. I could not understand why you would want to do that and it made me very, very angry. I was wrong to assume you did it without giving you a chance to explain."

"Ahhh," he said, comprehension shouldering its way past the hangover.

"I just sat on the hall stairs last night for the longest time, feeling stupid," she said. "At first, I was too proud even to bother Mr. Stamper again, so he could unlock my apartment, but I knew I would be sitting there all night if I waited, so I had to wake him."

"Ahhh," Jerry said again, now staring easily into her beautiful, penitent eyes.

"He's going to call a locksmith later today," she added more conversationally, now that her difficult confession was over.

Marilyn sipped her coffee and fingered the cup nervously, working up to her apology. "I felt so bad about the way I'd treated you the other night that I just couldn't wait any longer to apologize. Jerry, I am truly sorry."

Jerry was suddenly feeling much better about life in general, despite recent disasters and the poisons still pumping around his system. He raised his coffee in salute. "Apology accepted. No harm done."

"Whew," she said, wiping imaginary perspiration off her brow. "I was afraid you wouldn't want anything to do with such a ditzy neighbor."

"Oh, I don't think you're ditzy."

"You don't?" She seemed relieved to hear this.

"Naw," he reassured her, though he really wasn't sure he knew what ditzy meant. She seemed to want to hear more of what he thought on the subject, so he improvised. "You're a little high-strung maybe," he said. "But a woman on her own in this town has every reason to be high-strung."

Jerry could see complex machinations underway behind those big dark eyes of hers, while she sipped her coffee and thought about his evaluation of her. He could guess she must be struggling to make sense of the little she knew about him, that he was clumsy, that he drank in excess, that he tended to set off fire alarms, and that he worked in a porn shop, none of it flattering. Apparently, she decided to overlook all of that and not be insulted by his characterization of her as 'high-strung,' because she bounced out of her chair, and returned from the kitchen with baked goods.

"Would you like a muffin?"

They visited then, as neighbors would, sharing the muffins and a few superficial facts about one another. When the topic turned to Mr. Stamper, Marilyn said, "I'm really concerned about his health."

Jerry shrugged as if to suggest poor health should be expected in someone that old.

"He's so pale," Marilyn said.

"It's probably nicotine poisoning," Jerry suggested.

"Maybe it's because he stays indoors so much;" Marilyn said, "I've only seen him go out at night."

"Maybe, he's a vampire," Jerry offered, stupidly trying to be clever while she was trying to have a serious discussion, causing a lull in their conversation. Jerry made a mental note to never again attempt being clever.

"Plus," she eventually continued, adding this new revelation about Mr. Stamper with obvious reluctance, "I don't think his mind is very clear sometimes. For example, the other day he told me I haven't changed a bit."

"I've noticed something like that too," Jerry said, eager to make a serious contribution. "Sometimes it's as if he doesn't recognize me and sometimes it's as if he has known me for years. Perhaps it's the first stages of dementia."

They both pondered having a senile boss and landlord. To keep the conversation going, Jerry added, "We had an old-timer in my hometown who used to have long, heated conversations with an aspen tree." Jerry didn't feel he had known Marilyn long enough to reveal that the old-timer was his Uncle Harold.

"I don't think he has any family," Marilyn said, returning to the topic at hand. "His wife died years ago."

"His twin brother died too."

They both nodded solemnly at their coffee cups.

Then Marilyn said something that had not occurred to Jerry: "I don't know what will happen to our jobs if Mr. Stamper's health gets much worse."

- - -

NEW OWNERS

Mr. Stamper's Apartment

A few days after Marilyn's confession/apology, she met Jerry on the landing for what might have been their first date, though they were only going so far as Mr. Stamper's apartment, ostensibly to choose the pair of finches Mr. Stamper had offered Marilyn.

"You really haven't been inside his apartment before?" she asked Jerry after knocking on Mr. Stamper's door. As they waited, all he could do was shake his head "no," her question prompting a lively duet between Jerry's constant companions of anxiety and self-doubt. He wasn't sure he wanted to go inside, even with Marilyn, and he wasn't sure why. Marilyn had visited Mr. Stamper's apartment several times that he knew of, getting keys, admiring finches, and delivering baked goods. He wondered if he looked as anxious as he felt.

The door opened wide to reveal the silhouette of Mr. Stamper, faintly backlit by a distant natural light in what was otherwise a darkened room.

"Good morning Mr. Stamper," Marilyn bubbled at the silhouette.

"Welcome," Mr. Stamper said and stepped aside to let in his guests.

Jerry followed Marilyn through the door and toward the dim light at the back of the apartment, walking in the trail of cigarette smoke wafting through the backlit frizz of Mr. Stamper's hair.

While Marilyn had forewarned Jerry that Mr. Stamper's apartment smelled bad and was, as she said "over-furnished," he hadn't realized her capacity for understatement. A pervasive, nauseating, cigarette funk combined in sensory overload with another dank lemony smell Jerry realized must be furniture polish. On both sides of their path were jumbled walls of furniture stacked to the ceiling, fitted carefully together like Chinese puzzle pieces, so tightly warehoused into the available space none of it could have been in use. Jerry followed Marilyn closely, fighting the smells violating his sinuses, walking hunched inside the narrow walls of furniture to better manage his claustrophobic alarm.

"I invited Jerry to help me pick out my finches," she told Mr. Stamper as they walked, evidently needing to explain Jerry's presence.

Mr. Stamper gave Jerry a reappraising glance over a shoulder that incorporated a low-wattage twinkle and the faintest of smiles, as if approving of his tenants together. Jerry smiled back uncertainly, not feeling at all like the rascal Mr. Stamper's glance implied, wondering if the glance was a flash of lechery from this porn shop owner.

Marilyn continued her nervous chatter; further explaining Jerry's presence. "I wanted a second opinion. I wasn't sure I could pick ones that would get along. I know, I know, you said Society finches always get along, but I think it's so important that they do because they have to stay caged up together like that and it would be just horrible for them if they squabbled all the time. I don't know anything about birds, so I certainly don't know how I'm going to choose. I'm hoping you can suggest some guidelines, maybe, or..." etc., etc.

At that point in their budding friendship, Marilyn was still a complete mystery to Jerry; he had no idea why she occasionally talked so much. He accepted it as one of her eccentricities, like her need to bake things. Or, maybe she caught the twinkle in Mr. Stamper's eye too, and was embarrassed by it and having second thoughts about inviting Jerry.

Mr. Stamper appeared fascinated by her blather, eagerly listening to her every word as he slowly led them toward the light, looking back over his shoulder and smiling his yellow-toothed smile at Marilyn while she talked, slowing their progress through the hoard of looming furniture.

Jerry was impressed by the sheer size of the apartment, more than twice that of his own. While it smelled like an ashtray, from what he could see of the furniture in this murky, wooden graveyard it appeared to be of exceptional quality. Most of it was heavily carved hardwoods, dark and solid. Sideboards, armoires, dining tables, and china cabinets defined their path through the room. Plant stands, footstools, end tables, and tiny writing desks were fitted into the empty spaces. Ornate, glass-beaded, floor and table lamps were incorporated into the walls of furniture on either side of the aisles, but none of their lights were on. It was dark except where light flooded in from the back of the apartment. Cut-pile carpet runners underfoot protected the wall-to-wall underneath, thoroughly muffling their progress through the room. It was like walking through the warren of some smelly, burrowing animal, tunneling into the Hobbit's home.

They exited the warren into a bright oasis, a glass atrium across the width of the second story, an alley-side feature of the building Jerry had never noticed. He immediately felt better with evidence of blue sky through the frosted overhead glass. The atrium was filled with patio furniture, houseplants, birdcages, and the quiet flutter and chirp of birds. It was like a garden with lots of ashtrays, littered with signs of daily use, newspapers, reading glasses, coffee cups, cartons of cigarettes, and slippers kicked under the chairs. This was clearly where Mr. Stamper spent most of his time.

The open atrium did wonders for Jerry's claustrophobia, but he still felt anxious and out-of-place. Marilyn and Mr. Stamper hovered around the largest of the cages, while Jerry lurked behind them, grinning as Marilyn excitedly peppered Mr. Stamper with questions about the birds and the old man did his best to keep up, obviously delighted by Marilyn's enthusiasm. Jerry felt a hopeless laggard in their rapid, bird-centered banter. How had the two come to be so close so quickly? He'd lived there almost as long as Marilyn, yet he still wasn't comfortable around his landlord. Why was that? Why hadn't he become good friends with anyone in this town, or in *any* town? He'd left no friends behind in Kilgore. Jerry had wanted to show Marilyn on their "date," that he wasn't the dullard she had seen so far, yet he was standing back like a scarecrow, swamped by a cold crisis of confidence.

Maybe the rest of the world wasn't out of step; it was just him!

Was he one of those people who didn't fit anywhere, who disliked or distrusted everything and everybody? The writer in him tried to find the right word for that.

Miscreant?

Misanthropist?

Misogamist?

Misogynist?

Mycologist?

Marilyn grabbed his arm, pulling him up beside her, closer to the cage of finches.

"Here they are," she said proudly, as if she had just finished setting them up for display.

Jerry watched them without comment until Marilyn evidently thought he might need a formal introduction. "Jerry, these are all young society finches. Finches, this is Jerry."

Jerry was grateful for her rescue of him, for pulling him out of his navel and into the moment, and for giving him something to say.

"How do you do," he greeted them, more than willing to play along with Marilyn's silliness.

She rewarded his participation with her giggle.

"Well, you see the problem," she said to every creature present. "How can I possibly choose two from all these beautiful birds?" When she looked to Jerry for guidance, he could only shrug his dismay at the overwhelming nature of it all.

There were about ten or twelve birds in the big cage and some fewer numbers in each of the other cages. It was impossible to know how many altogether since some of them were inside the little, round wicker nests in each cage and those outside the nests were constantly flitting around or hopping along the perches. What's more, they all looked exactly alike to Jerry, right down to the last feather. He had no idea how to choose a pair.

"Would you like me to help?" Mr. Stamper wheezed the question and then broke into a prolonged, fluid coughing fit that sent the birds atwitter.

"Oh, please do," Marilyn said with great relief when he recovered, either relieved he'd offered to help or relieved he *had* recovered.

"Well let's see…" Mr. Stamper studied the problem, rubbing the silvery stubble on his chin. "Could I ask you some questions first?"

"OK. Ask away," Marilyn said.

"Do you want to have kids?" Mr. Stamper asked, sneaking a quick, mischievous glance at Jerry.

Marilyn saw the glance too and faltered a moment, almost rendered speechless by the double meaning in Mr. Stamper's cheeky question, but she recovered nicely. "Well, I don't know," she began, stalling to think. "I'm not sure the cage I bought is quite large enough to raise a family. How much room do they need for that?"

Mr. Stamper could not suppress a smug little smile over his zinger of a question. "It doesn't require much space to raise a family, at least at first," he said. "As the kids grow up, of course, you'll need more room, but I think you'd be just fine with what you have for now."

"Well, then *yes*," Marilyn said boldly, choosing to think he was talking only about birds. "I'd like to have a nest full of eggs. I think that would be exciting. Don't you Jerry?" Jerry could tell she was immediately sorry to have involved him in the subject of families. A delightful flush of color moved up her neck and into her cheeks and she began to prattle. "I can always get a larger cage if I can't bear to part with them after they've grown up," she said. "I don't have a lot of room for more than one cage, but I guess I could sell the smaller cage and put them all together in the bigger cage, but of course then they'd be all the more likely to lay even more eggs and I'd need another cage when they hatched, or maybe…," etc., etc.

Marilyn was locked again into non-stop chatter. She appeared close to panic. Her eyes darted to follow the frenetic birds, her eyebrows pinched together in her effort to maintain the flow of words.

Jerry was bothered by her escalating anxiety and wanted to do something to help her. Instinctively, he lightly touched her forearm. It was the first time he had touched her and it stopped her mid-sentence, like flicking a switch. She turned to face him, looking a little disoriented, as if awakening from hypnosis.

"What about inbreeding?" Jerry asked Mr. Stamper in the ensuing silence.

The effect of his touch on her had made him feel like some kind of powerful magician, come to her rescue. She was clearly grateful to have been interrupted and to have him shoulder some of the conversational load.

"That's a very good question," Mr. Stamper said, looking pleased and maybe a little surprised Jerry would have come up with such a good question.

"Inbreeding shouldn't be a problem," he said, "*if* you are careful to choose one bird from each of the two hatchings in this cage, because I know they have unrelated parents. You can tell the two hatchings apart because the latest one doesn't quite have its full plumage. There, look around the eyes and beak on that one. See?" He leaned forward to point it out for them with one long yellowed fingernail.

Marilyn leaned in to see the difference and asked with a shy grin, "How do you tell the girls from the boys?"

"It's not so easy with birds," Mr. Stamper said, standing upright again and looking down at Marilyn's butt while she leaned over. He saw that Jerry noticed this and smiled at him with an ancient wolfish leer. Once again Jerry was reminded this was a man who owned a porn shop. "The easiest way," Mr. Stamper continued, "is to put two of them together. If one of them sings then you have one of each. If neither of them sings then you have two of the same sex.

"How romantic!" Marilyn said. "When there's love, there's music."

Mr. Stamper and Jerry looked at each other over Marilyn's head and shared a special moment, their expressions exactly alike as they each marveled at the wonderfully alien nature of the female mind.

Freeing the Birds

Old Man Stamper came out of a dream. He had been laying with Emma, holding her close, sharing memories of their courtship, just as he had so often done during those interminable nights in her final years, trying to calm her agitation, not sure she was listening anymore. He continued his dream conversation in an empty bed. "Remember the notes we used to pass in class? Don't you wish we still had them? I'll bet we'd laugh at how silly they were." Stamper swung his bony legs to the floor and sat for a long time on the edge of the bed, as if waiting for something from Emma about their note-passing. He became chilled and draped his robe around his shoulders and legs as best he could without standing. "OK, so you can't talk to me anymore, but I know you can hear me."

In that dark and quiet moment, he decided.

He got up, tied his robe, clicked on the bedside lamp, lit a cigarette, and found his reading glasses. "I'd like to read you something." He found the book he wanted and returned to sit in the lamplight. He thumbed through the pages until he found the passage he had in mind. He read the few brief lines softly in the quiet, sharing them with Emma. When he finished, he left the book open on his nightstand, took a last, long draw on his morning cigarette, and pressed it out in the ashtray. He then retrieved a bottle of pills from the top drawer of his nightstand, stood up, found his slippers, and carried the pills into the kitchen.

He made a pot of coffee, sat on the lounge while it brewed, and reviewed his planning. He'd made a list somewhere; it was so easy to forget anymore. But, never mind; he'd tied all the loose ends he could think of. Simon would take care of anything else. Lawyers were good at that.

The coffee was done. He poured a cup and returned to the lounge. He took his time with the pills, swallowing a couple with each warm sip. When the bottle was empty, he lay back against the lounge pillow, folded his hands across his chest, and closed his eyes.

His eyes opened. With great effort, he swung his legs to the floor and stood up one last time.

"I almost forgot my babies."

It's Mr. Stamper!

Two mornings later, Jerry was reeled in from the depths of Mowdabb by a pounding on his apartment door. He found Marilyn standing there with her face screwed up in an unattractive manner. Before he could react to this remarkable sight, she flung herself at him, melding her warm, soft torso to his scrawny midsection, and began sobbing into his chest.

Jerry had no previous experience with such behavior, so remained motionless except to pat the neutral territory in the middle of her back. He let her go on like that for several moments longer, instinctively saying "shhhhh" to no effect whatsoever. Her sobbing settled into a steady, quavering "waaaah" that lasted until each breath was exhausted.

Carefully timing his question during her inhale, Jerry asked, "Marilyn, what is it?"

She struggled for a measure of control, taking deep breaths, finally able to squeak the words, "It's Mr. Stamper! I think he's... passed on." It was all she could manage to say and, having said it, let go again.

Jerry translated "passed on" to mean dead and experienced an assault of emotions unique in their combination. He was ashamed that his first concern was how Mr. Stamper's death might affect his own immediate future. More to his credit, his second concern was with Marilyn, who had to deal with the shock of discovering the body.

Nowhere in his thinking was the least measure of surprise Mr. Stamper had died; it was something he thought might happen in the brief pause after every raspy breath the man took. Jerry tried to give

Marilyn a more comforting hug, though she couldn't have been closer. "How did you find him?" he asked, hoping to get her talking so the crying could stop. It worked.

"I went to ask him a question about the finches," she said, with little gasps for air as she attempted normal speech, "but there was no answer. I hadn't seen or heard him all weekend and he's been in such poor health, poor thing, that I became worried. I used the emergency key he gave me to let myself in and... waaaah."

Jerry wondered if Marilyn might be wrong, if Mr. Stamper might have merely suffered a seizure, or a stroke, or something of that sort. Perhaps he had fallen into a coma, or a faint, or a funk, or into any other state not as final as death.

"I'll be right back. OK?" He led her to his couch. "I won't be long. You just wait right here."

Jerry went to Mr. Stamper's open door and began the dark, claustrophobic walk through the furniture. Approaching the light, he saw birds out of their cages, bravely flitting around the dimly lit room, watching Jerry's progress from lampshades and chair rungs. More of them were in the atrium, perched on the dish drainer by the kitchen sink, and in the ficus tree. All the cages were empty, their doors standing open.

In the middle of this bright, energetic setting lay Mr. Stamper's body, arranged on a chaise lounge. It was unmistakably a body, no longer Mr. Stamper. The labored breathing stopped, his face not the color of a living man.

It was Jerry's second dead body. His Grandma had died sitting upright, eyes open as if in horrified astonishment. Mr. Stamper was peacefully reclined in his robe, eyes closed, big-knuckled, tobacco-stained fingers deliberately interlaced across his chest. Apart from the deathly pallor, his ultimate relaxation made him appear to be enjoying the sunshine, comfortable and tranquil. While Jerry's Grandma had displayed nothing to recommend death, Mr. Stamper seemed to demonstrate it might not be a bad thing, the noisy effort to breathe no longer necessary. His last cigarette lay burned out to a gray relic of its former shape, a limp worm of ash.

A finch flew onto the toe of Mr. Stamper's slipper, accepting the body as part of the landscape.

The empty pill bottle was on the stand beside the lounge. Jerry picked it up to read the label and to think about things. After a moment, he pushed it down among the empty wrappers, soggy coffee filters, and food scraps of Mr. Stamper's kitchen garbage can. It felt right to hide the evidence of suicide, as if he might be doing the old man a favor.

When he returned to Marilyn, who was now under more control, dabbing at tears with her shirttail, she looked at him expectantly, probably hoping the same thing he'd been hoping, that she might have been wrong about Mr. Stamper.

He sat down beside her and said, "It looks like he just let the birds out and laid down to die." Her tears started again. This time she cried more quietly.

Jerry held her in his arms, knowing just how she felt. After he found his Grandma's body, he sat nearby and cried quietly, just as Marilyn was doing, feeling more lonesome than he ever had. He cried for his Grandma, from the shock of it, and from the sense of loss that is a part of death, but mostly he cried for himself, feeling truly an orphaned child, with crazy Uncle Harold now his only living relative, away somewhere at the time and not there to provide any comfort.

Jerry did not cry this time, though he felt the loss of Old Man Stamper. Marilyn was with him; he was not so alone. He held her in his arms for a long time before getting up to call an ambulance.

- - -

Mr. Stamper's body began its final gurney ride as Marilyn and Jerry clutched one another on the landing outside the big apartment.

"What do we do now?" Marilyn asked.

"I don't know," Jerry admitted.

"What do we do now?" she asked the ambulance men as they lifted the gurney wheels to manage the stairs. They paused long enough to give the semblance of a thoughtful answer. "Well, I reckon you just do whatever you would have done if this old gentleman hadn't died when he did." When neither of them responded to this folksy sagacity, the ambulance men returned to their grim labor.

The outer door closed behind them, shutting out the clatter of the gurney and the huff of their exertions. Marilyn and Jerry were alone in what now seemed a large and empty building, still clutching one another in the quiet.

"I don't want to sleep alone tonight," she whispered against his chest.

When she heard his heart begin to pound, she clarified, "I didn't mean that to sound like it did." She said this softly, still talking to his chest. "I wonder if you would stay with me tonight, sleep on my couch like you did when you lost your keys. I just... I just need to know someone is close by."

"Sure," he said, eager to be that someone. He didn't want to be alone either, but he didn't say it. Jerry was foundering in an unfamiliar sea, awash with new emotions, near tears, sad to see the end of Mr. Stamper and anxious about the probable loss of his job and apartment, but he had never felt more grounded and peaceful than he did at that moment with his arms around Marilyn. This was enough for him. Of course, he wanted to spend the night with her, even if only on her couch. He was happy to live next door to her for however long it might last. Anything closer than next door was even better.

Long before he could have verbalized any of that, Marilyn clarified her invitation, "It's just for tonight. I should be OK alone by tomorrow."

"Glad to be of service," he said, knowing as it left his mouth it was the inanest thing he'd ever said. Again, he was thinking too slowly, verbally stumbling when he wanted to say so much, that he liked having her as a neighbor and that it felt so good with her in his arms. It felt as if he was absorbing comfort. He wanted to prolong their embrace as long as possible, but his stomach growled loudly and spoiled the mood before he could put the right words together.

Marilyn graciously made no comment.

The grumbling reminder from his gut, which had always effortlessly wielded control over him, gave him something to say. "I'd invite you to dinner at my place, if I had a second chair in my apartment, or any clean dishes, or any edible food."

"Oh," she said, and no more.

This was disturbingly uncharacteristic of her to say so little; Jerry had begun to enjoy how Marilyn easily filled their conversations, her wordiness nicely complementing his own grunted contributions.

"Maybe we could walk down to the café on the corner?" He had been emboldened by his hope to forestall another embarrassing stomach growl and by his desire to stay with this woman as long as he could.

Still, she didn't say anything. This was embarrassing. He was cowering inside for fear of rejection. Had he been too bold? He didn't know what was going on inside her head, but the outside of it changed; her cheek altered its shape against his chest after he made his suggestion. A grin or a grimace? She was too far below for him to tell. At last, she spoke. "It would be nice to get out for a while."

"I should shut down my computer and change my shirt," he said, his relief at her acceptance had him thinking more quickly. "Maybe we could meet right here in about ten minutes."

She looked up at him, her smile leaving no doubt. "Make it a half hour and it's a date," she said.

The mood in the building was suddenly much brighter.

Then Marilyn stepped back to look questioningly at him, losing some of the smile, evidently concerned she might have presumed too much by calling their rendezvous a date.

"Sounds good to me," Jerry said, in what he hoped was reassuring acceptance of her presumption.

A little of her smile came back, but brought dozens of questions back with it. They swarmed in her eyes like worrisome gnats. Jerry was eager to answer them all if only she would tell him what they were.

Standing together on the quiet second-floor landing, with his grateful arms around her, Jerry wondered why he felt so different around this mysterious little human? Conversations he'd had with other people now seemed like remote, muted exchanges compared with the multilayered subtleties of a conversation with Marilyn. Somehow, merely being in her presence left him tangled in bewildering nuance.

Tell you the truth...

The café was warm after their walk on the street. They found a booth near the front window. A neon transformer buzzed quietly over the table, powering advertising for Miller Lite and clearing an area of steamed window with its heat. They sat quietly, watching the people on the sidewalk outside.

They had walked the few blocks shoulder-to-shoulder (actually shoulder-to-elbow), keeping close to preserve the feeling of comfort between them. There was little conversation while they waited for their order to come. Marilyn then nibbled the edges of a Patty Melt while Jerry dove into a Meatball Sub.

He could tell Marilyn had something on her mind, but didn't want to press her to talk about it, thinking she would say it in her own time, whatever it was. He was preoccupied with the sub, but Marilyn pushed her plate away after a few more nibbles, and patiently watched him eat. He was hungry. She seemed to understand his need to work through the sub uninterrupted.

"Whew, that was good," he said, coming up for air when the sub was gone and pushing the plate away. "Would you like coffee?"

"Yes, please," she said, all reserved politeness.

Jerry went to the counter to order coffee and find toothpicks. When he returned, Marilyn asked, "What will become of our jobs?"

Prying beef gristle from his molars, Jerry didn't answer. He didn't have an answer.

"I know it's crass," she went on, "to talk of such things now, so soon after poor Mr. Stamper has…"

She could not say it.

"Tell you the truth," he said, stepping in to help her out, "I was wondering the same thing."

She seemed relieved to hear he was crass too.

Jerry thought about it some more. Marilyn waited patiently for his slower thought processes to wend their way to his speech center. "I'm guessing," he said at last, "the new owners, or the real owners, whoever they are, maybe a bank, are not likely to keep things the same." After a bit more thinking, he said, "They might even want to sell the building."

Marilyn soberly nodded in agreement. "We would lose our jobs *and* our apartments." She studied her hands in her lap for a while, fighting back more tears.

"Maybe not," he said, though there wasn't much hope in the words.

The coffee arrived and Marilyn pulled herself together for the sake of the waitress. When the waitress was gone, she asked, "If that happens, what will you do?"

Jerry could not remember the last time anyone had any interest in what he planned to do. Without thinking, he said, "Well, I've been trying to work my way to Alaska." He had not told anyone about this plan before. It surprised him he had told her so easily.

"Really? Why?" she asked, truly puzzled.

Jerry was stumped, and disturbed that he was stumped. How could he explain *why*? His erstwhile, far-fetched, Bush-Pilot-in-Alaska dream was difficult to believe now, he couldn't expect Marilyn to make sense of it. It was too embarrassing to share, even more so after his flight lessons. He didn't want to get into his philosophy of getting away from the crush of too many people occupying the same geography, because he didn't want Marilyn to think she might be among those people from whom he wanted to get away. Also, he would likely have even fewer prospects in Alaska than he had in Seattle. (His resume was not impressive: Librarian's Assistant, Handyman, and Porn Clerk.) Beyond the nebulous adventure of it, he could not give a truthful, understandable reason. So... he made something up, improvising as he talked, drawing from his fantasies of living on the frontier. "I thought I might write a travel guide," he said, "on life in the remote towns up there, maybe pick up some used camera gear and take photos to illustrate the book. You know, pictures of the buildings and the means of travel, planes and boats and such."

"Wow," she said, impressed either with his idea or his extemporaneous fabrication.

He couldn't tell which, so he asked, "Kinda unrealistic, isn't it?"

"No!" she said. "It's a great idea."

"You really think so?"

"Sure. That could be a great book. I've often wondered about the people who can live way up there all alone in that cold country, so far from other people. I mean, how do they stand it, being by themselves all the time? I know *I* couldn't live like that, so I've always wondered about the people who would choose that kind of life."

"Well, I wasn't thinking of making it about the people so much," Jerry said, "but that might be a good angle."

Marilyn was obviously more into the people side of things than he was; it hadn't occurred to him to include the Alaskan people in his lie. What did that say about him? He wondered how it might change what she thought of him if she suspected he was one of those people who thought he might like living alone, but he didn't want to get into that either. The up side of his lie was that he had gotten Marilyn talking and sounding more like her old self. That was enough for now.

She said, "Wow" once more.

Jerry was uncomfortable with her spending so much enthusiasm on his lie.

After a time, Marilyn plucked her courage again to ask, "So, if we lost our apartments, would you go up there right away?"

"Unfortunately," he said, still improvising, "the weather is at its worst about now, and besides, I don't have enough money for plane fare, let alone camera gear."

"Oh," she said brightly, apparently delighted with his dream deferred. "Maybe you could sell your computer," she suggested half-heartedly. "You could use that money for a plane ticket and camera gear. You could take the photos and make a few notes by hand while you're there and type it up later."

She wrinkled her nose and gave him a little negative headshake, encouraging him not to like the idea.

Jerry liked that she hoped he wouldn't like it, but had graciously turned her thoughts to a possible solution. He was impressed with her ability to see possibilities everywhere, even in his lies. But most of all, he was flattered she thought he was capable of writing such a book.

"Only problem with that is: My computer is about five years out of date, which is forever in the computer market; I don't think I could get five dollars for it." He enjoyed seeing her countenance brighten as he shot down her idea. "Anyway, I still need it. I'm writing something else with it now."

"Oh, really," she said, all innocence and interest. "What are you writing?"

Incipient paranoia raced in to protect Jerry's vulnerable spots. Was this why she was paying attention to him? More reasonable thinking followed immediately. What possible ulterior motive could she have? No one was that curious. The unhealthy suspicion passed.

He wanted to answer her question, but… Mowdabb seemed far, far away at the moment, pointless pulp fiction. His erstwhile dream of financing a bush pilot's lifestyle with writing seemed childish. Unraveling even one string of truth from that embarrassing tangle would lead to more questions from Marilyn he couldn't answer.

Yet, almost against his will, he found himself saying, "I'm working on a novel."

"Wow," She said, apparently impressed all over again. And then, after a moment's hesitation, she asked, "It's not a porn novel, is it?"

"No! Good God, no. I haven't done enough field research for anything like that."

She laughed.

He loved her laugh.

"I could hear a lot of typing every time I passed your door, but I guessed maybe you were writing letters to your family, or writing for a correspondence course, something like that. I had no idea you were so ambitious."

Jerry had no idea anyone would see his self-indulgence as ambition.

"Tell me about it," she invited, and settled her chin into a hand, ready for a long telling.

He'd never attempted an extemporaneous synopsis, but... he told her about it.

- - -

"... and, in the end," Jerry wrapped up the telling almost an hour later, "Mowdabb becomes a sort of spiritual retreat for people throughout the galaxy. The export of Popnuts® is closely monitored so the yield is sustainable. All harvesting is done by hand to minimize the impact on the vegetation. Pilgrimage to Mowdabb is severely restricted to prevent overloading the delicate environment and to prevent degradation of the spiritual experience of living with the moss. Everyone who makes a pilgrimage is required to sign a pledge of compliance with Mowdabbian Rules. The Rydgyd dynasty becomes a model of environmental stability and cultural well-being throughout all the worlds where man has learned to live."

"Wow," Marilyn said again, quietly, the only thing she has said for the last hour. "It's beautiful."

While "beautiful" was not a word he would have applied to his novel, he saw no reason to take offense. He was delighted to have found someone with whom to share it.

"Most of that last part isn't written yet," he said. "I'm not really sure how all of that will come about, but I can't wait to find out."

She was staring into his eyes with what he wanted to interpret as unabashed admiration. He was soaking it up, grinning like a fool. To get them beyond that embarrassing impasse, he suggested it was time to go home.

When he was helping her with her coat, she lightly took his hand. They walked out of the café that way. Jerry was a little uncomfortable with the contact, with the newness of it. He didn't know what it all meant. He didn't know exactly how to swing his arm as they walked. He didn't know what might happen next.

Within a block, Jerry's discomfort was gone; walking with Marilyn seemed the most natural thing he had ever done.

Within another block, Marilyn was comfortable enough to raise a topic she had long wondered about, careful to word it in a way that wouldn't offend. "I'm extremely curious about why you come home all wet sometimes, or drunk, but I've told myself it's none of my business, so I'm not letting myself ask about that."

"Good," he said, embarrassed about those nights and not sure he could explain them so she would understand.

She looked up at him, as if to see whether he might have been upset with any part of her indirect question. He gave her a little smile.

A few steps further on he volunteered, "My car was stolen. That's why I had to walk home in the rain."

"No!" she said, fully ready to commiserate over his loss until she remembered something. "It was that little yellow thing parked near our building, right?"

"Yup."

"Someone stole *that* car?"

"Hard to believe, but true."

To her credit, she did not probe for more.

Then, without warning, Marilyn mysteriously segued from his stolen car to, "The finches!"

"What about them?"

"They're still loose in the apartment."

She dropped his hand to hurry her stride.

- - -

On entering Mr. Stamper's apartment, they flicked on the lights to dispel recent memories, expecting to see birds startle at the sudden brightness, but they were nowhere in sight. The finches had abandoned their expanded world and crowded into the security of their wicker nests. Feathered heads and tails filled the round entrances, their beady, black eyes tracking the big creatures outside. Those that couldn't fit in the nests were shoulder-to-shoulder along the perches, as close to one another as they could get.

"Aren't they wonderful?" Marilyn said.

"Amazing," Jerry said. "I see why they call them Society Finches."

"They feel safe and warm when they're close together," she said.

"They wouldn't be happy in Alaska, would they?"

The Planet of Love is in Eclipse

Jerry woke up on Marilyn's couch to the sounds of breakfast-making.

"Sorry," she said. "I was trying to be quiet. Are you hungry? I'm making scrambled eggs with diced ham and salsa. I like my eggs with salsa. Do you? I've just got regular whole wheat bread if that's all right, or I could make some biscuits really quick if you like biscuits for breakfast. Sorry I woke you up; I wanted to have it all ready for you first thing, but this kitchen is so small and I don't have room for all these pots and pans, so every time I try to pull one out of the cupboard it makes a heck of a racket." Etc., etc., etc.

Jerry managed a nod or a shake of the head at her questions, attempting an appropriate change of expression for each new topic. Marilyn was evidently nervous about having him in her living room, or excited about making breakfast for him. He guessed mostly the former.

"Good morning," he said.

"Oh yes," she said, took a deep breath, and smiled, "Good morning." As she said it, she pushed an undisciplined wisp of hair from her forehead with the back of her wrist in a way he liked very much.

Everything smelled so good he was instantly starving. Last night's meatball sub was a distant memory.

"Is there some way I can help?"

"No, thanks for asking, but, like I said, this kitchen is so small, there's no room for two cooks. It's almost ready anyway."

Jerry busied himself by folding up the blankets and washing his face in the bathroom until called to breakfast, where he shoveled down a mound of scrambled eggs, drank two big glasses of orange juice, and piled jelly on slices of whole wheat bread. He could not remember breakfast ever tasting so good.

"What should we do today?" Marilyn asked when he finally leaned back to enjoy a second cup of coffee. "About the two stores, I mean."

"I think I'll just put a sign on the door," he said.

"What kind of sign?"

"I don't know, maybe something like 'Closed Today - Make Do with Your Fantasies' or 'The Planet of Love is in Eclipse.' What does it matter?"

"I don't know; maybe it does matter," she said.

"Well then maybe I'll just say, 'Closed Due to Personal Tragedy.'"

"No, that's not what I mean," she said. "Maybe it matters that we should keep the stores open."

"What for? We may never see another paycheck and I'm not providing any vital services."

"I'm thinking of the new owners, whoever they are," she said. "Maybe they would be more likely to keep things the way they are if they can see the stores continuing to operate, bringing in the income we produce for them."

Jerry could see she had a good point.

"Anyway," she continued, "I have customers coming back today to pick up copy jobs; I can't simply put up a sign. They'd be furious with me."

"I guess I was hoping to focus on my writing today, but you're probably right." Then he found he was getting angry. "I don't know why in hell I even work there; I hate that damn store."

"It *is* pretty grungy," she agreed, smiling a little, evidently pleased to learn he didn't like the store either.

Jerry fumed a little longer, trying to think of a word to top her choice of "grungy." All the while, Marilyn appeared to be thinking.

"Why don't you open the store as usual and bring your computer to the shop, set it up behind the counter and write the whole day. I doubt if your customers would care."

"Yeah, I could do that! That's a great idea," he said, amazed he hadn't thought of it himself. He could have been doing that for months instead of the notebook to computer conversion each evening.

"Sure, then even when the new owners walk into the store," Marilyn added, "they'll see you working on something. They won't know what you're doing; they'll just see you're still there, keeping the place open for them."

- - -

Jerry set his computer right on the glass counter top of the dildo case. He perched on his stool, as usual, but had to open the back of the case to make room for his knees among the dildos. He was soon slipping away to Mowdabb, issues of his future in the real world all but forgotten.

The writing of the novel began to pick up speed from that day forward since there were no intermediate steps between thinking about it and typing it up. Everything seemed to be coming together.

The residents of Mowdabb were coming together too:

Slicker

All of Mowdabb's children are working together on a giant slide. It is their biggest ever construction project. They'd made smaller slides before, but never on this scale, a construction site covering a hundred meters of gentle winding slope in the shape of an S. The children have already cleared the area of all overgrowth and loose rocks. Now, they are working to cover the clearing with a mosaic of moss slabs of a special type the children call "slicker," a dense, cushiony moss with the rare property of being slippery, as if greased, even when perfectly dry. Once repositioned, the contiguous slabs will continue to grow, weaving themselves together into an unbroken, living playground.

Their work on the slope looks like a child-labor camp, except there are no adults around and every child appears to be enjoying the labor. They cooperate in the construction without question or complaint. They all know what to do. Even the youngest of them understands they are making a place to play and they play as they go; there is no timetable for completion. Slicker already covers the outrun at the bottom of their giant slide, where the edges curl up to contain plunging sliders. The youngest cannot resist sliding on what has been assembled so far, but many more slabs will be needed before the mosaic reaches the top of the slope and they can all enjoy the full length of it.

Adam is working a distance away from the construction site, harvesting slabs of slicker wherever it is found growing naturally. He is the only one of the children with the size and strength to peel slicker off the rocks. When a slab is harvested, a few assistants roll it up and lift it onto the shoulders of the next two children waiting to carry it to the construction area. At the other end of the moss brigade, the two oldest girls receive the slabs, unrolling and positioning them on the cleared slope. The two oldest girls, though half-sisters, look and act as if they are twins like their mothers. They are unconsciously synchronized in their movements as they fit the slabs together like pieces of a quilt.

Adam is their natural leader, born into the role, the oldest and the largest of them. He is confident, even-tempered, poised beyond his years, and protective of the little ones. The children all do as Adam says, not because he demands it of them, or threatens them in any way, but because he always seems to know what should be next, and he is the oldest.

Most siblings would not work with such unity and cooperation, but the children have no way of knowing that; their way is all they have ever known.

Adam watches the other children carefully, not to keep them working, but to judge when they are beginning to tire. When he sees the youngest members slowing, he stops the construction and leads them to a place to rest in the shade, drink from the waterlogged moss, forage for food, and otherwise spend the balance of their day playing together, lost in the ancient, idyllic pursuits of unfettered childhood. When the slide is finally assembled, they will leave it alone until the slicker slabs grow together. When Adam declares their play will not damage it, he will lead them back to this place for many afternoons of play.

The children return each night to the home cave, the youngest first, the oldest trail in just as the fog begins, their exhausted bodies smelling sweetly of humus and the mossy perfumes of Mowdabb. The youngest sleep around their mother's beds, in peaceful, innocent exhaustion. The older children begin to adopt neighboring caves.

At regular intervals though, for four nights in a row, the younger children have their bucolic routine disturbed as their parents are overcome by another sexual storm. During those four nights, the children either migrate to a "puppy pile" in an opposite corner or sleep in separate caves with the older ones. They are not upset by the mysterious noises adults sometimes make in the night; that is simply the way it is with adults.

- - -

POOLING BUDGETS

Nuzzle

Jerry's growling stomach pulled him back from Mowdabb and made him think it was lunchtime, the clock over the door said 5:45! He'd spent the whole day lost a glorious Mowdabbian fog. He was exhilarated by the progress he'd made, numb from sitting so long, and starving.

He counted out the register, but didn't know what to do with the deposit. He called Marilyn in COPY/COPY to see what she planned to do with hers.

"I think we should carry it to the bank tomorrow and deposit it in the same account Mr. Stamper used," she said. Jerry could hear the copier whirring and chunking in the background.

"What about our next payday?" he asked. "How are we gonna pay ourselves?"

"I don't know yet," Marilyn admitted, "but I think this is the right thing to do until we figure that out. It's what the new owners would want."

Jerry knew she was right, but they couldn't buy food without a paycheck. He hadn't saved much since the piece-of-shit car and flight lessons fiascos. "My finances are pretty tight."

"I know. Mine too; I spent too much on a birthday present for my Aunt Irene. Then there was that new outfit I couldn't resist. You know how that is."

Jerry didn't know, but said, "sure," anyway.

Marilyn said, "Maybe we could pool our food budgets and share our meals."

When he did not react immediately, she raced ahead with the idea. It was obviously something she'd thought about. "I don't mind cooking for the two of us. We could buy larger quantities and get better prices on things. Cooking for one is wasteful. It would be much less expensive if we shared."

She was talking fast to get all her arguments in before he could object.

"Besides, I love to cook," she added, "and, it's much more fun to cook for two than for one and you seem to enjoy my cooking and there are lots of dishes I would love to try but they just can't be done for small servings, like a pot roast for instance or almost any kind of baking or..."

Jerry wished he could reach out and touch her arm, to help her out of this, but, over the phone, the only way was to interrupt, "You'd like to cook for me every day?" He couldn't imagine anyone loving to cook that much, and wanting to do it for him.

"Oh sure," she said. "It'd be great. Maybe you could do the shopping and I could do the cooking. That'd be great."

"If I may borrow a phrase, 'Wow!'" he said.

Marilyn giggled.

"So, what's for dinner?"

She giggled again. "I have enough groceries for tonight and maybe for tomorrow night, but you'll need to go shopping soon."

"OK, we'll plan it out tonight over dinner."

Closing time. Jerry locked the door to The Planet of Love, tucked the day's measly take into the deposit bag, and went to his room to clean up.

Colonel Sanders Night

She made fried chicken. The smell of it cooking had Jerry salivating even before she responded to his knock on her door. There was coleslaw and mashed potatoes and brown gravy. She called it Colonel Sanders night. Jerry ate a lot of everything.

After dinner, they talked about many things, a philosophical conversation to discover where they stood on things that really mattered. The only thing on which they disagreed was that Alaska would be an exciting place to live. Marilyn conceded it might be an exciting place to visit. It was a conversation marked by honesty, pleasant and comfortable.

Jerry did not want to be anywhere else. He was too full to move for a long time anyway. When he finally could move, he helped to clear the table and do the dishes. He washed and she dried and put them away. She stood beside him on a little kitchen stool while they worked, in order to reach the higher shelves of her cupboard. The stool brought them eye-to-eye, an intimate difference.

"Where did you grow up?" he asked, setting a squeaky-clean plate in the drainer.

"Well, the simple answer," she began, "is that I grew up in Oceanside, but it's more complicated; I was a military brat. My dad was stationed in three or four places while I was little, but I was mostly raised in Oceanside. I didn't feel connected to anywhere we lived, but now I do. Since I got this job I've met a lot of people in the neighborhood, customers I see regularly. It's nice."

"Did you move here from Oceanside? I mean, what brought you to Seattle?"

She didn't answer right away and he was afraid he had asked too many questions. "Well…" she said, her face full of unspoken things.

"Sorry," he said, "I didn't mean to get too personal."

"No, no. It's not that at all." She went through a series of dismissive gestures and took several deep breaths, all false starts, trying to find the best way to tell him. "I came here to get away from my boyfriend." She glanced across, to see his reaction.

Most of the pleasure he had been feeling with the evening and in her company drained out of his face, down his arms, and into the dishwater. He was sure it showed. Her face softened a bit, incongruously pleased by his crestfallen reaction.

"I didn't know you had a boyfriend," he said, lamely.

"Oh, I don't anymore," she said, eager to clarify. Then she hesitated again, trying to decide how, and how much, to tell him. "I want to avoid him. It's difficult for me to explain. I don't want you to think badly of me for the way I behaved, but if we're going to be friends…" She leaned on the countertop now, turning her face close to Jerry's. His face flushed. It was the nearest he'd been to those big dark eyes and he found himself getting lost in them.

"*Jerry Garcia Gustafson*," he thought, "*you had better be careful.*" He wanted to be her friend, but, true to form, his reaction to her words, and to her proximity, was a spike in anxiety.

"…I should tell you about Coby," she said.

Without knowing more than Coby's name, Jerry deeply hated the sonofabitch. The sudden intensity of this reaction surprised him, as if a big switch had been thrown on his emotional console, putting him into full-blown protection mode, ready to wrap his soapy hands around Coby's neck to defend Marilyn. He returned his eyes to the dishwater, hoping Marilyn wouldn't notice how upset he was.

"I met Coby at the gym where we both worked out. He was a Marine, just like my father and brothers. I thought I had sworn off Marines, but..."

Visions of hard, stalwart men surrounded Jerry.

"I guess he charmed me at first," Marilyn continued, checking Jerry's face with each sentence to monitor his reaction.

Jerry kept his eyes on the dishwater.

"At the time, I thought he seemed so sophisticated and worldly, just like I thought I wanted to be. I was unhappy living at home, so... I spent a lot of time at an apartment Coby sometimes shared with a few other marines."

Underwater, Jerry's hands were scrubbing the same plate over and over, as if trying to get through the shine

"Anyway," she continued, "I didn't really move in with him, but I spent more nights at that damn apartment than I like to admit."

They were both quiet for a time. She waited for the next clean plate, aware of how hard Jerry was trying to show no reaction at all.

"It didn't last long between us. Coby was possessive and soon became abusive. When the abuse turned physical, I got on the train for Seattle without telling anyone I was leaving. I didn't even tell my dad where I was going."

When she didn't say any more, Jerry stopped scrubbing the plate, rinsed it, and handed it to her. She dried it and he returned his hands to the dishwater because he didn't know what else to do with them. He had a thousand questions, but didn't really want most of them answered.

"Did he hurt you?"

"Yes, a few bruises, but mostly my pride."

When Jerry turned to look at her, she was studying his face. He saw tears were welling.

"I'm so sorry," she said.

"Why? You've done nothing wrong."

They worked slowly on the dishes after that, her waiting quietly for the next item to dry, him hardly stirring the dishwater as he adjusted to the news of Coby.

"I don't think Coby knows where I am," Marilyn continued, "and I'm not sure he would come looking for me if he did know, but he might. I still worry about that. He is... very controlling."

Jerry wanted to say, "I'll protect you." But that sounded stupid, and presumptuous on several levels; she hadn't asked for protection and he wasn't sure what kind of protection he would be against a possessive marine.

"Do you still love him?" he asked.

"Hell no!" she almost shouted. "I never loved him. I hate him. He used me for sex. That's all it was to him."

Jerry was ready to begin stalking the sonofabitch.

"'We've done it all now, Punkin,' he told me one time in bed. You know... after. Then he laughed at me when I blushed, the bastard. It was like he'd been working from a checklist."

Jerry was too embarrassed by her admissions of intimacy and by his own limited sexual experience to want to know any more about Coby's checklist. Instead, he asked, "'Punkin'?"

"Yeah, I hated that, and he knew it."

Jerry was angrier than he had ever been, and at a person he had never met. He wanted to put his arms around Marilyn, and might have done so if he knew it would be consoling, and if his hands had not been soapy. He wasn't sure of their bond yet, maybe there was none from her perspective. All they had done was hold hands.

"So," she said, trying to move beyond the mood, "when I got to Seattle and went looking for a job, Mr. Stamper found me in line at the unemployment office."

"What? Wait a minute. Do you mean he found you through the unemployment office?"

"No, he picked me out of the waiting line. He just shuffled over and asked me if I knew how to run a copy machine. He said an apartment was included in the deal, handed me his business card, and walked away. It was just dumb luck on my part; I probably didn't know any more about running a big copier than the next guy in line, but he offered the job to me so I had to check it out. I wanted my own place and the unemployment office wasn't likely to offer anything better. So..." Marilyn shrugged.

"That's weird," Jerry said. "That's how it happened with me too. I mean I wasn't standing in line, but I was at the unemployment office when Mr. Stamper just walked up and offered me the job."

"Really? That is weird. Why would he pick the two of us out of the crowd?"

"He told me I reminded him of someone."

Neither of them could imagine any better explanation.

"I guess we'll never know," Jerry said, and was immediately sorry when Marilyn began to tear up.

Marilyn dried her eyes on the dishtowel and handed it to Jerry to dry his hands. The dishes were done. She stepped down from her kitchen stool and carried it to its place in the corner. Jerry hung the dishtowel to dry on the oven door handle. When he turned to face her, she had her hands on her hips and a smile on her face. "Thanks," she said.

He knew she meant for listening to her story. "Thank *you*," he said, meaning for the fine meal and for her willingness to confide in him.

She knew.

"How about some pumpkin pie?"

The woman's timing was flawless. Jerry had digested enough of dinner that he was able to hammer home a big wedge of pie and wash it down with a fresh cup of coffee. Afterwards, he was full to the brim again. More than that, he was grateful for her company.

"What about you?" she asked. "What brought you to Seattle?"

- - -

With only one reservation, Jerry told her everything. His lengthy confessional across her kitchen table started with Ms. Nervan's collapsing chair. He summarized his time on the street and the work he'd found before he got lucky with The Planet of Love. He ended with his abortive flight lessons. She was a great listener, appropriately sympathetic in all the right parts of his tragic adventures, especially when he talked of his failed dream to be a pilot.

"Oh, you'll find something even better," she said, confident, as if she could see into the future. Her certainty made him smile. He wasn't going to spoil the mood by doubting her.

Summarizing his life for Marilyn was the most he could remember ever having talked about himself to anyone. He told her a little about his mother, his grandmother, and his crazy uncle, but he didn't mention the doubtful story of his father. He made it clear his mother was unmarried and left it at that.

When Marilyn attempted to stifle a yawn, he said, "I should go now. I can probably get in a couple of hours of writing before bedtime."

She relaxed just a bit. He had not been able to notice that little bit of tension in her until it was gone. She must have been concerned about how to wrap up the evening. "Yes," she said. "That'll give me time to wash my hair and work out a menu plan for next week."

"Oh, yes. I forgot about that," he said. Her mention of menu planning reminded him of their plan to pool the food budgets, so he stood up, opened his wallet, and cleaned it out. "Look, all I have is thirty-three bucks right now and that isn't nearly enough the way I eat, but we're due for a payday on Friday, if we can figure that out, so, if you can cover the difference..."

"No," she said. "You don't need to give me this now. If you'll agree to do the shopping and keep all the receipts, we'll keep a running account of our food expenses for the week, divide it down the middle, and even everything up after payday."

"Sure."

"I'll just give you some cash to go with that," Marilyn said, "so you'll have enough for this first time."

"OK," he said, putting his money back in his wallet, "but I'm already indebted to you for all the good food I've eaten here."

"Oh no," she insisted. "You've been my guest. I enjoyed feeding you. I like watching you eat; you seem to enjoy it so."

"Well, yes, I guess I do," he said, wondering if he should be embarrassed about his enthusiastic table manners. "I certainly enjoy eating with you and... getting to know you."

He was a little uncomfortable as soon as he said it, even though it was true; he thought it sounded lame and perhaps too forward. However, the look on her face told him it had not been a mistake to say; she was pleased. Neither of them knew what to do next. Marilyn broke the awkward moment when she spun around to get her purse where it hung from a closet doorknob. She pulled out $30 dollars and handed it to him.

"This should help to cover whatever we'll need for the week."

Jerry took the money, all the while, for some reason, feeling ill at ease for doing so.

"I'll work out a menu plan and shopping list," she said. "I'll get it to you tomorrow morning, so you can go to the market after you close."

"OK."

It didn't seem right to be standing there with her money in his hand after he had been so heartily packing away the grub at her expense.

"Are you sure you want to trust me with this?" he did not want to take advantage of her; he was beginning to realize she was the best thing in his life right now and was terrified of screwing it up somehow.

"Of course," she said. "I know where you live."

They both smiled at the truth of it.

The awkwardness followed them to the door. Marilyn unhooked the chain for him, but let him turn the knob. Jerry did not go out right away; he wanted to tell her about all of the complicated things he was feeling, but he didn't know where to begin or even whether he should. What he ended up saying was not adequate, but it was better than his previous attempts at conversation. "I'm glad you're here," he said.

She put her arms around his middle and hugged him close. "I'm glad I'm here, too," she said.

Then, they sort of... nuzzled. He leaned down to her, so their cheeks came together. He could hear her breath in his ear. It was not a kiss, but it was about as close as you can come to a kiss without actually kissing and it was good. In fact, for the circumstances, it was just right.

- - -

That night, as he wrote, it was hard to keep his mind on Mowdabb. His thoughts kept returning to Marilyn. He was beginning to like this woman a lot and it scared him because these feelings were unprecedented. What's more, he was beginning to dare to think she was beginning to like him too.

Jerry's only other relationship with a woman had been the physical play with Karen. She had been fun, but he could not really have said he liked her personally. He had known little about Karen except that she was the only daughter of the manager of a ski lodge not far from Kilgore, and that she was so bored with living at the lodge she thought it was exciting to drive into Kilgore. He also knew she had two large moles, one a few inches above her belly button and the other halfway between her belly button and her pubic hair. He thought it looked like a row of three buttons. Jerry also knew that several of the young men around Kilgore were familiar with Karen's buttons. He never expected anything more from his relationship with Karen than playful, energetic sex, which, if she was in the mood, she never failed to deliver, so there was no reason for him to dislike her either. He had felt fortunate to be one of those upon whom she turned her attentions. She asked nothing of him but an erection, so there was never a problem between them, and nothing at risk.

With Marilyn, there was something at risk. Jerry didn't know what it was yet, but he wanted to find out. The fact there would most certainly be consequences from a relationship with Marilyn was a little frightening because he suspected it might already be too late for him to decide whether he wanted to risk them.

From Old Man Stamper's yet undiscovered library, Jerry would eventually learn that Shakespeare wrote the following:

Journeys end in lovers meeting.

Twelfth Night, act 2, sc. 3.

A Quick Kiss

Jerry knocked on Marilyn's door the following evening, his arms full of groceries. When she opened the door, he leaned down so she could take the bag he was about to drop. As she took it, she stood on her toes to give him a quick kiss on the cheek.

That was a first; one small step beyond their previous nuzzle.

She began unloading the food, behaving as if kissing him was unremarkable. "Didn't you shop at Safeway?" she asked, noticing the generic, unmarked bags.

"I went to Louie's," Jerry admitted.

"Louie is a rude barbarian and a pirate," she said vehemently, evidently having had a significant encounter with Louie. "Why do you go there?"

This was a difficult thing for Jerry to answer with any brevity, so he didn't try.

Marilyn fished the receipt out of the bag and tried to make sense of it. "I can't even tell what things cost; this is just a list of numbers. But, the total is at least ten bucks more than it would have been at Safeway, maybe twenty." Marilyn was delightfully furious. "I tell you, the man's a pirate."

She was right, of course; Jerry could defend neither Louie nor himself. His reasons for paying premium prices to endure Louie's prickly nature were complicated and sentimental. For one thing, Louie was better kept safely occupied behind a counter, holding food for ransom rather than acting out his hostilities on the street, but mostly the little market reminded Jerry of the one in Kilgore.

Marilyn's indignation over Louie's overcharging was, of course, also her way of indirectly pointing out his poor shopping skills. Jerry admired her diplomacy.

"You're right," he said. "Next week I'll shop at Safeway," already dreading the crowds.

"We can't afford Louie's prices," she said, unnecessarily underscoring her point, probably thinking about their uncertain finances.

Jerry nodded his agreement. With that, Marilyn returned to her campaign, now nearly won, to fill the kitchen with wonderful smells.

While Jerry put away the groceries and Marilyn attended to a big pot of pasta, she cautiously initiated another topic. "I had an idea today," she said as she stirred. "It came to me while I was working on one of those endless, monotonous jobs. You know how your mind tends to wander when the work is tedious. Well that's the kind of job I spent *hours* on today. I thought I would go nuts! But it gave me lots of time to think about your book."

"My book?" Alarm flags went up in all quadrants. Where was this going? Was she going to be critical? Was he wasting his time?

"Here, would you set that on the table?" she said, handing him a dish between a pair of hot pads. "Watch out, it's hot."

"What about my… Mmmmm, is that spaghetti? That smells good. What about my book?" He set the dish on the hot pads.

"Here, could you open this?" she asked when he came back to the kitchen, handing him a bottle of wine and a corkscrew.

"Sure, but what about my book?"

"Well, I need to ask you some questions first and, right now I need to toss this salad and put a few perishables away before we eat." She said all of this in a rush, clearly still running at high speed from her busy day, doing what she did so well, madly and magically multitasking, whether juggling paper in COPY/COPY or skillets on the stovetop.

Jerry opened and poured the wine, forcing himself to keep quiet while he watched her work.

"There," she said when the kitchen was straightened to her satisfaction. "Dinner's ready."

Surprise

They clinked glasses and dug in. When his feeding frenzy was over and he was again able to entertain conversation, he poured them each a second glass of wine, leaned back in his chair, and anxiously gave himself over to curiosity. "Now… about my book?"

"Yes," she said. "But first, a couple of questions…"

Jerry was impatient with her delay; he could not imagine where this might be headed.

"First, I need to know how long before you think it'll be finished."

"Till it's finished?" Jerry had never thought about finishing it and didn't have a timetable. How far into the future did he want to imagine Lurk's clan living on Mowdabb? What would constitute an appropriate ending? These were not easy questions. He could sense the end was near, but he'd need to review everything and cleanup details.

"I don't know." It was going to be difficult to let go of such a long-held project.

She waited for something more.

He gave her a vague estimate. "It could be another month or two, maybe a little longer, maybe six. Why?"

"OK," she said, absorbing that information, calculating something in her head, and moving on to the next question. "How were you planning to get it published?"

Another question he'd never considered... Jerry answered with sheepish honesty, "I don't have a plan for that. I've been focused on writing. I guess I planned to think about that later."

She nodded her head thoughtfully, studying him, weighing something behind those big, dark eyes. "I think maybe it's too early to talk about this; it might be better to wait until the manuscript is finished."

"Why not now? What's the mystery?"

"It's not a mystery so much as a surprise... maybe. OK, I guess *that* was a little mysterious." Seeing his rising impatience, she went on. "I've ordered something for COPY/COPY that should be here in a couple of weeks that might be used for my surprise, but I won't even know if my idea will work, exactly, until it gets here. I don't want to tell you about it, and then have you be disappointed if it doesn't work."

Jerry was becoming annoyed with her roundabout approach. "I'm already disappointed I don't know what you're talking about." His book was a precious and fragile thing he didn't like her trifling with.

"Oh," she said, her pouty bottom lip beginning to protrude in regret. "I shouldn't have mentioned it at all. I am sorry. I don't mean to be mysterious; it's just that I didn't want to be presumptuous... and if it doesn't work anyway..."

"If *what* doesn't work?" Jerry labored to keep his voice down. He was too curious by that time, and too irritated by having been made so curious; he could not let the topic drop.

She reluctantly said, "A book press. OK? I ordered a book press."

"A book press? What the hell is a book press?" Jerry was still irritated.

"It's really just a big clamp," she explained. "I plan to use it in the store for binding notepads and small booklets for customers. I was just thinking maybe I could figure out a way to bind a copy of your book for you, if you aren't offended by the idea, if the book isn't too big, if you are even interested..." She shrugged sadly, as if to apologize for making such a big deal out of such a little idea.

Her explanation generated even more questions. Jerry was trying to decide which of them to ask first, when he noticed how dejected she was. He realized he had browbeaten her into telling him about her idea. He finally stopped thinking about himself.

"Sorry," he said, but that sounded lame. "I'm not used to people being thoughtful."

The bottom lip retreated a little and she looked up to see if he was serious. "It was silly of me to think you'd be interested in such a thing. I'm sorry," she said.

"*No,*" he said, a little too forcefully. "No, you shouldn't be sorry; I *am* interested. I am the one who should be sorry. I was being a jerk." Suddenly filled with self-loathing, Jerry poured the rest of his glass of wine down his throat, gulping it quickly to deny himself the pleasure of tasting it and to put down an installment on a later, well-deserved headache.

It was quiet around the table. Jerry stared at his empty wine glass, but he could feel Marilyn staring at him.

A boom-box car passed by outside. The vibrations clattered the tableware.

It was quiet again.

When Jerry looked up to meet those big dark eyes of hers, they were steady and wide open. He had never felt so vulnerable. Tears were welling in her eyes, and then in Jerry's. Something in the air between them was changing, and something in him. A dizzying blend of hopeful expectation and fearful hesitation filled every wretched part of him. His tears embarrassed him, causing him to look away again, trying to find somewhere less daunting to focus.

No one had ever looked at him the way she did, as if she could see the real Jerry hiding behind the prickly bluster and haughty pretension with which he usually protected himself. He forced himself to meet her eyes again, attempting to match her open, unconditional look. He could not hide from her if he wanted to, and suddenly he did not want to. Incredibly, even though she could see clear through him, she was still here, still looking, evidently still interested.

The question was out of him before he had time to decide whether he should ask it. "Marilyn, why are you so nice to me?" Jerry sounded angry.

She looked down at her hands and then back at him. "I like you Jerry, very much."

"I can't understand that," he said.

She did not respond. How could anyone respond to that?

"I can't understand that," he said again, softening, "but I like it."

She smiled. The release of his tension in seeing her smile was almost debilitating. Every part of him relaxed, his body, his mind, everything.

"I like you too, Marilyn." He sounded so childish and shy, he could feel himself blushing.

She got up from her chair and stood close beside him, hugging his big dopey head to her chest. He put his arms around her, which, from his sitting position, put them around her butt. He hadn't planned to be that bold, but his arms were so long they easily wrapped clear around her anyway, putting his hands into less brazen terrain. It was not your classic hug, but it was a good one.

This time at the door, he kissed her. It was a little awkward at first because he had to lean way down and she had to stand on her toes, but once they had accomplished the lips-to-lips connection, all differences in height and thoughts of awkwardness were forgotten. Their positions had the added benefit, from Jerry's point of view, of keeping his embarrassing erection from throbbing up against her belly. Any contact down there was at risk of being premature and might well have ruined an otherwise perfect end to the evening.

Back in his own room, it was impossible to think about Mowdabb.

Simon

The next morning, Jerry sat behind the counter of an empty Planet of Love, trying to calculate on an already cluttered scratchpad the potential reproductive rate, over time, of three women and one man living on a Mowdabbian diet, on a planet with a 21-hour day. When the brass bell tinkled an entrance, he hardly noticed, but he heard hard-heeled shoes striding smartly toward him, all business. The man wore an expensive, well-tailored, chocolate brown suit. He was lean and, by Seattle standards, tan. A lavender tie was held in place by a gold clip matching a gold watch and ring. A perfectly bald head topped the polished appearance, giving him a mildly villainous Lex Luthor look. He carried his nose high over a strong, square jaw, his eyes focused on Jerry, taking no notice of the store's merchandise.

Something told Jerry there was trouble on the way and his defenses came up like a drawbridge.

"Are you Jerry Gustafson?" the man asked in a tone like he was expecting more than he saw.

"What are you selling?" Jerry asked in full defensive wise-ass mode. It gave the man a moment's pause.

"My name is Walter Albert Simon," he said, recovering nicely. "I am Mr. Stamper's lawyer."

This was suspicious news; Jerry wasn't aware Mr. Stamper had a lawyer.

"Now that he's dead, what are you?" Jerry countered, recovering nicely himself.

"I represent Mr. Stamper's estate, Mr. Gustafson," Simon said simply, ignoring Jerry's snappy repartee. "I am here to inspect the property and to arrange a meeting with you and Miss Gladkowski."

"Who the hell is Miss Gladkowski?" Jerry asked, without thinking.

Simon was almost able to hide a sneer at Jerry's evident social retardation. "Your neighbor," he said.

"Oh, you mean Marilyn," Jerry smiled knowingly at Simon, smoothly (he thought) letting the man know he and Marilyn were definitely on a first name basis, while hoping Simon couldn't tell how stupid he felt for not knowing Marilyn's last name.

"If you and Miss Gladkowski could meet me at my office at this address, we can get this settled." He handed Jerry his business card. "You'll both have to be there, so would Friday at six p.m. be a good time for the two of you?"

"Get what settled?"

"I think that will all become clear at our meeting. Just let me know if either of you can't make it."

Jerry was struggling with the logistics. "The stores close at 6:00; how about 7:30?"

"Fine." Simon turned away to end their conversation and begin his inspection of the building. He pulled a large set of keys from his pocket and went through the hidden doorway at the back of the store, displaying a familiarity with the building that Jerry found disturbing. Simon never glanced at the merchandise.

"The owners are taking control," Jerry thought. "It's starting to hit the fan."

With the occasional sounds of Simon clumping around upstairs in his hard-soled way, and with thoughts of a looming return to street life, Jerry had a difficult time on Mowdabb for the rest of the day.

Visitation

Lurk's uncounted Mowdabb years of peaceful domesticity and unfettered propagation come to an end when two hovercraft land in front of their cave in an early morning blitzkrieg of noise and wind. Lurk and the women have only enough time to gather in the cave entrance to watch a camera crew jump out of the nearest aircraft, all wearing identical orange coveralls. They are setting up tripods and pointing lenses and microphones like weapons. A similarly clad crew from the other aircraft begins unloading cases of equipment.

Lurk instinctively pushes the women into the cave behind him and centers himself in the entrance, effectively filling the opening. Several of the smaller children run past his legs and into the cave, seeking their mothers. The majority of the children fade into the moss.

The orange-clad crew continues arranging gear around the cave opening, ignoring the fierce expression of the big man who stands his ground. When a smallish man among the crew, intent on adjusting his recording equipment, comes too close. Lurk barks, "Back off!" The man startles, as if surprised Lurk could speak. All the other crewmembers stop their work, and look for direction from a tall, slender, and perfectly bald man bringing up the rear. The bald man steps forward, directly confronting Lurk. He nods to his crew to resume their work.

"I am Doctor Walter Albert Simian," he says. "We are conducting a study of the planet."

Lurk maintains a steady stare from his stand in the cave opening.

Dr. Simian continues. "We have long-term funding to make this the most comprehensive study yet conducted on Mowdabb. That study will include all flora and fauna. Since you have adopted this planet and have been sustained now for many years on a purely Mowdabbian diet, the study of this planet's fauna must include you, the women, and any children born here."

Lurk's heart is pounding, his senses on full-defensive mode. No one moves a muscle for the longest time. The cameras and microphones all center on Lurk, poised to record his response. When the smallish man moves to adjust his equipment, Lurk's stare snaps his way, startling everyone except Dr. Simian, who merely waits impatiently, as if observing a recalcitrant specimen. Lurk quickly returns his vigilance to Dr. Simian, to what his instincts tell him is the embodiment of danger.

Lurk's mind is racing. Though he has known, and dreaded, that such a day would come, he has no idea how to handle their intrusion now that it is here. He senses Eve and the twins are standing quietly behind him, comforting the littlest ones. He is not concerned with the children hiding in the moss; he knows they will remain there as long as these strangers are around. His single, overriding concern is to defend the women in the cave.

Finally, Lurk comes up with an appropriate response for Dr. Simian's comprehensive study of the local fauna. "Fuck off," he says.

The smallish man appears shocked to have recorded it, but Dr. Simian continues as if Lurk had not spoken. "We need to know if you've had any medical problems, what sort of parasites you've picked up, skin rashes, infections, that sort of thing. We need to know if you've encountered any life forms or obvious evidence of previous life forms beyond the ubiquitous rock carving. We need to know if you've discovered any unusual mineral deposits or other natural resources. But we especially need to know what you're eating."

Lurk maintains his motionless stare; he has said all he wants to say.

Dr. Simian's impatience grows more evident. "I'm sure you've enjoyed your little vacation here, with three women all to yourself," he says, a lurid smile momentarily corrupting his face, "but it's over now. You don't own this place. The greater good of science cannot be denied access."

In his travels, Lurk has seen many evils done in the name of the greater good and will not condone having any of them done in his domain. Lurk's menace is obvious to everyone. He is on high alert, determined to deny this arrogant, bonehead doctor and his minions access to anything. In defense of his family, Lurk is prepared to do whatever it takes, even to kill anyone foolish enough to come within his range. Eve reaches forward to place a concerned hand on Lurk's shoulder, but no one else moves.

"We expect to be here for three hours," Dr. Simian continues as if addressing a less hostile reception. "We will need blood, urine, and stool samples from each of you." Dr. Simian turns slowly and carefully beckons a young, dark-skinned man who steps forward so Lurk can see him. "Dr. Milky will be conducting interviews to work up preliminary psychological profiles on each of you."

"How do you do, Mr. Rydgyd," Dr. Milky says.

Lurk does not respond to Dr. Milky, he has already returned his attention to Dr. Simian.

Lurk is determined to plug that doorway until his last breath, to stand his ground and deny them access to the women, to the children, to anything, but his mind is racing through a limited list of tactical possibilities: With hand-to-hand combat, he knows he could handle any of them one-on-one, but they aren't likely to come at him that way. They might have weapons; they probably do, though he cannot tell with the camera lights in his eyes.

If he could maintain this standoff, he could wait them out; they probably don't know the cave is a food warehouse, full of Popnuts® that would last longer than the expedition's supplies, even with two hovercraft shuttling supplies for them. The expedition would eventually have to leave; their reserves could not be inexhaustible and it is an expensive and time-consuming proposition to resupply from off-planet.

Lurk's mind races on. If he can get the visitors to leave, even for a short while, his clan could escape, traveling under the moss along secret trails, the way the children do. They would be invisible from the air and leave no tracks Dr. Simian might follow. Moving under the moss is more difficult for adults than it is for the children, but it is possible. Lurk has spent hours under the moss playing with the older kids, him being the big, slow-moving monster and they being the nimble attackers circling him at will, squealing in to "count coup" as the plains Indians once did back on Earth, tagging Lurk for the prestige of it and darting quickly out of range of his tickling fingers.

"Will you cooperate?" Dr. Simian asks, clearly nearing the end of his patience. Lurk does not answer; he is still in turmoil, struggling with his limited options, but certain none of his options involve cooperation.

Lurk decides a standoff is their best option. He snuggles back into the cave opening a little more, the better to avoid anyone moving in on him from the side. He will wait them out.

If Lurk's band can avoid the unwelcome probing of these invaders and steal away into the moss, it wouldn't be a bad life. They would become ever-vigilant refugees, living like exiles on their own planet, but it would be better than living at the mercy of Dr. Simian and his comprehensive study for the greater good. Lurk's confidence returns. It's a big planet and the moss will provide.

Lurk announces his final decision. "Fuck off."

Dr. Simian does not speak or change expression. Instead, he slowly raises his right hand and tugs on his earlobe. Immediately there is a "phhttt" sound from beyond the lights and a sharp sting in Lurk's left thigh. He has time to look down at the dart and back to Dr. Simian's leer before he begins to feel the first wobbly effects of the drug. His rage propels him out of the cave and across the distance between them. He loses consciousness with his hands around Dr. Simian's neck.

Violation

Lurk regains consciousness amidst a discordant chorus of crying children. He jerks awake, ready to throw himself into the defense of his family, but finds his wrists are taped together behind his back and he is on his stomach. His wrists are taped to his ankles. He has been set aside, like an overlarge suitcase, into a corner of the cave to sleep off the effects of the tranquilizer, out of the way of busy scientific processes.

It appears to be all over. Dr. Simian and his men are packing their equipment and sample cases. The women are in a huddle across the cave, trying to console the distraught children. Lurk senses someone on the other side of him and turns his head to find young Dr. Milky squatting beside him, watching him struggle with the lingering drug.

"I'm very sorry for this, Mr. Rydgyd," Dr. Milky says, giving every appearance of meaning it.

"Fuck off," Lurk tries to say once again, definitely meaning it, but finding it difficult to say clearly. The tranquilizer makes it sound more like "Fuh-gaw."

Dr. Simian hears the rumble of Lurk's voice and comes over to squat beside him. Lurk is pleased to see deep red bruises on Dr. Simian's neck. "If you had cooperated, Mr. Rydgyd, this wouldn't have been necessary," he says. "We had a limited amount of time and simply couldn't have gotten all of this done with you resisting us."

"Duck-um-baa." Lurk says, trying to sound as threatening as he can with no control over his mouth.

"I, personally, have no need to come back, Mr. Rydgyd, but members of my staff will be back in six months to take follow-up blood and urine samples. I suggest you cooperate with them. Otherwise, they will be forced to use the same methods."

One of Dr. Simian's crew steps forward. "We're all packed up, Sir."

"Strap in, I'll be right there," Dr. Simian says and then turns back to Lurk.

"Dr. Milky here will be staying with you for ten days, to make observations for his research. He will have a radio and is armed with a tranquilizer gun just like the one we used on you. He has been instructed to use the gun if you threaten his well-being and to use the radio if, for any reason, he determines that he, or you, needs to be physically extracted. If that becomes necessary, you will be quarantined at the airfield until Dr. Milky's study of the women is complete. I suggest you cooperate peaceably, simply answer his questions. In ten days, I'll send a ship back to get him and it will all be over for you until we return in six month's time."

Lurk glowers at Dr. Milky, sizing him up. Milky is built like a distance runner. His slender body is almost a hundred pounds lighter than Lurk and several inches shorter. His presence in their domain would likely be more of an irritant than a threat. Lurk returns the full focus of his hatred to Dr. Simian.

"In the meantime," Dr. Simian continues, "the Federation's Council of Exploration has decided you are free to remain on this planet indefinitely, even though it is now closed to further colonization. They decided that, since you volunteered to stay here in the first place, and since you've already invested so much time in this experiment for them, it is a perfect opportunity to study human adaptation. If you want the council to continue tolerating your presence on a planet closed to colonization, I suggest you do nothing to jeopardize our study."

The hovercraft engines begin to whine.

Dr. Simian smiles unpleasantly at Lurk and gets up to leave. "Dr. Milky," he says before exiting the cave, "don't untape him until we're airborne."

Milky's Welcome

As soon as the invasion party leaves the cave, the women surround Lurk. The tearful twins flutter uselessly, but Eve strips off the tape, eyeing Dr. Milky, defying him to stop her. She helps Lurk shake off the drug by massaging the circulation back into his stiffened legs and arms and then by helping him to his feet.

"Is everyone all right?" Lurk asks her.

"Just peachy," Eve says, her anger smoldering dangerously near the surface. "Can't remember a better time."

"Sorry, I couldn't keep them away."

"No one could have, Love."

"What did they do while I was out?" Lurk asks, not really wanting to know.

"Oh, you didn't miss much, just your complete, standard physical exam, in public, by tag team."

"Shit."

Eve is silent for a while until the still-whimpering twins get on her nerves. "Knock it off," she barks at them. "It's over." This sets the children to crying again and occupies the twins to quiet them.

When Dr. Milky, watching at the cave entrance, sees the hovercraft fade into the haze, he turns to Eve, standing protectively between Milky and the still-groggy Lurk. "I want to apologize for all of that," he says. "I think Dr. Simian was a little heavy-handed. I knew they were ready to tranquilize you if you didn't cooperate and I told them it would make my job harder if they did, but..."

In a reprise of the same uncontrollable rage that launched him toward Dr. Simian's throat, Lurk makes a similar move for Dr. Milky, but the effects of the drug have still not worn off and it is more of an awkward leaning stumble. Eve is there to steady him. Milky takes a cautious step back and draws the tranquilizer gun from his holster with gunslinger ease. Eve circles Lurk's neck with her arms and whispers discouraging words into his ear. "Take it easy, big fella. We're OK. Don't make it worse." Lurk stands as still as he can, his muscles trembling from the tranquilizer and from the effort of restraining his fury.

Eve turns her head to Milky, her arms still around Lurk's neck. "Could we have a few minutes?"

Milky holsters his weapon and steps outside.

Eve smiles up at Lurk. "What do you say we dump this Bozo, huh?" she asks.

"Good idea," Lurk says, calming as he thinks about her idea and coming to like it more and more. "He might get lonesome all by himself for ten days," Lurk says this with sarcasm as virulent as he can muster with still-slurred speech.

"Aw, it'll be good for him." Eve's smile is radiant.

"I hope he brought plenty of food." Lurk says, "I'd hate it if he had to experiment with the local vegetation and spend ten days with the screaming shits."

"Yeah, I'm sure you'd hate that."

Lurk finally smiles.

"Let me take care of Milky," Eve says. "I'll buy us some time. You stay here and hug the twins, OK?"

He doesn't like to think of her "taking care of Milky" in any form his addled mind can imagine, but he doesn't ask what she has in mind. He nods agreement and the twins swarm around him to receive their hugs.

Eve steps to the doorway and says, "Dr. Milky, could we take a short walk together? I'd like to talk to you privately."

Before Eve leaves the cave, she turns back to Lurk and says with mock severity, "Stay," as if he were a dog. Her face is stern and her manner is domineering enough to set Lurk back, but she gives him a wink Milky cannot see.

Tit for Tat

Outside the cave, Eve leads Dr. Milky away from the entrance, looking back furtively as if to be certain they are well enough away to avoid being overheard.

Milky keeps his distance from her and his hand on the butt of his tranquilizer gun. He has no idea what to expect from this rather large woman (relative to him), but is excited for the opportunity to establish a relationship with his subjects so soon after arriving.

Eve leads him well away from the cave. Keeping an anxious eye on the cave entrance, she whispers urgently, "Can you take me with you when you leave?" She is clearly terrified. "Please, I have to get away from that man. He is an insatiable, manipulative tyrant. You've no idea of the hell we've had to endure."

Dr. Milky is unprepared for this. He had expected her to plead to be left alone, not to have her reveal this seamy undertone of coercion in the social structure of Mowdabb. To a Social Psychologist this was fascinating stuff. "We thought you were all here voluntarily."

"I am. At least I was," Eve explains. "But, things changed. We all changed. Now, he has some kind of control over us. I don't understand it, but we thought we were making our own decisions and yet, all the while, he was really deciding for us. He's very controlling. He plays us, one against the other. In a way… It's hard to explain, but we had no choice."

"Why didn't you say something earlier, when we first got here?"

"What if you had refused? He would have been furious with me."

"Why didn't you say something while he was tranquilized? That would have been the time to…"

"Oh no, he can hear everything," Eve said, nervously checking the cave entrance. "He can even hear what we say when he's asleep. It's spooky. He's done it before. I tell you, the man is very scary."

"Still, with him taped up like that, I would have thought…" Milky was still unconvinced.

"You have no idea how strong he is," Eve explains, taking Milky's upper arm in her two hands as if to measure his strength and pulling him closer to her still-naked breasts, "I was afraid he would break that tape. You saw what he did to Dr. Simian. I didn't want to see another one of his rages."

Dr. Milky was softening, but still not wholly convinced. "Certainly, with all of us there, he wouldn't have been a problem. If necessary, we could have simply kept him sedated until you were safely off-planet."

"Maybe," Eve said, "but I'm just terrified of the man when he gets in a rage. You have no idea of what we've been through. We've had no one to protect us from him." Eve edges closer, putting Milky's upper arm between her breasts. "You've just got to take me with you when you leave."

"Of course, I'll take you with me." Dr. Milky seemed affronted she would doubt his humanity. "The council would never have allowed this to continue if they had known you were here against your will."

"And not a word of this to Lurk?" Eve asks anxiously. "We can't let him know our plans, or anyone else. He even has some of the children spying on us, reporting our every conversation back to him. He's a dangerous man.

"Absolutely," Dr. Milky promised. "This is just between you and me. I will simply abort my study and radio for a ship to come get us tomorrow."

"No! No, don't do that. I think we should just stick with the schedule for now, at least until we can find the best way to call without alerting him. That way, you can interview us a little, but if Lurk should learn you called for a ship early, he would know I had asked you for help and was trying to get away from him."

"Well, I don't see how he would necessarily make that connection, but very well. I'd like the chance to conduct at least some of my research project. You have no idea how difficult it was to be included in this expedition. So, if you are sure you and the twins will be OK for a day or two, we'll come up with a safe way to extract you, without alerting Mr. Rydgyd."

"As long as he never knows what I've told you, and we're gone before he knows we're leaving…

"I'm curious, Eve." Dr. Milky is still finding it difficult to understand this radical departure from what he had expected. "What does he think you are saying to me right now?"

"I told him I would tell you how to keep a respectful distance from him and from 'his women.'"

This was fascinating stuff! Dr. Milky could hardly wait till he was alone so he could begin making notes.

"All right," he agrees, "This will all be over soon. Don't you worry. If worse comes to worse," he pats the tranquilizer gun, "I can always sedate him again and we can keep him tied up."

"Oh, thank you," Eve gushes, giving him a long, full-body hug. "I'm so glad you're here."

Dr. Milky was a bit flustered being hugged by a semi-naked woman, but in no hurry to end it.

"Now," Eve says, stepping back to take charge again, "the next step is to get you two together; you need to get along for a while."

Eve explains her plan to Milky while they walk back toward the cave. "I suggest you wait outside. I'll show you a good spot where you will be comfortable. You may have to wait awhile; I'll have to get him calmed down enough for you two to talk. When I think he's ready, I'll bring him out so you two can make your peace. OK?"

Milky was not convinced Eve's plan made much sense, but was willing to play along with this neurotic and traumatized woman.

Eve led Milky to a large moss recliner just outside the cave. "You sit here," she directed.

He sat down and found it quite comfortable.

"You might as well lie back and relax. Here's something for a pillow," she said, reaching across him as he lay down, her breasts dangling deliciously in front of his face. Not wanting to gawk, Dr. Milky looked toward where she reached for the pillow. Consequently, he did not see her slide the tranquilizer gun from its holster with her other hand. He was positioning the pillow under his head when he heard the "phhttt" of the gun and felt the sting of the dart. He did not struggle; he knew there was no way to resist the speed and power of the drug. He just had time to give Eve a disappointed look and fold his hands across his stomach before the drug began to have its effect. He let consciousness slip away, reflecting as it did that this was likely to change everything.

- - -

COBY BLOOM

Punkin

Coby Bloom came to COPY/COPY by hopping a Navy cargo flight headed to Seattle out of Miramar Naval Air Station. He had recently been handed a transfer to The Marine Corps Logistics Base in Barstow, California as part of a disciplinary action after he wrecked a dance hall in Fallbrook and left the son of one of Fallbrook's leading citizens with a broken nose and wrist. Broken noses had become a Coby Bloom calling card in the communities around Camp Pendleton, so the Camp Commander transferred his problem to Barstow. Coby was pissed about it.

As he said goodbye to his more recent squeezes around Pendleton, he began to think of Marilyn once again. It still galled him to remember the way she walked out on him. He had a one-week leave in which to get to Barstow, so he decided to hop the flight to Seattle in the hope of finding Marilyn.

While he had known Marilyn's approximate whereabouts for three months (an independent copy shop somewhere in Seattle), he hadn't had the inclination or opportunity to find her until he was presented with the leave and found connections that could get him on the flight to Seattle.

Finding Marilyn's approximate whereabouts had been easy. All he had to do was to buy her father a few beers. Marilyn herself had provided the breech in her security; during the one brief call she'd made to her father, just to reassure him she was doing all right; she told him she had a job at a copy shop. Then, when he laughed at her for being a "Kinkos weenie," (weenie being one of her father's favorite labels for civilian employees of any kind) she feebly defended herself by saying, "No, it's an independent copy shop." Marilyn had hoped to ease her father's mind with the call, not wanting him to worry about her, but, by the time she hung up, she knew he hadn't been worrying at all and resolved never to call him again. Only later did she realize she'd made another mistake in the call; she mentioned how much her aunt had helped her get settled. Her dad knew her aunt lived in Seattle

Once Coby got to Seattle, he found the nearest phone book and tore out the several yellow pages that listed copy shops. He rented a car and began driving around the city, locating independent copy shops. COPY/COPY was his fifth stop. He didn't have to go inside to know he'd found her; he could see her blond curls behind the big copy machine from his parking space across the street. Coby noted the closing time on the door and drove off to find something to eat. By the time he'd finished a Whopper and a double Latte, he'd worked himself into an angry state of indignant impatience that wouldn't let him wait for the store to close. He considered it an intolerable personal affront the way she'd walked away. He wanted to hear her explain to his face how she thought she was too good for him. He went back to COPY/COPY, saw no customers through the window, and entered, turning the OPEN sign around as he closed the door.

"Sorry, we're about to close." Marilyn said from behind the copier.

"You bet you are, Punkin."

- - -

Jerry was getting out of the bathtub when he heard voices in the hall outside his apartment door. He pulled on his Levis and padded to the door to listen.

"Open the damn door," a man's voice was saying, not angry, but impatient.

Then Marilyn's voice: "Let go of my arm and it might be a little easier to open the damn door."

Jerry's stomach tightened; he knew immediately who had a hold on Marilyn's arm; it was that Coby sonofabitch.

Jerry boldly opened his door wide with no plan in mind except to make an appearance.

Marilyn and Coby turned to look at him. Marilyn had the key in the lock and Coby stood close behind her. There was an awkward pause while they adjusted to Jerry's sudden appearance. He saw a flicker of relief on Marilyn's face that quickly reverted to a look of anxiety.

He took that look to mean, "I'm glad you are here, but stay away." Jerry couldn't be sure.

Coby was obviously irritated by Jerry's intrusion and then contemptuous of his scrawny physique, his disdainful look traveled down Jerry's naked chest to his big bare feet and back up again, making Jerry feel more undressed than he actually was. In turn, Jerry was intimidated by Coby's appearance, as, he assumed, most people were. Coby's Marine haircut emphasized the size of his neck and the tight camouflage t-shirt did everything to show off his chest and arms. Jerry felt frail and wobbly by comparison.

"Is everything all right?" he managed to say as calmly as he could with his heart pounding as it was.

Marilyn tried to diffuse the moment with formality. "Coby, this is my friend and neighbor Jerry Gustafson. Jerry this is Coby Bloom."

Neither of them was pleased to meet the other.

Without taking his eyes off Jerry, Coby said exactly what he had said before: "Open the damn door."

Marilyn opened the door. Coby ushered her in and shut it behind them.

- - -

Jerry was stunned motionless in his doorway until overwhelmed by the need to do something. He padded forward into the hallway on bare feet, making it half way to Marilyn's door before realizing he had no plan. He stopped and padded back.

Maybe he was being presumptuous. Marilyn had just described him as a friend and neighbor. Maybe that's all he was to her now that Coby was back. She had let Coby into her apartment, giving Jerry no real signal she didn't want to be alone with the man.

But… Jerry padded out into the hallway again. Marilyn said she hated Coby and he'd physically abused her. He could think of no reason for her to say that if it wasn't true. Maybe she was so afraid of Coby she couldn't deny him entry and was hoping to diffuse the situation on her own.

Should he force himself into this… situation? How? He hadn't defended himself well in childhood playground conflicts. Could he defend Marilyn? What could he do against a man built like Coby?

Jerry crept to a midway point between the two doors, trembling with indecision and with damp nakedness in the cold hallway. He hustled back to his apartment, jerked on a sweatshirt and snatched up his shoes. Back in the hallway, now looking like an interrupted intruder, shoes already forgotten in his hand, he edged forward, propelled by ugly visions of what might be happening behind Marilyn's door.

Fond memories of the night before, of their kiss, made him raise his fist, ready to pound on the door. He would not wait for Coby to start slapping her around; he'd much rather Coby slapped him around. Then he heard their voices. They sounded peaceable, though he could not tell what they were saying. At least they were not yelling. He hesitated and then, again, slowly retreated.

Backed into his own doorway, he realized he was still carrying his shoes. He sat down on his doorsill to put them on. One shoe was tied when he heard Coby raise his voice. It sent an electric charge through Jerry, propelling him to his feet. He still could not understand what was being said, but it was no longer peaceable. He hurried back to Marilyn's door, one set of shoelaces flailing wildly. Once there, he still didn't knock. Instead he brazenly put his ear against the door.

"What the fuck's the matter with you?" Coby's angry words came through the door loud and clear.

"It's *over* Coby!" Marilyn yelled right back at him. "Get over it and go away."

"I'll tell you when it's fuckin' over," Coby growled back.

Jerry knocked on Marilyn's door with no plan in mind except to interrupt the escalating anger... three quick knocks.

Heavy footsteps approached the door, which was pulled open with such force that Jerry was almost sucked into the room. Coby glared up at him without a word, as if counting on the menace of his glare to communicate for him. His face was red with the effort to control his irritation. Jerry looked over the top of Coby's head and into the room, to meet Marilyn's eyes. She was standing by the dining table with both fists clenched at the base of her throat, her lips pressed tightly together as if holding her breath.

Jerry asked her again, "Is everything alright?" He used the same words as before, but was clearly pleading to know if she needed help.

Before she could answer, Coby said, "Piss off," and slammed Jerry in the sternum with the flat of his hand. The blow propelled Jerry backward, off his feet, and clear across the hallway. The loud bang of his head hitting the wall was followed by the slam of Marilyn's door.

Jerry was stunned by the blow to his head and unable to inhale. He sat on the floor in a limp heap, moving his mouth like a fish out of water and listening helplessly to Marilyn yelling again at Coby beyond the door.

"Get out of here! Get out of here! Get out of here!" she said in a voice much closer to screaming. Coby was chuckling.

Jerry struggled to control his legs and make it to his feet, while still trying to restore his breathing. The throbbing on the back of his head felt wet. He reached back and found blood. Standing now, but still wobbly, he looked at the wall behind him and saw where his head had hit the top of the wainscoting and then painted a bright trail downwards as he slid to the floor.

Marilyn screamed, "Get out of here!" as forcefully as Jerry imagined she was capable of screaming, desperation now in her voice.

With no plan except to take away their privacy, Jerry braced against the opposite wall of the hallway to launch forward, slamming the sole of his still-untied shoe into Marilyn's door between the doorknob and the deadbolt. The doorjamb splintered and the door flew open, crashing against the folding screen Marilyn kept behind the door. While the door shuddered on its hinges, reverberating from the crash, the screen, folded flat by the impact of the door, teetered for a second and then fell like a tree into the middle of the room, adding more noise to his dramatic intervention.

Coby and Marilyn were staring at him open-mouthed and frozen in place. She was pushing against Coby's chest; he had his big, meaty hands around her back and under her blouse, evidently trying to undo her bra.

Marilyn reacted first, squirming quickly out of Coby's grasp.

Coby reacted more slowly, startled by the noisy reappearance of Marilyn's scrawny neighbor. Jerry enjoyed Coby's look of surprise almost as much as the grateful relief he saw on Marilyn's face.

Instead of running to his side, as all white knights might expect of fair maidens, Marilyn went from the clutches of evil directly to the telephone on the wall by the door. While she moved, she was talking. From the moment she left Coby's clutches, all the way across the apartment to the phone, and all the while she dialed 911, Marilyn was rapidly jabbering something directed at Jerry. Her words were wasted on him however, because his head still throbbed like a hammered thumb and he was involved in maintaining his macho e macho stare-down with Coby. Jerry understood the essence of her message though and it was hardly necessary; she was warning him to stay away from Coby until the police arrived.

Jerry stepped further into the room and to one side in order to get Marilyn at his back while she was on the phone, putting his unsteady body in harm's way. He had every intention to stay between them for as long as he could to keep Coby from touching her again. Jerry squared himself, spread his feet apart a little, and, for once in his life, tried to appear as tall as possible. He looked down to meet Coby's flat stare, hoping to transmit his resolve.

"Oh Jerry," Marilyn said behind him, "your head is bleeding."

Before Marilyn could give the Emergency Operator their address, Coby moved, and with such amazing speed that Jerry only had time to flinch at his sudden approach. A casual swipe of a brawny forearm sent Jerry flying sideways across the apartment, rolling into the kitchen cabinets, and banging his forehead on a cabinet handle. With Jerry out of the way, Coby stepped past Marilyn and pulled the phone off the wall.

Jerry lost track of any further action that might have taken place. The next thing he knew, Marilyn was kneeling beside him, dabbing with a dishtowel at the new flow of blood from his forehead.

Jerry was unreasonably happy. Even though he lay on the floor with a throbbing head, he was once again in direct contact with Marilyn; everything was all right; the confrontation must be over. Then he saw Coby still standing in the middle of the room, fists on hips, amused at the bloody mess he'd made.

"Well, Punkin'…" Coby said, "you've certainly fallen a long way. If Bones here is the best man you can find, you'd be better off goin' lesbian."

Jerry stupidly wondered how Coby had learned his childhood nickname; he thought he'd left Bones Gustafson back in Kilgore.

Coby stepped closer, put his big hands on his knees, and leaned down to take a closer look at him. "Don't you Seattle pukes ever get outside? You're white as a goddamn mushroom."

"Get out of here," Marilyn said quietly to Coby. "You've shown us who you are."

Coby turned his head to study Marilyn's face. He had a blank expression, as if trying to decide if he should be offended. Without changing expression, he turned back to watch Marilyn's attempts to staunch the blood leaking from the front and back of Jerry's head. Coby finally snorted in disgust and then stood up. "Waste of my fuckin time, the both of you." He swaggered into the hallway before turning back to examine the shattered doorframe. He pulled down one of the larger splinters and tossed it into the room. "Looks like your wimpy-ass hero has some maintenance work to do."

Coby was turning to leave when Jerry called out his name. Coby turned back and leaned his meaty shoulder against the doorframe, as if weary from his exertions. His expression was a contorted mix of amused annoyance in anticipation of whatever pathetic thing Jerry might have to say.

"Don't come back," Jerry said.

"What!?" Coby was instantly enraged. He surged back into the room, swiping Marilyn to one side, sending her reeling into the kitchen chairs. He stood astride Jerry's prone body, reached down to gather the entire front half of Jerry's sweatshirt into a wad in the middle of Jerry's still-aching chest, and lifted him off the floor with no apparent effort. Coby's grip on the sweatshirt seemed to collapse his lungs; Jerry could not resist. He was lifted straight up until their noses were at the same elevation, his toes dragging on the floor behind him. "What the fuck you say to me you maggoty piece of shit?"

Jerry could smell the coffee on Coby's breath and see the bloodlust in his eyes.

Jerry knew he was going to get hurt, but he still had a message for Coby. "I'm not going away. If you come back, I'll get between you and Marilyn again, for as long as I'm able to move."

Coby lifted Jerry the rest of the way off the ground, pressing him directly overhead now, locking his arms straight, easily bearing Jerry's full weight on his big knuckles and on Jerry's already tender sternum. Held aloft with such ease, Jerry felt like a feeble child. His skin was painfully pinched up under his arms, his sweatshirt seams ripping from the strain, and he could not inhale.

"And then what asshole?" Coby asked, "When you can't move any more, what the fuck you gonna do then?"

Jerry could not speak, but he had nothing more to say anyway.

Coby dropped Jerry's feet to the floor and, with a disdainful shove, sent him reeling backward. Traveling now in the opposite direction from his first trip across the apartment, Jerry flailed his arms to catch his balance, but his heel caught on the fallen screen and he landed hard on his lower back. The back of his throbbing head banged on the floor, leaving a wet splat of blood and stunning him once again. When his eyes were able to focus, he saw Coby was standing upright over him, straddling his body once again. While he grinned down at Jerry, his big stubby fingers were unzipping his fly. Marilyn was repeatedly lunging against Coby's shoulder with both hands, trying to dislodge Coby from his stance over Jerry, but having no effect whatsoever. "Get out of here! Get out of here! Get out of here!" she resumed screaming, timing each ineffectual lunge against Coby's bulk with the word "out."

As Coby's penis appeared overhead and Jerry saw the evil grin spreading across Coby's face, he knew what was about to happen.

"I told you to piss off, Motherfucker," Coby said.

Just as Coby leaned back slightly, relaxing to let the urine flow, Jerry reacted to stop the humiliation about to befall him. He punched violently upward, using both fists together and all of his strength in both long arms, driving from the solid floor at his back. More from luck than intention, he connected decisively with Coby's testicles.

A tiny spurt of urine left the tip of Coby's penis as his knees buckled. A faraway look of abject pain filled his watering eyes. He began to wobble like a slowing top, little-by-little hunching his back, effectively retracting his abused privates into his pants. It looked like Coby might collapse in any direction, but a final lunge by Marilyn directed his fall toward the doorway. Her lunge also introduced a slight rotation to Coby's bulk, causing him to land on his face with a resounding crunch that suggested another broken nose.

Marilyn seized the advantage by roughly sitting on Coby's neck, facing his feet, showing no concern for any pain she might be adding to the man's nose. She pulled each of his huge arms, one at a time, behind his back until his wrists were crossed. She put her feet outside of his elbows to help hold his arms in place and gripped both of his big wrists as best she could with her interlocked hands. She leaned back hard, pulling Coby's wrists towards his head.

"Quick, there's some duct tape in the kitchen drawer by the phone."

Jerry was impressed by Marilyn's command of the situation and understood the need for tape, but not the urgency; Coby did not look likely to move soon; he gurgled wetly with each breath, but otherwise remained limp. Jerry, necessarily, took his time standing up. When the room had stabilized, he brought the tape to Marilyn, whose face was red from the effort of pulling on Coby's wrists, as if straining to dislocate his shoulders.

Together they wrapped multiple layers of the silver tape around Coby's wrists and forearms. There was still plenty of tape on the roll and they both knew the power in Coby's arms, so they just kept wrapping, adding tape around his upper arms, pulling his elbows close together behind his back. When they finished, it looked as if the man's arms were joined together behind his back inside a large section of aluminum pipe. Marilyn then moved to sit on the back of Coby's knees while Jerry used the last of the tape around the man's ankles.

- - -

The police so admired the tape work on Coby's arms they didn't bother with handcuffs. The paramedics cut the tape off Coby's ankles so he could sit at the kitchen table while they packed cotton into his broken nose and wiped blood off his face. Coby was quiet through the whole process, staring at the floor through puffy eyelids already beginning to darken. He said nothing to the police except his name, rank, and serial number.

The paramedics were still working on Jerry as the police lead Coby down the back stairs to a waiting patrol car. They cleaned the blood off the front and back of Jerry's head, examined his assortment of cuts and contusions, and repeatedly flashed a bright penlight into each of his eyes. A small butterfly strip was enough to repair the ragged cut on his forehead, but the double blow to the back of Jerry's head earned him an elaborate gauze headband and made the paramedics want to take him to the emergency room for observation and proper stitches. Because the bleeding had stopped and his pupils were the same size, Jerry was able to persuade them he would come for stitches when he felt a little better. He really didn't want to go anywhere, ever again.

As the paramedics were packing to go, Marilyn asked them to examine her left ring finger. She wondered if it might be broken. During the mêlée, when Coby shoved her away, she had dislocated it on the rung of a kitchen chair when she tried to break her fall. She had reset it herself before beginning her final assault on Coby. The paramedics said it looked fine and simply taped her swollen finger to its neighbor. They also wiped disinfectant on a scrape centered on a bruise, already forming, over her cheekbone. Marilyn's injuries were a surprise to Jerry because they had happened while he was aloft on the platform of Coby's knuckles, focused on trying to breathe.

When the paramedics were gone, Marilyn and Jerry were alone in her apartment, quietly trying to adjust to recent events. They sat apart on isolated kitchen chairs that still faced in whatever direction the intruding violence had left them.

"I'm so sorry," Marilyn said, staring at her taped fingers. "I never should have brought him upstairs."

"Why did you?"

"I didn't want to have a scene in the store. I was hoping to make him understand it was over between us, but he didn't care what I had to say; he wouldn't let it go."

Jerry did not know what to say.

"I'm sorry," she said again. "I didn't want to get you involved, but thank you for being here. I don't want to think about how it might have gone if you hadn't kicked in the door."

Jerry's head throbbed with each beat of his heart, but he was happy.

"Don't be sorry," he said. "I want to be involved."

Marilyn met his eyes.

"I couldn't let him hurt you again," Jerry said.

Marilyn came over to lean down and give him a kiss. Jerry pulled her onto his lap. They kissed as they never had before, with gentleness and affection Jerry had not known was possible between two people.

After a time, Marilyn stood up and reached out for his hand. "Come with me," she said, and led him into her bedroom.

- - -

His tender sternum made it difficult to take off his bloodstained sweatshirt, so Marilyn helped him with that. As he sat on the edge of her bed, she wiped the blood from his neck and back where the paramedics had not done a thorough job. The warm washrag, in her hands, was the most sensual experience of Jerry's life to that point. While Marilyn carried the bloody shirt and washrag out to the washing machine, he leaned back on one elbow, resisting the urge to rest his still throbbing head on her pillow. When Marilyn returned, she stopped at the bathroom door and held up one finger before going inside to take a shower. She came out of the bathroom wearing her blue chenille bathrobe and, as it turned out, nothing else.

Escalation

After they found positions compatible with their injuries, there was a brief time of clumsiness during which they each adjusted to how different their bodies were, Jerry's long, lean, and hard, Marilyn's short, round, and soft. But, after solving the logistics and finally reassuring one another with words and deeds that they each, in actual, miraculous fact, reveled in those differences, they were able to release the surly bonds of inhibition and soar. Their first intermission came so quickly Marilyn hardly had time to appreciate Act One was over, but Jerry did his damnedest to be certain Acts Two and Three were memorable. What he lacked in experience, he made up for in fervent ardor, tempered by a gentle eagerness to please. It was a combination Marilyn had never found in previous lovers.

Their first union was a revelation for each of them, the first time either of them had felt the heady combination of sex and an affectionate touch.

Jerry was making love for the first time in his life. His few, brief encounters with (what was her name?) Karen, back in his former life, long ago and far away in Kilgore, had been nothing more than the execution of sexual congress. With Karen, it had been difficult to know if she was enjoying their friendly couplings; she had participated well enough, but always seemed somehow distracted. This was not the case with Marilyn who was consummately involved in the moment and, as always, vocal about it, talking him through it the first time and leaving no doubt about her physical pleasure or about her joy at discovering new levels to their compatibility.

They enjoyed themselves thoroughly in that first night of love, from beginning to end and from one end to the other.

- - -

Later, long before Jerry could have moved, Marilyn returned from the kitchen with two glasses of wine. He struggled to a sitting position.

They clinked glasses and drank. Marilyn heaved a quick heavy sigh, and said, "I needed that."

"The wine?" he asked, with a stupid, happy smile.

"No," she laughed that honest female laugh he liked so much. "I didn't actually *need* the wine."

They were quiet for a while, basking in the afterglow of their new intimacy, amazed at how easily they had fallen into one another's lives after such a difficult start and how good the world now seemed to be.

"This changes everything doesn't it?" he asked.

"Only if we both want it to," she said. "Everything can stay the same, or everything can change, or anything in between."

- - -

Jerry's life had been improving steadily since he accepted Mr. Stamper's job offer, but from that moment in Marilyn's bedroom the improvements began to escalate in ways he could never have imagined, each new and wondrous improvement soaring beyond the previous one in a breathless exponential spiral.

The Longest Day

Jerry sat behind the counter in The Planet of Love the next morning with his thoughts rocketing from the alien terrain of Mowdabb to the puzzling new world he found himself inhabiting in Seattle. Every customer was a much-resented interruption. The clock over the entrance seemed not to be moving. Delicious memories of his night with Marilyn were roiling the waters of concentration. Long-tamped hormones had been revived and now intermixed with the first stirrings of desire for a future with her.

In just one night, she had become the most important component of Jerry's life. Fortune/Fate/Destiny had been unusually kind to him, despite his bumbling ways. Chances were slim he would ever get this lucky again.

A future with Marilyn was little more than a dream-in-waiting at this point, one he could not yet allow himself to dare. If he was brave enough to try for this dream, he would need to make some big adjustments to his life plan. Primarily, he would need to stay put, maybe forego his dream of living in Alaska altogether, just as he had quit his dream of flying. The idea was difficult for him; walking away from Kilgore had closed a door to his past, but abandoning Alaska would cut another major chunk from his imagined future.

He'd finally begun to sense the weasel's influence; it seemed to have led him, after all, to The Planet of Love and to Marilyn. He was desperate not to lose sight of the little bugger now.

Another bit of Shakespeare from Old Man Stamper's library:

> There is a tide in the affairs of men
>
> Which, taken at the flood, leads on to fortune;
>
> Omitted, all the voyage of their life
>
> Is bound in shallows and in miseries.

Julius Caesar, act 4, sc. 2.

Destiny's visit that long-ago night in the Kilgore Library was the beginning of Jerry's flood tide, one he would never regret taking. Instead, he shuddered to think of the lonely, miserable life he might have had if he had remained bound in the shallows of Kilgore.

By mid-afternoon, he was finally able to make occasional, though still intermittent, forays into the damp atmosphere of Mowdabb, allowing him to focus, instead, on Lurk's problems.

Vanished

Dr. Milky lays unconscious on the moss cushions until darkness and its accompanying warm fog have settled onto Mowdabb. When he opens his eyes, he sees darkness as absolute as the sensory deprivation tanks he experimented with during his years at University. He becomes aware he is all wet and still cannot move.

While he waits for mobility to return, Milky applies his considerable deductive powers to his new situation: There is no reason for anxiety; anyone wishing him harm would have had their way with him. There is no reason for urgency; whatever has happened to his reluctant subjects is long ago done and nothing he is capable of doing now will alter that situation. Having thus reviewed his new circumstance and efficiently distilled it to "no worries and no hurry," Milky relaxes, allowing the tranquilizer to work its way out of his system.

He has made a mess of things: On his first real assignment after getting his doctorate, on his first trip into the field, at his first opportunity to make a mark in the annals of pure research in his specialty of human psychological adaptability to physiological change, within minutes of first contact, he is neutralized by his subjects. Even though he knows negative thoughts are damaging to the psyche, Dr. Milky concedes the situation really pisses him off.

When his body is capable, with great expenditures of wobbly willpower, Milky swings his legs to the ground and sits upright. His equilibrium sloshes as if at sea in a small boat. Gradually, the boat begins to feel larger. He listens for sounds of life around him, but there is only the gentle white noise of countless accumulating dewdrops falling from countless mosses.

He considers walking, or more likely crawling, in the direction of the cave, but realizes he might have been moved while he was out, carried onto similar cushions in order to disorient him further. He has no choice but to wait for daylight. He didn't expect anyone would be inside the cave anyway and there is no reason to find it for shelter because he is as wet as he can get. He lies back down in the warm fog and goes to sleep.

Scuttling

After Milky's anesthetization, Lurk's clan comes together in the home cave. Children materialize out of the moss and begin milling around the adults. Everyone is eager to get as far from Dr. Milky as they can before daylight. Lurk's main concern is to leave without a trace. That requires they disguise their point of exit from the home clearing. While the clan waits in the cave, at the first hint of dawn, Lurk and Adam begin a search of the perimeter for the right location for their disappearing act.

There are a few obvious openings in the moss, larger ones near the home cave used by the adults for food gathering or for needs of the toilet, and smaller ones used by the children to enter their secret network of paths under the moss. It has proven easier to navigate under the moss canopy than to walk over the spongy moss surface, so banks of moss between these entrances are surprisingly pristine.

When Lurk finds what he is looking for, an extensive growth of dense moss extending right up to the smooth rock, he and Adam carefully work their hands under the edge of the mat and lift it overhead so Lurk can duck-walk under, letting the bulky elastic carpet slide over his broad back. A few meters in, the rock surface slopes downward, revealing thick, supporting moss stems rooted in eons of rich humus. Lurk squeezes between the stems, working deeper into the dank greenery, encountering larger and longer stems with more space between them, making it progressively easier for him to move. He has to move slowly, feeling his way forward, because little light penetrates the overhead. When he intersects one of the well-traveled tunnels created by the children, a relative thoroughfare through the deepest parts, he backs out the way he came in. Lurk and Adam adjust the moss mat carefully to leave no evidence of their exploration.

Lurk assembles his clan, stresses the need for quiet, and leads them to the chosen point of exit. Lurk and Adam go first to hold the mat on their backs, serving as human doorposts. One by one, Lurk's clan quietly disappears into the dark, wet tunnel. When everyone is under the moss, huddled together in the darkness among the moss stems and staying in close physical contact with one another like a tribe of nocturnal monkeys in a bamboo thicket, heads are counted and the mat is carefully repositioned.

Adam takes the lead without being asked; this is his terrain. He organizes the group into a train of humans with himself as the engine. The women and the two oldest girls are next, each carrying the youngest of the children. The rest of the clan follows in line, smallest to largest, with Lurk acting as caboose, keeping his big hand on the tiny shoulder of whoever is ahead of him, one of his youngest ambulatory daughters.

Within a few minutes, they intersect with an established children's thoroughfare and traveling is easier. Lurk is forced to move in a full crouch and the heavier adults sink into damp humus uncountable centuries deep. The muffled giggling of the younger ones at the bumbling adults is the only sound they make. Considering their bulky caboose, the train makes good time.

Adam stops them for a rest after what Lurk estimates is about two hundred meters from their home cave. They huddle together against the wet and dark. After a brief, whispered conference, it is decided they will get some sleep and wait for daylight to resume their exodus. They have traveled far enough Dr. Milky will not be able to hear them or see any movement their passage might cause in the overhead canopy.

As Lurk drifts into sleep, he begins to feel secure once again. They could travel this way anywhere on the planet. If they're careful in their journey and keep a low profile wherever they resettle, they won't be found before Dr. Simian's supplies run out. Dr. Milky is likely to spend the next ten days trying to figure out where they went.

Reconnoiter

When Milky wakes, the sun is already burning off the morning fog. He can't remember the last time he's slept so well. He is still on the same cushions where Eve had tranquilized him the night before. The cave is where he remembered it to be and, upon inspection, as empty as he expected. He inventories his personal equipment. The radio and dart gun have both been removed from his belt, but his pallet of supplies is undisturbed except that the batteries have been removed from his backup emergency radio, probably thrown deep into the moss. They might as well have been launched into space.

Milky unfolds the solar stove and prepares breakfast, while considering the issue of his vanished research subjects. By the time his meal is finished, Milky has a plan.

He begins at the right edge of the cave entrance and walks slowly around the convoluted edge of the clearing, examining the dozens of openings into the network of tunnels into the moss. It is a tedious and daunting task, but he is methodical; he has nothing else to do.

Slow Going

Even before Dr. Milky finishes breakfast, Lurk's clan is moving away from their bivouac. Their progress is still slow, but they can see well under the green glow overhead. At each rest stop, Lurk and Adam confer over their general direction and whether they might double-back or create false pathways to confound the most persistent follower. Periodically, Lurk finds places in the overhead canopy where he can reconnoiter by standing upright on the nearest rock and pulling the moss down to peer across the surrounding terrain. On one such reconnoiter near the end of the day, he spots a storehouse cave almost identical to their original home. When all the children are settled in for the night, the adults confer, now including Adam in their conference. They decide on one more grueling day of travel to be certain they are well away.

By the end of Milky's first day alone on Mowdabb, he has examined the perimeter of the clearing twice and found nothing to indicate where Lurk's clan exited the area. He has crawled into each of the many tunnel openings, looking for recent disturbance. He is wet, dirty, and exhausted. He fixes a meal, inflates his mattress, and beds down in the empty cave. The next morning, having come up with no better idea, he starts at the left edge of the cave entrance and begins the circuit again, in the opposite direction.

At the end of their second full day of travel, they exit the moss carefully to minimize any sign detectable from the air. The cave Lurk has chosen for their new home is fully stocked with Popnuts®. The children are eager to explore their new home, but the adults are exhausted. Lurk enlists Adam and the two older girls to teach the smaller children the new game of walking only on the rocks and to avoid disturbing the moss. They are all soon jumping from rock to rock like a tribe of lemurs.

Halfway through the second day of searching, Dr. Milky realizes Lurk's clan must have lifted the moss and gone under it. He is upset with himself for failing to understand the obvious earlier, attributing it to the after-effects of the tranquilizer. He begins exploring likely exit points, shoving under the heavy mats and low-crawling forward. He soon discovers a trail of many large footprints in the faint green glow from overhead.

- - -

INHERITANCE

If you'll just sign here...

Simon said, "Which would you prefer? I can read it word-for-word, or I can summarize it for you."

Marilyn and Jerry have been invited into matching leather chairs in Simon's office, facing his massive oak desk. They look at one another, but cannot come up with an answer to Simon's simple question. They didn't know Mr. Stamper had a will, especially one requiring their attendance at its reading.

Simon doesn't wait for them anyway. He rattles papers on his desk, searching and sorting, getting ready to do what he'd planned to do anyway.

This pissed Jerry off. *The sonofabitch is gonna 'summarize' it for us, figures we might have trouble with the big words.* Jerry couldn't have explained his hostility toward Simon, a gut reaction to the man, but it was evident on Jerry's face if Simon had bothered to look up from his paperwork. It also pissed Jerry off that Simon was wearing another expensive suit, this one a different shade of brown and faintly pen-striped, nicely complimented by a rose-colored tie.

"In a nutshell," Simon began, "you two have been awarded co-ownership of Serendip Incorporated, a private corporation that owns the building and all contents of the building except for the leased copier. It includes the two businesses: COPY/COPY and The Planet of Love."

"Oh my God!" Marilyn said.

Jerry was dumbstruck.

Oblivious to their shock, Simon continued his summarization of the will. "There is only about $3600 in Serendip's business account, but you each have a 50% share in that as well as the entirety of Mr. Stamper's estate, free and clear. The estate comprises all assets and inventories of the three apartments and the two businesses and the building itself. Simon looked up from his papers only long enough to consider each of them in turn, reacting not in the least to their obvious astonishment. "Neither business is worth much," he confided, trying for a sympathetic tone. "COPY/COPY returns a small but steady profit. The Planet of

Love should probably be…" Here he worked his mouth, his expression implying he might be sorting through various distasteful words, finally settling on "…converted." He returned to the paperwork. "Not insignificantly, Mr. Stamper's apartment contains a large number of fine pieces of quality furniture that will bring a considerable sum at auction. I have seen the majority of them, but it is too much a jumble in there to produce anything like an official inventory. I can come up with an estimated value for tax purposes if you wish, or you can opt for an expensive, official, item-by-item appraisal. Nothing is very old in there, no antiques, but most of the pieces are of excellent quality. Let's see, what else…" Simian turned a few pages, reading the details before continuing. "All the appliances are included, etc. etc. Nothing too valuable there, but it all adds up. The real value, of course, is in the building. The big copier is leased, of course; you will have to arrange with the copier company to get that lease changed to reflect the new owners of the corporation if you want to continue using it. I can advise you in that negotiation if you like, but all the other business equipment is fully owned. There are no encumbrances, no leans against anything, nothing owing, no outstanding bills related to building maintenance, nothing like that. It appears to be a clean transfer of Serendip Incorporated from Mr. Stamper's estate to joint ownership by the two of you. You are, of course, free to dissolve the corporation, dispose of the property however you choose, and to divide the money between you. Again, I can advise you with that process if you would like me to continue as the administrator of Serendip Incorporated, or you can retain another administrator. My fees as executor of the estate are to come out of Mr. Stamper's personal accounts, so that means we don't have any further business between us after we're done here today unless you'd like to contact me for the advice I've mentioned."

Simon held out his long black desk pen and pointed to a couple of blank lines on the will. "If you'll just sign here to acknowledge your attendance at the reading of the will, I'll prepare copies for each of you and draw up the necessary papers to transfer ownership. After that, as you wish, let me know when you'd like to liquidate and I can put you in touch with several estate auction houses that do a good job."

Marilyn and Jerry looked at the pen and then at one another and then back to the pen. Mr. Simon shook the pen up and down, in an impatient attempt to break their spell. "If you could just sign here where I've made the Xs…"

Marilyn took the pen, signed, and handed it to Jerry. While he signed, Marilyn asked Simon, "Why? Why did he give all of this to us?"

Simon got his pen back and checked the signatures before answering. "I have no idea."

"He didn't say anything to you?" Marilyn asked.

Simon shrugged. "I was hoping one of you might explain it to me."

Marilyn and Jerry shook their heads in perfect unison.

- - -

There was little conversation in the taxi as they left Simon's office. They each stared out opposite windows, trying to digest the news of their inheritance. Jerry was feeling a little wobbly, as if Destiny had kicked out his underpinnings once again, as if somebody had pushed the NEXT button in a cosmic slide show and replaced his former perception of The Big Picture with a new reality. He was certain of absolutely nothing except that this turn of events would send his life spinning off in some new, unforeseeable direction. At first blush, his inheritance appeared to be a windfall of unprecedented proportions, but who could tell; in all of Jerry's previous experience, there had always been a "gottcha" underlying what would first appear to be good fortune. Why should this be any different?

He was awash with imponderables: What next? What were his options? What were the decisions ahead of him? Which of the decisions ahead of him would be the most urgent? Was anything urgent? Why did Mr. Stamper include them in his will at all? What did Marilyn think of all of this? What the hell was Serendip? [*Originally, Serendip was an old name for Sri Lanka. The word became associated with serendipity, the faculty of making fortunate discoveries by accident. When the English author Horace Walpole coined the word based on a fable entitled* The Three Princes of Serendip *in which the princes were always making remarkable accidental discoveries in their travels.*]

Of all the questions that rode with them in that taxi, Jerry realized there was one for which he *could* get an answer: He could find out what Marilyn thought of all this.

"What do you think of all this?"

She was perfectly silent, simply staring out the opposite window of the taxi, not jabbering with excitement, or with anxiety, or with anything else. The silence was not like her at all. She gave him a little shrug of one shoulder at his question, as if to dismiss it as nothing at all, as if inheriting things from virtual strangers was something that happened to her all the time.

"We are property owners now," he said, trying to make it real for her, and for him. "This means our net worth just probably quadrupled, hell more than that, it probably quintupled, or sextupled, or even..." he could not think of what was after sextupled. Septupled? Since he really had no idea what the whole thing was worth and, since his own net worth had been close to nothing, it was pointless to think in multiples of nothing, but he scoured his memory for the right word nonetheless. Sestupled?

"This means you can afford to go to Alaska now," Marilyn said to the window, speaking for the first time since they left Simon's office and obviously fighting to control her voice.

"Wow! You're right." He *could* go to Alaska. He could live wherever the hell he wanted to now. He was suddenly soaring with the possibilities, thinking this might be a real windfall after all, one without any gottchas.

Marilyn turned to face him. There were tears in her eyes that brought his thoughts back inside the taxi.

When Marilyn saw the joy still on his face at the reinvigorated prospect of Alaska, a single whimper escaped her control and she turned back to the window.

"What's wrong?" he asked. "Are you sad for Mr. Stamper?"

She turned her big, tearful eyes his way and gave him a forlorn look. "No, you big dope."

Finally, the reason for her tears penetrated through the dizzying news still swirling in his head: In the midst of all this good fortune, what mattered most to Marilyn was that he might soon leave for Alaska. This was unprecedented in his life; someone would miss him if he left!

Jerry was ashamed; he had only been thinking of himself, as usual, considering the value of the inheritance for his own purposes. It was sobering to realize that there were now other considerations at play, and other people.

There *was* a gottcha.

"What about you?" he asked. "What do you want to do?"

"I want to stay here," she said, control rapidly slipping away. "I don't want anything to change." Her voice was rising in pitch with every word. "I want things to stay exactly the way they are." She finished in the high, squeaky registers. "I was really starting to like... this life." With that, she folded. She buried her face in her hands and her hands in her lap. She sobbed so loudly the taxi driver started to pull to the side of the road.

Jerry was devastated; he had never seen her this upset, not even after Old Man Stamper died. To him, she had always seemed poised and... strong, even in the face of Coby's assault. "Marilyn," he said, touching her shoulder. At his touch, she unfolded, wrapping her arms around him and sobbing against his chest. He made signs to the taxi driver in the rearview mirror she was OK and he should continue driving. Jerry then wrapped his arms around her and tried to absorb her unhappiness.

"I don't want you to go," Marilyn said, talking fast into his chest and through the tears, "I like the way things are right now. I want to keep the copy shop; I like running that little business, and it's something I'm good at. And, I like cooking for you. I like knowing you're close by. I don't like the idea of being alone to face all the changes I've been through lately."

"Shhh," he told her, straightening her hair at the side of her face where it was sticking to her tears. "We can talk about all of this. Nothing needs to be decided right away. We can keep things the way they are for now and take our time making any changes."

She pulled away from his chest. "You don't want to... sell?" She looked in his eyes, embarrassed by her tear-streaked face, but needing to see the truth of whatever he would say. "I mean, right away?"

"No, not right away," he said. "Anyway, selling is probably just one of many options. My point is that we have all the time we need to think about this. I don't know what I want to do. This is all too new for me."

"You said this wasn't the best time of year to go to Alaska anyway," she reminded him hopefully.

"That's right. It'll be months before things warm up in Alaska."

Her bottom lip still quivered, but she managed a small smile.

The taxi dropped them off at the entrance to the alley behind what was now, suddenly, their building. Jerry paid the driver while Marilyn unlocked the door. They walked up the back stairs with their arms around one another.

"I guess it's back to the old routine for the time being," he said.

"You'll be here for dinner, then," she asked, "tomorrow night?"

"Looking forward to it," he said, meaning it.

"Great." She could not hide her relief and Jerry was touched by the fact she didn't even try.

At the top of the stairs, he held her close. The kisses were easy. The hug was full-length and nowhere near close enough.

"I'm thinking of asking Simon's advice about getting a restraining order on Coby," Marilyn said.

"Do you think you can trust him?"

"Who? Simon?" Marilyn asked.

"Yeah," Jerry said. "He's a lawyer." It was the best objection he could come up with.

"Sure. I guess so," Marilyn said. "Mr. Stamper trusted him."

Jerry had to admit she had a good point. "Do you think Coby might come back?"

"No. I don't think so. But he wouldn't dare if he's served with a restraining order."

"Is that OK with you?" Marilyn asked.

"What? A restraining order?"

"No. I mean is it OK that I use some of our money to hire Simon?"

It was the first time they'd had to deal with co-ownership. They had been pooling the food budgets, but this was completely different. "Sure," he said, "anything that will keep the sonofabitch away."

Jerry tried to find something about their new arrangement he didn't like, but came up with nothing. Marilyn would make a good business partner for him because she was practical, exactly what he wasn't. Her thinking was enchantingly different from his in ways he still didn't understand. The more he thought about it, the more he suspected this was probably the best thing to have happened in his life; the partnership even more than the inheritance. He knew he should have said exactly that to her the instant he had the thought, that she was the best thing that had ever happened to him in his life, but he didn't; he still wasn't good at sharing things that mattered. Instead, he said, "Marilyn, I think that is the best possible first use of *our money*." He emphasized the last two words and held her away from him so he could smile at her, trying to show her how much he liked the sound of it. She evidently got the message he intended because she smiled back and resumed the hug.

They stood like that a while longer without talking, but, in time, they both felt the need to think things through on their own and went into their separate apartments.

Once inside, Jerry felt a new desolation in his green dump. Even though it now really was *his* apartment, it seemed emptier. All he had ever done there was eat, sleep, and write. Now that his computer was down in the store, and now that Marilyn was cooking for him, there was nothing to do in his apartment except sleep and he was far too wired up to attempt that. He could think of nothing to do with his nervous energy except to deflect it into his writing. He left his apartment and tiptoed down the inside stairwell, just as he had heard Mr. Stamper do on so many nights. He let himself into The Planet of Love and powered up the PC. Lighted only by a small desk lamp and the glow of his screen, he settled down for another trip to Mowdabb.

Three Options

Lurk and Eve lounge on moss cushions on the top of a pyramid close to their latest home cave. Together, they have been watching Dr. Milky's progress for about an hour. From their vantage point, they can see the moss move and shake above Milky as he noisily labors through the underlying stems. He is obviously following their footprints. At times, they can even hear Milky swear unintelligibly at some hazard in the trail, but he always plods on.

"Persistent bastard," Lurk comments casually.

"A little clumsy too," Eve says. "He must be getting tired."

"I would be."

"Shall I dart him as soon as I can get a clear shot?" Eve asks eagerly. She still carries the tranquilizer gun on a strap around her waist.

"You like carrying that gun don't you?" Lurk accuses her. "You like having that power in your hands."

"You bet I do. I've had dates where I could have used it, but in this case, I was thinking it would give us another good head start; we could do it again, hide our trailhead, and be miles away before he regains consciousness."

"No, there's no point in that," Lurk says, "except for the fun it would give you of course. As soon as he wakes up he'd find our trail again, now that he knows our technique, and keep following. He has no choice now."

"What do you mean?" Eve asks. "He could turn around and go back couldn't he?"

"Yeah, he could, but he won't. He's been on the trail for two days now. Unless he's carrying a lot of food with him, which I doubt, he's very hungry. If he were to turn around now, he might be too weak to make it back to the pickup point."

"He's passed the point of no return," Eve says.

Lurk smiles at her dramatic phrasing. "Yup. That's about it. That's why he doesn't care about being quiet. Even if he doesn't know it yet, he is hoping we will have mercy on him and let him join us. He's starting to feel desperate."

"You think we should?" Eve asks.

"Should what?"

"Have mercy on him."

"I think having mercy on him, in this case, is in our best interest," Lurk says. "If the damn fool should die, we'd be blamed for his death. Simian and his organization would never rest till they found us and got their vengeance."

"So how should we handle this?" Eve asks, suddenly nervous at the idea of another man in their midst.

"I suppose we just let him hang around, but on our terms, away from any connection to Simian and his buddies. We can show him what is safe to eat so he doesn't die. I think I can tolerate him till they come back to get him."

"You think they will find us when they come back, don't you?" Eve asks.

"Yes."

"What if you can't?"

"What if I can't what?"

"Tolerate him."

"Then you tranquilize him," Lurk says with a smile.

Dr. Milky is nearly delirious with hunger and exhaustion when he realizes there are no more footprints to follow. The mulch ahead of him is undisturbed as far as he is able to see in the gloom.

"Shit!" He says this loud enough for Lurk and Eve to hear.

Milky now has to backtrack to find where the trail of Lurk's clan must have left the relative openness of the natural tunnel to veer into the denser growth to one side. When he finds the footprints again, heading away from the main tunnel, the going is much more difficult. He has to get down on his knees and lift the branches ahead of him, letting the mat of moss slide over his back. In places he has to get down on his elbows and crawl forward. The effort of working his way forward under the heavy damp blanket of moss eventually forces him to stop. He rests his head on his forearms, breathing in the heady odors of decomposition, easily imagining this could be where his life ends, his body gradually decomposing into the mulch below. Then it occurs to him Lurk's troop would only put themselves through this low-crawl ordeal for one reason; they must have wanted to leave the moss. This thought reenergizes him. They must have been trying to exit the moss as stealthily as they entered it, without leaving a trail that could be seen from the air. They may have wanted to leave the moss for a cave where they could shelter. They must be close by!

Milky rolls over on his back and uses his arms to tear through the dense mat above him. He doesn't care if the moss is disturbed. Hell, he wants to disturb the moss. He is fed up with moss. Once he has made a large enough hole, he sits upright, pulls the moss down around him with his arms, and stands up. After a little more work, he can see the sky! When his head is above the moss, at first he sees nothing but blue sky and miles of rolling green. Then, when he turns around to look in the direction he had been crawling, he sees Lurk and Eve sprawled comfortably on top of a nearby pyramid.

Eve smiles and wiggles her fingers at him.

Dr. Milky is sufficiently pathetic, smeared with the grime of two days under the moss, to be worthy of the solicitous mothering the twins cannot resist providing. He is too weak and hungry to be any threat to them. In fact, they decide he is kind of cute. The twins adopt him as they might an orphaned child. They give him his first Mowdabbian meal and then strip him to the skin, ignoring his protestations, to give him a thorough cleaning with pads of damp moss.

What begins as solicitous mothering by the twins, rapidly grows into something more. In their four, perfectly matched eyes, Dr. Milky is fascinating and attractive, a striking contrast to Lurk. Milky is fine-boned, slender, chocolate-skinned, and well-educated. Lurk is none of those things. Milky is also nearer their own age. Over the next few days, the twins begin to spend much of their time with Milky and he begins to revel in their attentions.

What the twins do not know about Milky is that he has always been fascinated by the subtle psychological differences between twins. He is as enthralled by them as they are by him.

His digestive system takes a couple of days to adjust to his new diet, but under the attentive care of the twins he soon regains his strength.

Lurk has no trouble dealing with Milky's presence among them. Without his tranquilizer gun, Milky is no threat. The twins keep him safely occupied and usually far away from Lurk. What's more, Milky's travails on the trail have humbled him. He has been outwitted, and now drawn into an alien environment where his considerable intellect is of little value. Even though he knows his IQ is probably double that of Lurk, he is perfectly willing to be told what to do, by anyone. He is preoccupied with the attentions of two beautiful women and happy not to be decomposing under the moss.

On the fifth day after his resurrection from the mulch, Dr. Milky's relationship with the twins is eternally forged. A sex storm sweeps through their encampment. The twins feel the storm coming and draw Milky aside before it begins, wanting to keep him all to themselves. He does not feel it to the extent the others do, perhaps because he has not been eating a Mowdabbian diet very long, but he is none-the-less swept up in it, blown away by the sex storm tornado like an innocent tourist. He enthusiastically participates, accommodating the twins to the limits of his strength.

Eve is left with Lurk. No one complains.

Dr. Milky, still not fully recovered from his exhausting two-day journey, is almost consumed by the seemingly inexhaustible physical appetites of the twins. He survives all four days and nights, but barely. When it is over, he feels like a changed man at every level of his being.

Once the storm is past and after they have had time to rest and recover, Lurk addresses Dr. Milky for the first time. Up to that point, he had ignored Milky's presence completely. On the second day after the storm, Lurk simply walks over to where Milky is lounging in the sun, sits down beside him and says, "We're leaving this place. You have three options. Option one: You can remain here to wait for Dr. Simian or his people to find you. Option two: You can, if you accept our one, non-negotiable condition, go with us."

"Go with you!"

"Yes. The twins seem to like you," Lurk says simply, by way of explanation, giving no sign of the intense lobbying the twins have done on Milky's behalf for the last two days.

Milky looks across the clearing where the twins are lounging with the youngest children and sees they are anxiously watching the conversation he is having with Lurk. Milky smiles at the twins, then hesitates. "But, you said I had three options."

"Yes, I did. You have three options because there are two ways you can remain here to wait for Dr. Simian: You can remain here either conscious or unconscious."

"I don't get it."

"It's very simple," Lurk explains. "If you don't accept the one condition under which you can continue with our group, you cannot go with us. If you do not accept that condition and you try to follow us again anyway, we will know it. We will find you and you will be tranquilized and left behind. We'll leave you laid out nicely where the hovercraft will find you, but you will be left behind. You won't see us again."

Milky looks at the twins and then back to Lurk. "What's the one condition?"

"You must pledge that you will stay with us for the remainder of your life."

Milky's jaw drops.

"It's all or nothing," Lurk explains. "You can choose to become a part of us, or you can stay behind. You can stay behind either willingly or unwillingly."

Possibilities

Jerry gave her "Shave and a haircut" without the two bits and heard her sing, "Come in," right on the beat.

Once inside her apartment, he could hear the water shut off in the shower.

"I'll just be a minute," she hollered through the bathroom door.

The apartment was filled with the heavy odors of something delicious he could not quite identify. His stomach rumbled in anticipation. He fished the corkscrew out of a kitchen drawer and opened the wine he had chosen for the evening from Safeway. (It was the cheapest one he could find with a cork.) Jerry had two glasses poured by the time she came out of the bathroom wearing her blue, chenille bathrobe outfit.

She gave him a big smile. He gave her a quick kiss while she was still adjusting her towel turban and then handed her the wineglass.

"Is this a 'special night'?" she asked, indicating the wine.

"If my luck holds," he said.

"You look lucky to me," she said and gave him another kiss, leaning into this one, giving it all the body English she could manage with them both trying not to spill their wine.

"Mmmmm," he said, "You smell even better than whatever you have cooking."

"It's curried lamb," she said.

"Odd name for perfume."

"What you smell is not perfume," she laughed. "It's my shampoo. It's called 'Strawberry Nights' or 'Strawberry Dreams,' something like that."

"I think I'd like some with dinner."

"Couldn't you wait till after dinner?" she purred.

"I'll do my best," he said doubtfully.

"If you'll set the table, I'll fix my hair and then we can serve up the stew."

"Deal."

In a few minutes, she came back with her hair combed and a few errant curls pinned in place. She was still wearing the blue chenille, but loosely tied now, revealing something underneath in pink satin. Jerry finished setting the table, topped off the wine glasses, and they dug in.

Jerry put away two big bowls of curried lamb stew without missing a stroke. There was little conversation. She took one small bite to each of his two big ones, spending most of her time watching him enjoy his meal.

"I think the simple pleasures are the best ones," she said after he had finished his second bowl.

"Complicated pleasures are no fun at all," he said.

"Would you like a little more of this simple wine?" she asked, lifting the bottle and presenting the label for his approval.

"Don't mind if I do," he said, all the while enjoying the sight of a still-damp strand of her hair that had come unpinned and now dangled in front of her ear as she reached across the table to pour.

"My pleasure," she said for no particular reason, putting down the wine bottle and then working to re-pin her hair.

"*My* pleasure," he argued, watching her work.

They each inordinately enjoyed their silly conversation, smiling comfortably at one another through it all. If Jerry had not been a participant, he wouldn't have been able to stand listening to their sappy banter.

"How did you do that?" he asked, nodding toward the kitchen behind her.

"Oh, it's simple really," she said, "once you learn how to use bobby pins."

"Yes, of course… I mean, how did you make curried lamb stew while you were working?"

"Oh, didn't you notice the cooking pot?" she said. "I went over to Mr. Stamper's apartment last night to check on the finches and borrowed it. It's electric. I saw it in his kitchen a long time ago and wondered what possible use he would make of such a big cooking pot. But it's perfect for our situation, where we work all day I mean. I just put all the ingredients in the pot early this morning and turned it on low. That's why the meat was so tender; it's been cooking all day."

"I guess you didn't really 'borrow' it from Mr. Stamper," he pointed out. "I mean, since we inherited all of this, I guess it's our cooking pot now."

"True." She was quiet for a moment, more somber. "You know it was strange going back over there. It was strange not to find Mr. Stamper shuffling around in his slippers."

"What are we going to do with all that furniture?" he asked, hoping to change the subject before Marilyn got too maudlin. "There must be enough in there to overfill a couple of houses. It looks like an antiques store."

"I know. The way it's stacked you can't even see what's in the back. But you saw that. I don't think you've seen the second bedroom; it's even more crowded; it's stacked tight all the way to the ceiling. There isn't even a path down the middle in there like in all the other rooms. Why do you suppose he owned so much? And it's all good quality stuff, too."

"Maybe he used to have a big house and kept all its furniture when he moved here."

"Yeah, maybe. It all seems to match too, like all the pieces were chosen by the same person." She paused for a sip of wine. "I spent a few minutes walking around in there last night," she admitted, "trying to get used to the place and, you know, to the idea that we own it all now."

"Kinda spooky," he ventured.

"Yes it was, a little, but I was *so* curious."

"About the furniture?"

"Well yes, about that and about everything else," she said. "I mean, the more I thought about everything, the less sense it made. Why would Mr. Stamper pack all of that into his apartment, using up all that living space? Why didn't he rent some storage or sell it through an auctioneer?"

"It's a mystery," he said. "Maybe it had some sentimental value and he didn't want to pay for storage somewhere else."

"Well, the biggest mystery of all," Marilyn said, leaning forward, her eyes wide with the delicious mystique of it, "is why would he give it all to us?"

"I don't understand it," Jerry admitted.

"I wish I'd gotten to know him better," she said.

"I thought you and he were pretty close."

"Not close exactly, but we got along well right from the beginning. He actually picked me out of the unemployment line. I told you about that, didn't I?"

"He probably liked your bathrobe too."

"What are you saying; do I wear this too much?"

"Yeah, I think you should take it off."

She smiled her inscrutable Mona Lisa smile at his eager display of her desirability and talked on. "When he mentioned the apartment was included in the job offer, I was ready to go. He needed someone to start right away and… that was it."

"I'd hire you on sight," he said.

She paused for a heartbeat to accept his silly endorsement. "It was strange though; sometimes he'd forget what he was doing, just go all quiet-like around me and, I don't know, kind of sad. I can't imagine what was going on when he got like that, but it happened several times."

"He was always a mystery to me." Jerry was thinking of the time he met him leaving his apartment in that strange trance.

"What was it like when you interviewed with him?" she asked.

"It was kind of a non-interview; he just offered me the job. He just handed me his business card and told me to come by the next day."

"Me too!"

"What do you mean?"

"I mean he just handed me his business card; there was no interview," she said. "Even when I showed up in the shop, he just put me to work. I didn't know what to make of that."

"Very strange," Jerry agreed. "It was the same for me; when I showed up at COPY/COPY in my grungy old field jacket, looming over him like a heavily insulated stork, he turned a lighter shade of pale than he usually was, almost gray. I was afraid he was going to die before he could hire me."

"Jerry," Marilyn said, "you are *not* a 'stork'. You are a tall and elegant man."

"Elegant?"

"Absolutely. 'Elegant' is the perfect adjective for you."

He was speechless.

She smiled at his discomfiture. "Except when you're eating," she added, to put him at ease. "Then words like 'intense' and 'lumberjackian' come to mind."

"I've had many adjectives applied to me," he said, "but never 'elegant', nor 'lumberjackian'."

"I only wish I were taller," she said.

"Why?"

"If I weren't so short and dumpy, you wouldn't feel so tall beside me."

"Marilyn," he began, echoing the tone of her declaration to him, "you are *not* 'dumpy'. You are short and Rubenesque."

"Rubenesque? What the hell is that?"

"That is the term used to describe the vivaciously healthy wenches and rosy-cheeked scullery maids Peter Paul Rubens preferred to paint, often in the nude. The women that is, not Rubens."

It was her turn to be speechless.

"I only wish I could paint," he said.

Marilyn became more rosy-cheeked.

There was a delightful intensification of Marilyn's rosy cheeks when he suggested, "Now let's talk about something in pink satin."

They repaired to the bedroom.

Afterwards, much, much later, it was agreed they would never get any sleep with both of them trying to occupy Marilyn's little bed, so, Jerry went back to his own apartment, where he collapsed into happy, dreamless sleep.

For once, concern for Lurk's problems never crossed his mind.

Archaeology

The next morning, Jerry rejoined Marilyn for a monster Sunday morning breakfast, after which they ventured into the cave of Mr. Stamper's apartment. They went in with business-like intentions, Marilyn prepared with notepad and clipboard to make a list of all the furniture. But, they were both soon overwhelmed.

They did accomplish a listing of the furniture in the living room; most of the pieces there were accessible from the main pathways and, while all jammed together and nearly unusable as they were, it was only one layer deep. Jerry shuffled some of the pieces around as necessary, so they could get a good look at everything, inspected it for damage, open any doors or drawers, and look for manufacturer's labels or for anything else to help them determine what the piece might be worth or how they might use it.

Marilyn followed Jerry around as he shuffled things, writing down a description of each item and getting excited over almost everything they found. "There must be a fortune in here!" she said about a half dozen times. Jerry had never been much of a furniture fan, but she soon had him excited. She was seeing possibilities for everything they found, either for selling or for putting to good use.

However, their systematic inventory ended when they came to the second, unused bedroom. It was, as Marilyn had said, *filled* with furniture. The door to the second bedroom swung inward and swept across the only section of carpeting in that room not covered with stacked furniture. The wall of furniture went clear to the ceiling and was so densely stacked that turning on the switch for the ceiling light did little to light the room; its glow was obscured behind a forest of wooden chair legs, elaborately carved nightstands, coat racks, turned ashtray stands, lamps, fanciful wooden plant stands, umbrella stands, picture frames, mirrors, and a bewildering assortment of other bric-a-brac. Mr. Stamper had obviously segregated all the smaller furniture pieces into this unused room, where they could be stacked and packed more closely together. Unlike the main room, there was a fine layer of undisturbed dust over everything in that second bedroom. Neither of them was ready to begin untangling that Chinese puzzle to inventory what was in there, so they turned out the light, closed the door, and moved on to the main bedroom.

The ghost of Mr. Stamper was present in the master bedroom, more so than anywhere else. Their intended inventory-taking soon became more like the exploration of a tomb. The room had obviously been in daily use and was reasonably furnished with the finest pieces in the apartment. A large bed was the centerpiece of the room. Its spiral-turned and sculpted wooden corner posts held a lace-draped canopy overhead. An elaborate headboard was covered with carvings of garlands of leaves and flowers deep into the dark wood. All the other furniture in the room, the nightstand, dresser, bookshelves, and a massive chest-of-drawers also gleamed from years of loving polish. A lemon/wax smell almost overcame the sour tobacco funk pervading the whole apartment. The bed itself was neatly made, the spread smoothed and tucked around the pillows. Beside the bed, several silver-framed photographs were on display on either side of a large-mirrored vanity. In front of the photos, arranged neatly in the middle of a crocheted doily, was a woman's silver brush, comb, and mirror set, looking as if they'd never been used.

Marilyn was first drawn to the beaded lampshades on end tables on either side of the bed, the shades held aloft by what looked to be pewter sculptures of naked women, but it was the books that commanded Jerry's attention. Every other horizontal surface in the room was devoted to books. They were not in disarray, but carefully aligned, either inside a freestanding, glass-fronted bookcase, as on one wall, or in two separate corner bookshelf units, all precisely filled. Expensive-looking, matched bookends aligned more books on top of the bookcases. He began to read their spines. Shakespeare was much in evidence, but there was also a fair representation of the poets: Yeats, Whitman, Auden, and especially Tennyson. Most of the books were leather bound and some appeared to be quite old. They were not on display for the impression their leather covers might make though; all the books appeared well handled and dust-free. It was obvious Old Man Stamper had treasured them, and had been reading them.

The Clark County Library system contained nothing like them. He couldn't yet appreciate what a treasure his new library was, but he admired the quality of their binding, their obvious age, and their variety. It was certainly not the sort of collection he would have expected from a man who also owned the "reading material" with which they had stocked The Planet of Love. Mr. Stamper was full of surprises.

Jerry's attention was drawn to four books stacked casually on the nightstand beside the bed. Three of them were lying closed, as if next on Mr. Stamper's reading list, but one small book was lying open, nearest at hand to the pillow. Jerry's first impression was that the open book must have been what Mr. Stamper had been reading, but, when his eyes caught on one particular line on the open page, he decided the book had been left open deliberately. The book was Antony and Cleopatra.

"Listen to this," Jerry said, then read the passage aloud to Marilyn.

> But he will be, a bridegroom in his death,
>
> and run into't as to a lover's bed.

> William Shakespeare, act 4, sc. 15.

Marilyn came to stand beside Jerry to read the lines herself.

"He left this laying open," Jerry said. "I think this is what he wanted others to find, after he was gone."

They were quiet for a long time before she said, "He was ready to die."

Jerry didn't tell her about the empty pill bottle he'd found beside the body.

Standing in Mr. Stamper's sanctum sanctorum, feeling evermore like intruders, they were getting a glimpse of the old man as neither of them had seen him, or at least a glimpse of how he had once been. The only things in the bedroom that seemed to fit the man Jerry thought he knew were the two pewter naked women lamps. The books, and all of his other sentimental treasures so lovingly displayed, were a somber discovery that filled Jerry with a deep, abiding sadness at the loss of the man he had obviously not known at all, and now never would.

- - -

Then… Marilyn discovered the photographs.

She had moved to the delicately carved vanity and was sitting on the small bench in front of it when she drew in a deep, shaky breath and whispered, "Oh, Jerry, look!"

Jerry turned to see both her astonished face reflected in the vanity's mirror and, over her shoulder, the small collection of photographs to which he hadn't paid much attention. The photos stood in a silver-framed arc around the edge of the doily under the brush, comb, and mirror set.

When he leaned down to look more closely at what Marilyn was pointing out with a trembling hand, he was staggered and moved to settle on the bench beside her. She took a ragged breath and covered her mouth with her hands. "Oh, Jerry!" she said in a high, squeaky voice on the edge of tears.

It was the biggest of all the photos, an old wedding picture in faded sepia tones, gray matted in an intricate silver frame. The newlyweds were holding hands to show their wedding rings. The man in the photo was obviously a proud, young Mr. Stamper, about Jerry's age, looking quite handsome in an old-fashioned double-breasted suit with huge lapels.

Mr. Stamper was holding hands with Marilyn.

"Holy shit," Jerry said.

The Marilyn in the picture had her hair teased into formal curls around her face, but her face was Marilyn's. Even her expression seemed to echo Marilyn's reflection in the vanity mirror. While the serious, wide-eyed young bride faced the uncertainty of the marriage ahead of her, Marilyn faced her stunning resemblance to the bride. A wedding veil framed the face of Mrs. Stamper. She was dressed in satin white and clutched a bouquet in the crook of her arm. She was beautiful.

"Oh, Jerry," Marilyn said again, "look." She was pointing to another photo, a small black-and-white in the next frame over.

At first, Jerry saw only a young man leaning, with studied nonchalance, against a 1957 Chevy, but when he focused on the young man's face, he saw... *himself!*

Still reeling from the first photo, the impact of seeing himself on the vanity tipped Jerry down the rabbit hole. All he could do was stare.

"Is that you?" Marilyn asked, a quiver in her voice clearly revealing her confusion.

Either of the photos would have rendered Jerry speechless, but discovering them one after the other like that...

When he could find his voice, Jerry said, "No, that's not me."

The resemblance was so great it appeared to be a photograph of Jerry made up to look like someone else, as if in preparation for a school play, rather than a photograph of a man that looked like Jerry. It was more than uncanny; it was disturbing.

The young man in the photo was tall, skinny, and about Jerry's age, maybe a few years younger. He was wearing a plain white T-shirt with a pack of cigarettes rolled into the sleeve. He was squinting against the sun and through the smoke wafting up from the cigarette dangling straight down from his lips. It was just as Mr. Stamper had always smoked, letting the smoke curl up past one eye. The young man's hair was long and greasy, carefully combed up and forward into a drooping lock that coiled down over his forehead. He had a tattoo of some sort on his right shoulder, just below the pack of cigarettes. Except for the long greasy hair and the tattoo, it was Jerry.

"Who could that be?" Marilyn asked.

Even if Jerry had known what to say, he was incapable of answering.

"That can't be Mr. Stamper," she said. "Can it?"

Jerry could see why Marilyn might wonder; he could see Mr. Stamper in that face too, though he had not been aware of any resemblance he might have had with the man until that moment. The same bones were behind their long and narrow faces. They had the same heavy eyebrows, and narrow, prominent noses. It would be easy to believe the young man in the picture *was* Mr. Stamper, taken when he was younger, before the stoop and wrinkle of old age.

"No, it couldn't be Mr. Stamper; when he was the age of the man in the picture, they hadn't yet made a 1957 Chevy."

"I know Mr. Stamper had a twin, but did he have a younger brother?" Marilyn wondered aloud.

"Or a son?" Jerry added, staring, mesmerized by his own face looking back at him from the past.

"Here he is again," Marilyn broke Jerry's spell, pointing to a smaller, color picture on the vanity, obviously the same young man, but the long greasy hair was gone and he had become a lean, tanned PFC dressed in Army green. In the uniform, he looked a little less like Jerry, and he was older than in the other photo. His expression was determined... or defiant.

"He hired us because we look like his family," Marilyn said, and then began to cry. It was too much to assimilate and she rushed out of the room and out of the apartment. Jerry numbly followed.

- - -

Once they were out of the apartment, they stood together on the landing for a long time, embracing without speaking, each absorbing comfort from the presence of the other, each trying to come to grips with what they had discovered in Mr. Stamper's sanctuary.

Marilyn was upset with how sad it all was, and especially upset to have learned so late the truth of it, that a lonely old man had chosen the two of them to have around him in his final days simply because they looked like his absent family.

Jerry felt that sadness too. He believed it was true what Marilyn had said, that Old Man Stamper had hired them because of their undeniable resemblances to his family. But, Jerry was struggling with something even more fundamentally upsetting, an outrageous possibility that he might have a more direct connection with Old Man Stamper, or more precisely, with the insouciant young punk leaning against the 1957 Chevy. The moment he saw that photo, Jerry somehow knew it was Mr. Stamper's son. He hadn't even known the old man had a son, and it might have been the photo of a younger brother, or a nephew, but Jerry *knew* it was Mr. Stamper's son. That was spooky enough, but when Jerry saw the second picture, the one of the same young man in an Army uniform, a stunning possibility elbowed its way into his thinking. He resisted the idea for as long as he could, but it was loose now, racing out of control around and around in his head, accreting a thin veneer of validity with each lap. Almost against his own will, he had already begun to believe Mr. Stamper's son, this doppelganger, might have been the despoiler of his mother, the father Jerry never knew.

It was a possibility that scared him for reasons he couldn't immediately identify. Questions clamored for his attention while he held tight to Marilyn, as a drowning man might hug a pier. Could it be true? Did he want it to be true? How could he confirm it? Or refute it? When were those photos taken? If he knew when those photos were taken, he might be able to figure it out. All he knew was the apparent age of the son in the presence of a new-looking 1957 Chevy. Without knowing more, it was really nothing more than a compelling possibility, but it would not leave him. The uncanny resemblance alone might make anyone believe he was related to Mr. Stamper's son; Marilyn had even wondered if it was somehow Jerry in the photo, but lots of unrelated people looked like they were related. That alone wasn't what made his skin prickle. The kicker was seeing the uniform, learning that the young man had been in the Army. All the secondhand stories about his father Jerry had been able to pry from his Grandma had always included the detail that he had been a soldier.

Was it enough to warrant his suspicions to see this uncanny resemblance wearing an Army uniform?

It frightened him on several levels to think his father was out there somewhere. He didn't know why that frightened him, but it did. He thought he had accepted his fatherless circumstance long ago, but now he wasn't sure he wanted to welcome that possibility. *If* that was his father, and if he was still alive, could he be found? Did Jerry *want* to find him?

The very unlikely circumstance that both he and Mr. Stamper would be in the same place, at the same time, by chance, frightened him too. The odds of that happening had to be astronomical! Had he been receiving guidance from the weasel during his odyssey?

Another possibility: Maybe Mr. Stamper had known about, or suspected, Jerry's connection to the Stamper family all along, from the beginning. Maybe he'd been tracking Jerry's wanderings. That frightened him too.

As these questions continued to pop up and then settle into a queue for long-term consideration, Marilyn heaved a big, sad sigh against his chest that made him begin to think of her. He couldn't tell her about this. He wanted to share everything with Marilyn, but he couldn't tell her he thought Old Man Stamper was his Grandfather. It was just too unbelievable to say aloud. He had to keep such wild ideas to himself. It would make him sound as crazy as some of the lost souls he'd met on the streets. He didn't want Marilyn to think of him like that. Even to his own mind, his suspicions smacked of lonesome desperation, a pathetic desire to restore his severed roots and find family.

"I think it's time to call it a day," Jerry said. "Don't you?"

"Yes, I do. Maybe we can continue with this tomorrow night."

They held one another close a little longer and then kissed goodnight, each retiring to their separate apartments.

As soon as Jerry closed the door, he knew he would not be able to sleep. He paced for a while, giving Marilyn time to settle, so he wouldn't disturb her. Then he tiptoed down the stairs into The Planet of Love, seeking distraction on Mowdabb.

He turned on the computer, found his place in the manuscript, reread the last few lines, and tried to get his mind on task, but the questions continued to overlay the words on the screen.

Was he still the last of the Gustafsons of Kilgore, Idaho? Or, was he a Stamper, maybe now the last of the Stampers? *If* his mother had obtained a marriage certificate during her Wildly Romantic Weekend, which he knew she hadn't, he would *not* be the last of the Gustafson's. He did not know what to make of that. He could not decide if one was any better than the other.

If only there was some way to date the Army photo...

After a time of staring at his computer, Jerry turned it off and went to bed.

Visiting the Ghosts

The next night, during a fine dinner of home-cooked hamburgers, dill pickles, and pan-fried potatoes, neither of them broached the subject of the previous night's discoveries; they talked all around it. When the dishes were done, Marilyn and Jerry returned to Mr. Stamper's bedroom to continue their "inventory."

They did not immediately go back to the vanity; they had to work up to it, but its pull was irresistible. They began by opening the drawers of the large dresser where they found little more than a musty collection of Mr. Stamper's clothes. Together, they admired some more of the books for a few minutes and then finally allowed themselves to be drawn back to the ornate little vanity where Mr. Stamper had kept his memories. They studied the inexplicable photographs, as if to confirm their memories of the night before. As before, a long-haired version of Jerry still stood beside a '57 Chevy in one photo and Mr. Stamper and Marilyn still held hands on their wedding day in another. The defiant soldier son stood off to one side. Without comment, Jerry and Marilyn succumbed to their curiosity and began to search the drawers of the vanity. The first few drawers were filled with many little things, obvious keepsakes and mementos that had no meaning for either of them, lapel pins from old causes, hair clips and ribbons, and a large cocktail ring with pink and blue Zircons. Then, in a neat stack in the vanity's large bottom drawer, Marilyn discovered two unmatched photo albums and a smaller scrapbook of newspaper clippings. Jerry and Marilyn sat together on the vanity's little bench facing their reflections in the vanity mirror and opened the first of the photo albums. While Marilyn turned the pages of Mr. Stamper's past, Jerry could not help glancing up to watch her in the vanity mirror and to steal unsettling glances at the framed photograph of Mr. Stamper's bride.

The first pages of the album were filled with black and white shots of young Mr. and Mrs. Stamper together, some obviously from their wedding party and others from what must have been a New Year party, where they were dressed in formal ballroom attire on a dance floor, draped with streamers and sprinkled with confetti. In another series of photo clichés, they were variously clowning in bathing suits at a crowded ocean beach, walking in the surf with an out-of-focus pier in the background, and sipping drinks under a patio umbrella, surrounded by several other couples trying to squeeze into the photo. As the album pages continue to turn, Mr. and Mrs. Stamper begin to show some aging. Mrs. Stamper looks progressively less like Marilyn. Abruptly, with no intervening pictures of a pregnant Mrs. Stamper, about halfway into the album, she is proudly holding a baby. Almost every photograph thereafter involves their newborn. One notable exception to the many baby pictures was a single photo that appeared to contain two Mr. Stampers. The two men were sitting around a poker table, holding their cards and grinning identically goofy grins at the camera. One man had a cigarette hanging down from his bushy moustache, while the other had no moustache and a thin cigar clamped in his teeth, canting it upward at a jaunty angle, like Roosevelt.

The baby fascinated Marilyn. She turned the pages slowly, studying the pictures with a mix of sadness and wonder. The new baby clutched the index fingers of people off-camera, slept soundly in a stroller, or smeared food around a highchair. Within a few pages, there was a little boy toddling around in his first pair of shoes and then smiling through assorted birthday parties and around various Christmas trees.

By the time Marilyn had reached the end of the album, there were tears in her eyes.

"Do you want to quit for a while?" Jerry asked.

Marilyn shook her head, pulled herself together, and opened the second album. The first few pages contained a few shots of Mrs. Stamper and her sullen teenager. After that, Mrs. Stamper seemed to fade away. She appeared occasionally in the background of photos taken of their son, but she was often turning away or out of focus. Her resemblance to Marilyn continued to lessen as she aged. Sometimes the resemblance was not there at all. In the last few photographs of her, she looked exhausted and... depressed.

Mr. Stamper had evidently been the one who recorded their memories, because he was not in any of the photos in the second album.

One snapshot Jerry found particularly disturbing was a longhaired young Stamper boy sitting at a picnic table by himself, clearly bored. It was taken at a lakeshore campground with a raft and diving board in the background, but the lake didn't seem to draw the young man; he obviously did not want to be there. There were a couple of basketball team photos and then, near the middle of the second album, the photos stopped; the remaining pages were blank. Instead, a stack of loose photos was tucked inside the back cover, never mounted in the album. Among them, Jerry found two photos that caused his heart to pound. One was a snapshot of a shorthaired soldier home on leave, and not looking happy. The other was a formal, studio portrait of the Stamper boy in his Army dress uniform.

Throughout the two albums, which seemed to contain the complete, agonizingly condensed, photographic history of a family, the young son's resemblance to Jerry was always there. Many of them were much like the few pictures Jerry had seen of himself at those ages, pictures that he now wished he still had, though he couldn't remember throwing any of them away. They must have been lost in the auction of his Grandma's possessions.

Next Marilyn opened the scrapbook. It started out to be a carefully maintained baby book, a chronicle of the life of the Stamper's only child, though there were many lapses in the recordkeeping. It began with a birth certificate and a formal birth announcement for Darren Ezra Stamper.

Darren.

What followed were pages from a journal that had been torn out and taped into place in the scrapbook. The journal pages had obviously been kept by the young Mrs. Stamper because they were filled with careful, feminine cursive. She had chronicled the minutest details of Darren's development through the early months, even recording nursing times, each entry followed by a capital R or L.

After the journal pages, it was much less carefully put together, many things were just stuffed into place in the scrapbook in roughly chronological order. There were colorful invitations to several birthday parties with accompanying party photos. There were Little League standings gleaned from newspapers and photos of uniformed players standing with their coaches. There were high school newspaper articles, the first announcing that Darren Stamper had joined the paper's staff. Several articles written by Darren followed the announcement. There was a debate about policy regarding hall passes, a report on a prom, and a poem authored by Darren Stamper. The poem had been cleverly printed in one long narrow column in the margin of the editorial page:

Lost

loose-leafed

margins,

gone and forgotten,

like leaves loosed

in summer's past,

decay

and when regotten,

are renewed;

spring's

loose-leafed

margins

in their turn

lost, gone,

and soon forgotten.

Photographs proved Darren made the basketball team, but, despite his obvious height, the accompanying newspaper clippings about their games did not indicate he got much playing time.

Abruptly, the scrapbook clippings began to chronicle Darren's course through the Army. He attended basic training in Fort Ord and underwent further training in Fort Hood, Texas. He was then assigned to an Armored-Cavalry unit in Vietnam. There was a single, one-page letter from Darren to his parents, the only thing in the scrapbook written in Darren's hand. In the letter, he said that whatever bizarre, tropical fungus had been growing on his feet was just about gone, that there were only ten weeks to go, and that he was beginning to believe he just might survive it all.

The last item in the scrapbook was a clipping from the Sacramento Bee dated June 9th 1971. The column regretfully announced that Army Specialist Darren Stamper, the son of Mr. and Mrs. Barry Stamper, owners of Stamper's Furniture, had been killed in a rocket attack on Firebase Storm where he had served for ten months as a mechanic.

Jerry felt a ghostly sense of loss at the news the man who might have been the father he never knew, was dead, and had been dead for a long time. Jerry now knew that if his theory was correct, he would never meet the father he had never known. He waited for some greater emotional reaction to this revelation, but felt none. He had never decided he would want to meet the man anyway.

- - -

"There's nothing else," Marilyn said, searching through the last blank pages of the scrapbook. They looked through the vanity drawers but found nothing that post-dated Darren's death.

"It looks like everything stopped with the death of their son," Jerry said. He did not say aloud the several less-romantic possibilities that occurred to him, that there may have been nothing more in the scrapbook because Mrs. Stamper died, or their marriage had fallen apart.

Marilyn must have been thinking the same way, because she said, "Maybe she died of cancer or something," It was a possibility of course and a reasonable guess because Mr. Stamper would likely have thrown out anything that reminded him of the illness.

"Yeah, maybe," he agreed. He didn't share his thought that the death of her son might have pushed Mrs. Stamper's depression over the edge into mental illness, or even suicide.

"Stamper's Furniture," Marilyn said.

"Yeah."

Neither of them had much to say in the presence of Mr. Stamper private miseries. It was too sad. In addition, Jerry was beginning to think about the other clue he'd gotten from that same clipping. The date of Darren's death was June of 1971, after serving for ten months. He would have been given some leave time before shipping out during which he may have attended a Grateful Dead concert in San Francisco. Maybe Jerry could research the Dead's performances around that time. Then all he had to do was go back another nine months to allow for gestation time...

Marilyn closed the drawers of the vanity and broke Jerry's concentration. She fiddled with the inventory clipboard, briefly toying with the thought of continuing their inventory of the master bedroom, but her heart wasn't in it. "I think I'm done here."

"OK." But, Jerry remained sitting a moment longer on the vanity bench, lost in the calculations, working in both directions in time, from his birthday forward and backward from Darren's death. It all seemed to fit; Jerry had been conceived not long before Darren went to war.

There it was... no hard evidence to support Jerry's theory except for "motive and opportunity," as they say in the detective novels. He doubted there would ever be any hard evidence.

A theory was all he would ever have.

- - -

They hardly spoke as they left the big apartment. The sad revelations gleaned from Mr. Stamper's memorabilia had left Marilyn near tears. Jerry didn't want to talk about any of it either; it was all too much to assimilate and there were, for him, too many imponderables he wasn't ready to share.

Jerry and Marilyn had become part of the larger tragedy that had been the Stamper family. They had come to know of it too late to provide any more comfort to Mr. Stamper than whatever he might have found in having the two of them around him in his final days. They were delighted with their inheritance, but the heat of their excitement over material wealth was quenched in knowing that all these fine furnishings had done nothing to bring happiness to the Stampers. On the landing, they hugged only briefly. Marilyn fixed Jerry with her tear-filled eyes and said, "Good night." Jerry wrapped her in his big, long arms once again and whispered "good night" in her ear. They each retired to their separate apartments.

Again, Jerry paced for a while, letting Marilyn settle, and then tiptoed downstairs to make a welcome escape from recent sadness to another world of his own making.

Milky's Quest

At first light the next morning, as most of the children begin drifting away to play in the moss, the adults gather anxiously around a basket of "fruit" to hear Dr. Milky's decision.

"I'm going to leave," he announces.

A twin clings to each of Dr. Milky's arms and each says, "Noooo," in perfect chorus. Eve clings hard to Lurk's arm in sympathy with the twins, but also, clearly, distraught in her own right over Dr. Milky's decision.

"But," Dr. Milky adds, "I hope to come back to stay."

"That's not one of the choices I offered you," Lurk says sternly, quickly dampening the hope that struggled to rise past the tears of the twins. "Once you leave here, you'll never find us again."

Dr. Milky nodded to himself, resigned to the chore of delivering what he had to say next, to reveal the true extent of their entrapment on Mowdabb. "Here's the part you don't understand," he began. "You can easily get away from me, as you've so ably proven, but there is no way to hide from Dr. Simian. No matter where you go, he will find you and he will do so easily. He has equipment capable of locating any endothermic creature larger than a mouse anywhere on the planet. That is how we were able to fly directly to your home cave when we arrived. Unless you are all willing to remain inside the caves, your warm bodies will show up as little pink hotspots on a dark blue screen, complete with longitude and latitude. There's no way you can hide."

Lurk's former lordly manner is wretchedly deflated when he hears his suspicions confirmed. He had been hoping their guerilla tactics were confounding Dr. Simian's search for them, but that wasn't the case; Dr. Simian simply wasn't ready to search for them. Lurk had always wondered how they had been so easily found in the first place; this explained it. Lurk stares at the ground between them as he says, "We're Simian's lab rats."

Dr. Milky did not disagree.

"I can see why you wouldn't want to join the rats," Lurk says.

Dr. Milky looks steadily at the twins as he says, "Ahh... but I do. I want to come back more than anything I have ever wanted. But..." He turns back to address Lurk. "I have to leave first. I believe there is a slim chance I can do more good for all of you, all of *us*, if I leave."

There are puzzled looks all around. Eve speaks first. "How could you help us by leaving?"

"I have a plan," Milky says. "I can't stop Dr. Simian from finding us, but I might be able to stop him from looking for us. What I'm planning to do is risky because it will make Dr. Simian my enemy. This is not an idea I relish. It is also risky because there is a good chance it will fail. Failure would mean I could never find a way to help the people I care about." Here, again, he looks pointedly at the twins. "My plan is to go over Dr. Simian's head. I'm going to make an appeal directly to The Federation of Planets."

Mowdabbian Rules

"If I approach the Federation Council with what I have in mind to propose, my career as a scientist will probably be over. Dr. Simian will fight my proposal with every bit of the considerable influence he has. The worst of it is that, if my proposal is denied by the Federation Council, I won't have any way to come back here." The twins begin, in unison, to cry. Milky holds the twins close and continues. "Dr. Simian alone has the coveted permit to study Mowdabb; he will simply replace me with someone else to finish my project here. You will have no peace until Dr. Simian has learned everything he can from you. That could take years. He might even be able to extend the study permit so it will last for generations."

"So, that's what you have in mind, you intend to appeal to the Federation to stop Dr. Simian's study of Mowdabb?" Eve asks.

"Not exactly," he says. "What I have in mind to propose, if accepted, will certainly put an end to Dr. Simian's study, but I'm going for more than that. I am going to propose that Mowdabb be granted sovereignty."

He could see that no one understands the implications of that and possibly not the word itself.

"It would mean Mowdabb would be given the right to govern itself."

This statement still does not generate much comprehension.

"We are already governing ourselves," Lurk says, "if they would just leave us the hell alone. How will you persuade them we have that right?"

"It's going to be a tough sell," Dr. Milky admits. "We need to prove this planet has its own indigenous higher life form, namely, all of you."

Incredulous looks pass among them, effervescing with tiny flickers of hope.

"If sovereignty is granted, Dr. Simian will be required to approach the planet by conventional diplomatic protocols; he can't simply insert himself and his research project into the environment as he has done so far. By law," Dr. Milky continues, "any planet with an indigenous higher life form is entitled to sovereignty. Dr. Simian will argue you haven't been here long enough to be considered indigenous, that you are really just castaways."

"I just want to get my hands on him again," Lurk says irrelevantly and for the hundredth time.

"Here's the problem," Dr. Milky says, ignoring Lurk's persistent hatred of Dr. Simian. "To be considered 'indigenous,' a higher life form must have three attributes. First, it must have a history of subsisting only on what is provided by the environment of the planet. I think we can easily demonstrate you've done that. Second, an indigenous higher life form will breed sufficiently to maintain its population. You'll forgive me for saying so ladies, but you have demonstrated no difficulty whatsoever with breeding. This brings me to the third and most important requirement, also the one most difficult to prove: I will have to prove to the Federation Council that an evolutionary process is taking place on Mowdabb, to prove that you all have somehow begun to change as a species."

"We have changed the way we breed," Eve says, her eyes twinkling with memories of the last sex storm. "I think you can testify to that yourself."

"I most certainly can," Dr. Milky admits, blushing slightly at the indelible memory of it. "But, it will take more than my testimony to convince the council that what I experienced was anything more than a wild weekend on a love-starved planet."

"What about our menstrual cycles?" Eve persists. "They've certainly changed."

"Yes, but that's a hard one to argue; the change could be dismissed as the result of diet and we don't yet have a menstruating second generation on Mowdabb to use for evidence, one way or the other."

Eve lets go of Lurk's arm and steps forward, getting right in Milky's face, as if to better read his eyes. "Let me understand this," she says. "If our children were to show signs of change because they've lived their whole lives on this planet, then there's a chance we could stay?"

Dr. Milky thinks about it. "Essentially, that's correct. It would not guarantee planetary sovereignty, but I could make a good argument for it. At least I believe I could get Dr. Simian's project stopped, or force him to adopt some other, how should I say it... gentler project plan. In either case, you'd be better off."

Eve seems to reach a decision. "OK," she says, "Milky, I'm going to trust you. Give me a moment." She turns slightly to one side to face the deep moss nearby. She doesn't say anything or make any other motion, she simply looks quietly into the rolling moss landscape. The children are out of sight, but the sounds of their play can be faintly heard. Simultaneously, the play grows quiet in all directions. Faces begin to appear in openings in the moss all around the gathered adults. Eve remains perfectly still. The faces of the children then vanish one by one as they duck below the moss, return to their network of tunnels, and then appear again as they leave their playground to come to their mother.

Dr. Milky is astounded. "You called them! How did you do that?"

The children continue to gather quietly around their mother, waiting expectantly to learn why they were called.

Eve does not answer Dr. Milky. Instead, she gives him one last hard look before saying once again, "I'm going to trust you." With that, she addresses her eldest son. "Adam," she says aloud for Dr. Milky's benefit, "you have to show this man what you can do."

Adam remains motionless, his dark eyes looking steadily at her.

"You know what I mean," Eve says. "It's important he understands you can do that thing, you know what I mean, that thing you were surprised I couldn't do."

Adam glances suspiciously at Dr. Milky then back at his mother.

"No, it's not a trick," Eve says quietly to Adam. "We have to trust him."

Adam studies his mother and then bravely turns his dark eyes to Dr. Milky. For a moment, they simply stare into one another's eyes. Then Dr. Milky reacts as if he's been slapped. The boy's lips did not move, but Dr. Milky clearly hears a voice in his head say "Hello."

When Dr. Milky realizes his mouth is hanging open, he closes it firmly and concentrates on forming a question in his mind, staring fiercely at the small boy. "Can you hear me think?"

When Adam nods his head up and down, Dr. Milky turns away and begins pacing around in a tight circle. "This is incredible," he says as if talking to himself. "Oh, my God, this is incredible!" After a couple of laps around his circle, he speaks directly to Eve, "This is incredible!" He then turns to Lurk and sees only confusion, so he doesn't say it again. Instead, he returns to walking his circle, stealing glances at Adam at every turn.

"What's incredible?" Lurk asks Eve.

Before Eve can answer, Dr. Milky suddenly stops and faces Adam again. He doesn't say anything, but just stares at the boy with such intensity that Lurk becomes concerned. "What the hell's going on?"

"Just a minute, just a minute," Dr. Milky says impatiently to Lurk, waggling a dismissive hand in Lurk's face while he continues to glare at Adam.

"The man's a fucking fruitcake," Lurk says to no one in particular.

Dr. Milky's concentration is complete.

Adam stands calmly through it all, steadily meeting Dr. Milky's ever-widening eyes. Dr. Milky spins away and says, "Whoo!" He is holding his head in his hands as if to prevent it from exploding. "This is incredible!"

"OK," Lurk says, stepping forward to grab Dr. Milky by the front of his shirt. "We're going to take a little time out now to bring Lurk up to speed." He has lifted Dr. Milky until he is standing on his toes, their noses almost touching. "Are we ready to do that now?" Lurk asks, the menace in his voice coming through clearly.

"Of course, of course," Dr. Milky says, mainly to calm Lurk down; he doesn't really understand why, or much care, that Lurk is upset and is too excited at the moment even to be afraid of Lurk.

Lurk waits, prepared to hold Dr. Milky on his toes all day if necessary.

"What is it you want to know?" Dr. Milky asks.

"What the hell do you mean 'What is it I want to know'?" Lurk roars. "I want to know what is so god-damned incredible."

With considerable difficulty, Dr. Milky strains to look around Lurk to Eve, questioning her with his expression.

Eve shakes her head, no.

"You didn't know?" Dr. Milky asks Lurk.

Lurk has become bright red with frustration and raises Dr. Milky another inch by way of an answer.

"OK, OK. Put me down and I'll tell you."

Lurk thinks about it and lowers the man to the ground.

- - -

Moving On

Moving In

Early the next morning, shortly after Jerry had turned the OPEN/CLOSED sign to OPEN, Marilyn made an unprecedented appearance through the front door of The Planet of Love.

"What's up?" he asked, immediately anxious about what might have caused her early-morning appearance and uncomfortable all over again to be associated with what he had to sell.

She didn't answer right away. Instead, she walked in a little circle with a grimace of distaste on her face, scanning the store's contents. When she came back around to him, she stretched up to give him a peck on the cheek and then looked him in the eye with just enough intensity to let him know something big was coming. "I have an idea," she said.

Her serious expression made him even more anxious, so he attempted to make a joke of it. "Looking at this crap makes you horny?"

"Hardly," she said. "This crap makes me unhorny, if that's even a word. My idea *does* have something to do with this crap though."

"Should I be nervous about this idea?"

"Yes," she said, and clearly meant it. "I came over this morning to suggest you get a real good bottle of wine when you go shopping tonight. That way we can drink the first half of the bottle to give us courage to talk about my idea and then, if the talk goes well, we'll have the last half of the bottle to celebrate."

"And if the talk doesn't go well?" he asked.

She had to think about that for a while. "Then I guess we'll use the last half to drown our sorrows."

"Now you're really making me nervous," he said. "Can't you give me a clue?"

"I'd rather not talk about it next to a display of dildos."

"OK." Jerry didn't want to repeat his last shameful response to her book press idea, so he suppressed his need to pummel her with questions and fought to quell his rising panic. He knew Marilyn preferred to share her ideas when she was ready, when she'd had time to think them through. He needed to honor that. Unfortunately, she had evidently decided he might be able to handle her ideas better if he was given *even more* forewarning. She didn't know him well enough yet to realize that was exactly the wrong way to do it; he handled surprises much better than he handled her announcements of an impending surprise, especially one about which he had been forewarned he should be nervous.

"Make it a good red wine," she said on her way out. "Maybe a Chianti; I made us a dynamite lasagna."

- - -

When he showed up at her apartment with a good bottle of Chianti from Safeway, (more than twice what he usually spent on wine) the smell of lasagna was almost more than he could handle. While he opened the wine and poured them each a glass, they talked of other things, the food, the wine, the customers she'd had that day, anything but her idea. Jerry did not press the subject even though his curiosity, and unshakable anxiety, had made it difficult to focus on his writing all day. He was determined to let her bring up her idea when she was ready, not to browbeat her again with his insistent, untimely questions as he had done before.

The mood was good as they prepared the table together and sat down to eat, but all through the meal Jerry could tell Marilyn was a little nervous too. Once he leaned back in his chair to recover from his third helping, having made serious inroads into what had indeed proven to be a dynamite lasagna, and after the wine bottle was a little more than half-empty, Marilyn began, obviously trying to keep it casual.

"I was just thinking the other day..." Almost immediately, her resolve to keep it casual began to crumble, her innocent beginning decomposed into something more resembling her usual nervous chatter, with all the points she wanted to make fighting one another for their place in her stream-of-consciousness. "There's a lot we could do along with all the other changes we're making, and with that wonderful kitchen in the big apartment, and with the finches in there already, they're all alone now and need some attention, and also with the fact that we're together almost all the time now anyway, I thought maybe we should talk about how we could use all this space better." She paused, either to recover her breath, or to review what she'd said so far, and evidently realized none of it had come out in the orderly, logical, indisputable way she had been practicing all afternoon. However, she jabbered on, the nature of the botched beginning of her presentation having made her sufficiently uncomfortable that now she couldn't do it any other way. She didn't wait for a response of any kind from him, not that a response was forthcoming since he still didn't know what the hell she was talking about. "I've been juggling some numbers, working with rough counts actually, and tossing around some possibilities I think might put us in a good position to, you know... to explore other arrangements for... well, for both of the businesses actually, how we might run them in the future and so on, other ways to make the best use of all this living space and the furniture and so on and so on." She paused again, took an anxious breath and attempted a kind of summary. "I have been thinking about how those possibilities might be better for our... living arrangements and maybe even for... you know... us."

Her use of the words "living arrangements" and "us" in the same sentence seemed to have completed everything she had screwed up her courage to say. Now that it was out there, on the table, so to speak, Marilyn nervously awaited his reaction.

Jerry knew only that she was expecting him to say something. Unfortunately, he was still well behind, without a clue about what she might have in mind and wondering why anything she had said might have been making her so nervous. He said nothing at all. He tipped his head to the right instead of to the left, which didn't give her much in the way of body language to interpret. She chose to read his attentive expression to mean, at least, that his curiosity was well piqued, which it certainly was. However, he was actually occupied with other thoughts entirely. What she interpreted to be the possible beginnings of comprehension on his part was, in fact, pure enchantment.

Jerry really loved this energetic little woman. He had become comfortable with her eccentricities. He could let her jabber on without feeling pressured to respond with an appropriate contribution at every hairpin turn in whatever conversation she might think they were having. When they first met, back with that plate of hazelnut cookies, Marilyn's nervous jabbering had made him uncomfortable, mainly because it underscored how his own speech center worked with excruciating sluggishness by comparison (since he tended to self-edit as he formed each sentence and before he let himself say it). Now, he viewed her particular form of nervous communication differently; it was reassuring to him that there didn't appear to be any editorial filters on the content coming out of her; nothing she said was ever contrived. He found that endearing.

Marilyn rolled on, taking courage from her misinterpretation of Jerry's neutral reaction and assuming he understood what she was driving at, relieved he hadn't rejected outright a discussion of the subjects of "living arrangements" and "us." As a result, her presentation slowed and became more orderly as she lost some of her nervousness and got into the details of her plan. "There are real possibilities with the furniture. If we sort out the most serviceable pieces, things that are well made, but wouldn't really bring much in a sale, we could use them to refurbish the two smaller apartments. We could keep the best pieces in the big apartment and sell off everything else. But, even after sorting out the best stuff to keep, I think there's more than enough to bring in quite a lot of money. Heck, there's probably enough in there to furnish six or eight apartments. I know it's heartless to think of selling off the things Mr. Stamper thought were precious, but I also think he would like to know the best of his favorite things would be used again." Here she raised her eyebrows in a way Jerry interpreted as an opportunity for him to indicate whether he agreed with what she thought Mr. Stamper would like to know. He nodded yes and Marilyn continued. "For example, I think we should leave the master bedroom set just where it is. I think it's the most beautiful set I've ever seen and, because it was obviously important to Mr. Stamper, it would definitely be wrong to sell it." Here she paused again to give him time to react. Jerry was catching up, but still a bit adrift. He had, however, noticed the conviction in her voice when she said, "it would definitely be wrong to sell it," and knew she was still talking about the bedroom set. He had no problem nodding his agreement to that. "I'm a little worried, though," she continued, "that it might be just a bit too strange for us in Mr. Stamper's bed. What do you think? Do you think it would be just... too weird?"

Now she had his attention. What was she talking about when she said "... us in Mr. Stamper's bed?" Her idea was finally coming into focus. She was talking about more than a one-time roll in a dead man's bed; she was thinking of them *living* in the big apartment... together. Without really knowing why, Jerry's anxiety increased.

Marilyn could see it on his face, but again she misinterpreted his reaction, thinking he was hesitant to use Mr. Stamper's bed, and quickly sought to reassure him with a rapid torrent of words. "Of course, I promise you the master bedroom will look *completely* different when we get things fixed up. I have some wonderful ideas about how to redecorate that I think you'll like, in fact, I have ideas for the whole apartment, so I promise you it would feel like our space." Anxiety wouldn't let her stop. "I mean, just to put some new paint on the walls and clean the smell out of the carpets and drapes would make a world of difference, but with a few houseplants and flowers around and with the right lighting, the place will brighten up so much you would not believe it. I just have dozens of ideas I know you would love. I promise you it would have an entirely different feel before we ever slept in there." Jerry's stunned expression apparently had not changed to her satisfaction, so she rushed on. "I'm sure it might be a little awkward at first; we'd have to do our best to adjust to the changes. But, the changes I have in mind would make other things possible that are *so* exciting it would be well worth it. If we shared the big apartment, we could rent out the two little ones and probably get enough rent to pay all our property taxes and most of our monthly expenses. Or we could do what Mr. Stamper did and hire some people to run the businesses, offer them free rent as part of their benefits, and you and I could move on to other things if we wanted to. Whatever! You could spend most of your time on your writing, if that's what you wanted."

Marilyn forced herself to stop, sensing something was wrong. The essence of her pitch had been delivered; she had only to wait for his response. This she did with a charming anxiety not entirely lost on him, but he now had anxieties of his own. To be certain he understood what he thought she was saying, he asked, "You think we should live together?"

Marilyn's countenance fell, either from her realization of just how far Jerry was behind in their conversation, or from his immediate lack of enthusiasm for her idea.

Jerry immediately regretted the tone of his question; it sounded like disapproval or incredulity, when all he was trying to do was clarify the topic.

Marilyn did not answer; she stared at her empty plate.

Jerry felt like shit.

"Sorry," she said quietly.

"Don't be sorry," he said, "And don't stop. I'm still reeling from all the other changes lately; you're just going too fast for me."

Marilyn looked up at him, her sad brown eyes making him feel even worse than shit.

"*Please*," he said. "Tell me more."

She studied him despondently before saying, "You're still thinking of moving to Alaska, aren't you?"

Jerry knew this was a pivotal moment and desperately wanted to get it right. He honestly wanted to let her into his life as much as he was able, but he had trouble knowing where the words and feelings inside him came together. He had never wanted to let someone else into his thinking before and didn't know if he could do it; he had always kept his own council and been proud of his self-sufficiency. Her empathetic thoughtfulness made him feel like a foolish child. Jerry stared at the red dregs of the wine in his glass for a long time, ordering his thoughts. It was important he say this right.

"Marilyn," he began, "I'm not thinking of the future just yet. I don't know what I want to do beyond tonight and maybe tomorrow. I *can* say I would be completely destroyed if I thought I couldn't see you tomorrow. Right now, that is enough for me. I am just happy to spend time with you, however and wherever you want to spend it."

This brought a welcome softening to Marilyn's face that encouraged him to continue, to attempt saying the difficult part. "You need to understand I have been by myself for a long time, forever really, so I'm not good at being a part of anyone else's life; you'll need to be patient with me."

Marilyn nodded.

"It's all so different lately…" Jerry trailed off, overwhelmed by memories of his quiet life in the library and of his lonesome and desperate time on the street. "I'm a small-town boy at heart; I still haven't decided if I can fit into life in the big city." Jerry paused again, both amazed at having been able to say so much of what he felt, and frustrated by not being able to say more. "I don't think I'm saying this well."

Marilyn dared to speak. "Are you still thinking you might want to leave in the spring?" she asked, still expecting the worst.

"I have *no plans*, Marilyn." he set his wineglass aside and leaned forward onto the table, getting as close to her as he could with the table still between them. "No plans," he said again. "I guess I just want to go slowly. Give me a few minutes to think about this. OK?"

She nodded, hoping it was a good sign all he thought he needed was a few minutes. They were quiet while he toyed with his empty wine glass.

"How long have you been thinking about this idea?" he asked.

"Ever since we left Mr. Simon's office," she admitted.

"OK," he said, now feeling justified in asking for time to get used to the idea.

He leaned back in his chair to think. His eyes darted around the table as if looking for a place to focus while he pondered the multifarious ramifications of what he had expected to be a rather simple, one-dimensional idea, like one he might have come up with. Instead, Marilyn's idea reordered every aspect of his present life and jeopardized every aspect of the life he had always imagined would be somewhere in his future.

Marilyn chewed her lip, watching him think.

Jerry stared at the red sauce mess he had made of his plate. In time, when he could not think of any way that any part of Marilyn's idea was not a good thing, his eyes settled on a tiny bit of the pasta that had somehow escaped the lasagna carnage. He forked it off the plate and into his mouth. As he nervously nipped the pasta into dozens of tiny pieces with his front teeth, turning it into semolina mush, he dared to look at Marilyn. He fell deeply into her eyes once again, like slipping into a warm tea-colored bath. He told himself he would need to learn to trust this woman; she was no threat to him.

Jerry took a deep breath. "First, let me say how I feel about Mr. Stamper's bed: It *is* big and beautiful. I'd have no problem being in that bed if you are there with me. In fact, I think there is something *right* about us making love in Mr. Stamper's bed. I think he would want that. If I made love to you in that bed, just once, that would make it *our* bed. That's all it would take for me."

Tears were welling in her eyes, but all she said was, "OK."

"Now, please, slowly tell me all about your furniture/apartment shuffle idea, step-by-step."

- - -

Marilyn took him through the logistics of her idea again, this time measuring his reaction to each part of it, learning his pace for assimilating new ideas. Jerry listened carefully, feeling slow-witted, holding his questions until he understood each part in turn, and nodding for her to go on when he had his mind around it.

"How long do you think this will take," he asked, "to finish all of this furniture moving and selling and apartment painting and redecorating and all the rest of it?"

"Well, I don't know, maybe two or three weeks. But..." Marilyn hesitated, not sure whether Jerry was ready for anything more. "I have some other ideas... about The Planet of Love."

"Weeks?" he was expecting more like months. Then he realized she had broached another subject. "What? What do you mean, 'About The Planet of Love'? Do I want to know anything about these other ideas?"

"I'd like to think about them a little more first," Marilyn said carefully, "if that's alright."

"OK, sure," he said, but he could feel the old, instinctive anxieties trying to muscle in.

Marilyn saw his struggle and tried to reassure him. "If I can work out the logistics of it, we might be able to shorten the time it would take to rework the apartment situation, but trying to rush the process might also just complicate things. Anyway, I promise we'll talk it all through together just like this and I'll get your full approval before we do anything. All of this belongs to *both* of us."

"OK," he said.

"I think you'll like it." Jerry saw a confident twinkle in her eye as she said this and it was enough to allow him to leave the subject at that.

There was a long silence between them. Jerry was feeling good about controlling his anxieties around Marilyn, about beginning to trust her. It was progress for him. He didn't feel stupid around her, just slow. He could put the right words together if given enough time, as in his writing, but he had trouble realizing in the moment, just what the right words were.

In their long silence, Marilyn was thinking of something else, returning to the critical issue that had kept her anxious for days. She screwed her courage to the sticking place and said, "I've never lived with anyone else either. Do you think we could be happy sharing the same apartment?"

"It makes sense to try," he said, though without enough conviction in his voice to give Marilyn the assurance she sought.

"I don't want to pressure you into a situation you don't want," she said. "If all you want to share is a bed and a dining table, then I can deal with that. I'm not interested in pushing our involvement to a new level."

Jerry was not sure what that meant exactly, her talk of levels, but he recognized it was time to let her know he was not with her just for food and sex. For once, he said what needed to be said... sort of. "Marilyn," he began, at last spontaneously prompted by his heart instead of his head. "Marilyn, I believe I am supposed to be with you." It was a strange thing to say, certainly not your classic endearment and probably not exactly what she wanted to hear, but it was enough to make her smile.

His statement had the additional weight of being literally true; Jerry had begun to believe he might have found where he was supposed to be, that maybe The Right Place he'd been seeking for so long had nothing at all to do with geography.

The Big Shuffle

So, it began. A week later, Jerry found himself carrying one end of a large dresser down the back stairway, toward a moving van parked in the alley. The man carrying the other end of the dresser was big enough to change the acoustics of a sizable room. Jerry thought of him as The Hulk, though he would never have addressed him that way. The man had arms bigger around than Jerry's legs. Most of the man's upper torso was squeezed into a T-shirt about the size Marilyn might have worn as a floor-length nightgown, though this T-shirt was so sweaty and food-stained Marilyn wouldn't have gone near it enough to throw it away. The Hulk carried his end of the load with one hand most of the time, looking bored and sorely put-upon to have to wait for Jerry on the other end of the dresser, who was wobbling slowly along behind, struggling with it, looking and sounding like a palsied old man.

When Marilyn finally got up the courage to tell Jerry all about her biggest idea, one that began with the closure of The Planet of Love, she did so slowly and carefully and after they had finished a big cheese and potato casserole. Just as she had predicted, Jerry liked her idea. He liked it a lot, but it was still strange to think The Planet of Love would be no more. As much as he had disliked the place, it had provided a necessary time of stability away from the vagaries of life on the street. The first big benefit of closing The Planet of Love was that Jerry was no longer required to suffer the interruption of customers. As a consequence, when he was not laboring under the weight of moving furniture, his writing was going well.

Marilyn had proven to be amazing throughout The Big Shuffle. Hiring muscle for the move was just one of the many details she had managed in preparation for it. She was in her element, planning and tracking the many activities in that week, handling far more than Jerry could have tracked even if his mind had not been preoccupied for most of that time with Lurk's travails on Mowdabb. Once Jerry had sufficiently reassured her he was comfortable trusting her judgment during The Big Shuffle, she took charge. She loved every minute of it, reveling in the busy management of a dozen things at once, organizing, planning, and directing traffic. She agonized over every decision involving the disposition of the furniture, striving to keep only the best pieces, those for which she had determined both a purpose and an appropriate location.

Mr. Simon, too, had proven himself useful beyond the restraining order he obtained against Coby by referring Marilyn to an appraiser, with whom she had then inventoried, valued, and tagged every piece of furniture in all three apartments and in The Planet of Love. Tags hung everywhere. Each one had the appraiser's estimated value for the piece to which it was attached, and was color-coded to indicate where the piece was destined to go. Red tags meant it would be kept in the big apartment. Only the best pieces got red tags. Yellow-tagged items were to be moved into Marilyn's old apartment. Green-tagged items were to be moved into Jerry's old space. White-tagged items were destined for the moving van and disposal through a wholesaler. A few pieces sported blue tags, which indicated they were to be left where they were. Most of the blue tags were in the space that had been The Planet of Love, destined to be repurposed in the shop's reincarnation.

During The Big Shuffle, The Planet of Love gradually became an alien, cavernous place, emptied of its entire inventory, of all of its lingerie racks, and of some of its shelving. Gone was every magazine, every bottle of "personal lubricant," every dildo, every tasteless coffee cup, every off-color birthday card, every tacky deck of cards, and every scrap of lingerie.

It had been Jerry's first assignment to oversee the three-day closeout sale for The Planet of Love. Anything that did not sell by the end of those three, hectic days, then had to be boxed up for wholesale to Blue Video in the north end of the city. The only remaining vestiges of The Planet of Love were the glass-topped counter that had once been full of dildos, the cash register, the stool on which Jerry had spent so many hours, and a few general-purpose shelf units. The clock over the door still hummed away the minutes, but the little brass bell hung quietly.

The big, hot-pink planet-rise of a sign was taken down from the front of the shop and, at Jerry's insistence, was reinstalled against the wall in a corner of Mr. Stamper's old bedroom, now most definitely *their* bedroom. Marilyn thought it was weird, but he thought it was the perfect place. The big pink sign now commanded one corner of the bedroom, dawning above the carpeting, demarking the space Jerry had decided would be his spot for writing.

He could write at his desk with the planet-rise at his back and look across the room to *their* bed, which they had officially made *their* bed during their first night together in the big apartment. Any misgivings Jerry might have had about occupying what had been Mr. Stamper's bed, were soon forgotten during that first glorious romp with Marilyn. Their lovemaking could have taken place anywhere in the world for all either of them cared.

- - -

The Hulk and Jerry lowered the dresser onto the floor of the moving van and Jerry followed the bulk of The Hulk back up the stairs for the next piece of furniture. On the way, he noticed that the man was trailing some serious fumes from the food stains on his T-shirt, or from… Jerry did not want to imagine what. The fumes had a heavy onion component and, of course, there was the sweat, but the balance of the odor was too unpleasantly complex to be deciphered. Jerry made a mental note to lead the way as much as possible.

With one hand, The Hulk patiently held up one end of the last big item to be moved into the van, a large walnut, drop-leaf table. He had gotten used to having to wait for Jerry to marshal his strength, to get his legs under him and shrug to loosen his aching shoulders before he could lift his end of things. When Jerry had the table off the floor, they headed down the stairs again.

Jerry's back and legs were killing him. Sitting on his ass all day in The Planet of Love, or now on a more comfortable chair between the big pink planet-rise and his computer, had not proven to be good preparation for a day of furniture moving. As he groaned under the weight and tried to keep the table legs from adding to the bruises on his shins, he noticed the white tag on the table they carried indicated it had been estimated to be worth $650. Jerry had long ago lost track of the running total he had tried to keep of the value of white-tagged things he and The Hulk had moved into the van, but he knew it represented a small fortune relative to the dollar values with which he was used to working. What's more, the wholesale deal Marilyn put together with Blue Video represented another considerable contribution to their working capital. Thinking about how good that grand total from The Big Shuffle was going to look in their new joint bank account was what had kept him going all day, that and not wanting to look too foolish in front of The Hulk.

When Jerry finally lowered his end of the table onto the floor of the van and leaned heavily on it, thinking he probably would not be able to get out of bed the next day, he caught a look of pure disdain from The Hulk at his obvious exhaustion. Jerry's first reaction to that look was shock at the man's arrogance. Jerry's second reaction was puzzlement at his own first reaction. He was suddenly, once again, awash with uncertainty and self-doubt. Wasn't he the one being arrogant? And why was that? Was it because The Hulk was fat? Did he look down on the man because his T-shirt was stained, because he smelled bad? Well... yes, on all counts, but what real justification did Jerry have for feeling superior to The Hulk? None. He didn't know the man at all. He was better able than most to know one shouldn't look down on a man merely because he was dirty and smelled bad; Jerry had spent several months on the street in that condition. Did he have an overriding prejudice against fat people? When he remembered that hellish bus ride out of Idaho Falls, he had to acknowledge he probably did. Jerry was the opposite of fat, but he was also much weaker than The Hulk and, even though at least ten years younger, evidently in much worse shape.

Feeling frail and humbled, he left the van and returned to the big apartment where he discovered Marilyn, clipboard in hand, checking the tags on the remaining furniture against her list.

"Jerry! You look exhausted," she said. "Why don't you take it easy for a while? We're about done with this anyway. There are just a few more little pieces to be sorted out. Morty can do that."

Jerry did not know who Morty was but figured it was either The Hulk or the appraiser and he was too tired to care which.

"Why don't you go write for a while?" She wanted to know. "I can finish up here."

Grateful for the opportunity to get away, Jerry snagged a beer from the kitchen, gladly lowered his tired body into the chair centered under the garish pink planet-rise behind his desk in their master bedroom, and orchestrated a return to Mowdabb.

Telepathy?

"It has to be something in the moss," Dr. Milky says as he walks rapidly in a tight circle, ostensibly beginning his explanation to Lurk, but it is more like thinking aloud. "It could be the ground water, or moss spores in the water, or in the air for that matter." He is more animated than anyone has seen him, gesturing wildly at each new thought, at each posit and each rejection. "Perhaps it's a unique trace element in the soil, something concentrated into the Popnuts®, or into one of the moss fruits, or in some combination of fruits and nuts, or maybe even a chemical reaction between elements after they are consumed."

Lurk is watching Dr. Milky as a cat might watch a carousel, and with about as much comprehension. He has heard nothing so far to explain what Dr. Milky has found so incredible. Nevertheless, he does not interrupt; Dr. Milky's circular discourse is mesmerizing and Lurk is still hoping he can make sense of it.

Dr. Milky completes a couple of silent laps and then stops dead as another question comes to mind. He spins in place to face Adam, glaring at him like a mad man. After a moment, he shakes his head as if to dislodge water from his ears. He resumes walking in circles, still with the gestures, though now thinking quietly. "No," he decides aloud. "with all the environmental pre-landing checks we did, air, water, radiation and such, it has to originate in the moss. But how? How does it work?" He thinks for a few laps and then races away on a tangent to run his fingers through the rich loam at the edge of the clearing. "I have to get this tested," he says to himself, acting as if he might stuff a handful into his pocket on the spot. Instead, he throws it down and returns to glare, once again, at Adam. Whatever he learns there frustrates him further. "So what is it? Is it telepathy?" He asks this question aloud, as if asking the cosmos more than Adam.

Adam stares pleasantly back.

"Of course," Dr. Milky says abruptly, exasperated with himself, "you wouldn't know that word."

"Telepathy?" Lurk says, trying to remember exactly what telepathy is. When he notices Adam is smiling up at him, he hears the word in his head, "Telepathy."

Lurk's jaw drops and Adam returns his attention to Dr. Milky.

"This is going to make all the difference." Dr. Milky is getting more excited with each lap. "Once the Federation Council is convinced this is for real, I am sure they will grant Mowdabb its sovereignty. The key is to convince them. I can't wait to get Adam in front of those stuffy council members; it'll blow their minds." Dr. Milky actually giggles.

"No," Eve says, bringing Dr. Milky up short.

"What do you mean, 'No'?"

"Adam doesn't leave Mowdabb," Eve says.

"But this can save you all from a life of..."

"Adam doesn't leave Mowdabb," Eve says again.

"I can't... How could I... But this is..."

Though Lurk doesn't understand Eve's resolve, he wants to support her, so he says it too, "Adam doesn't leave Mowdabb."

Dr. Milky throws his hands in the air and resumes pacing his circle, mumbling to himself.

"Why not bring the council here?" Eve asks.

Dr. Milky stops to contemplate such a thing. "These men are..." he is almost unable to describe them. "They are the most powerful, the most unapproachable... They determine the fate of planets! They don't travel for days to some remote, barely inhabited planet in order to meet with a small boy, and certainly not on anything more than the fevered endorsement of some recently marooned, obviously delusional junior scientist."

Eve shrugs her shoulders as if to say, "It can't be helped." What she does say, with a big, confident smile, is, "I'm sure you can convince them."

Getting it Together

Dr. Milky spends his last two days with Lurk's clan in an effort to gather as much evidence as possible to take back with him to the Federation Council. There is only so much he can think to do. Even working closely with the patient, even-tempered cooperation of Adam, he has nothing he can call irrefutable evidence. He encounters the same problem researchers have always encountered in proving telepathy: It is impossible to devise a test that will confound explanation by a skeptic. Without watching a live demonstration in person, or better yet, actually experiencing telepathic communication, people remain unconvinced. In the end, his notes and personal testimony are all he has, nothing likely to make believers of the Federation Council members. Despite Dr. Milky's best arguments, Eve and Lurk remain adamant Adam is not to leave Mowdabb. After two days of effort, Dr. Milky believes the only, faint hope of success is to convince at least one of the Federation Council members to come to Mowdabb in order to experience direct, personal communication with Adam.

When Dr. Milky can delay no longer, after a last, unforgettable night with the twins, followed by a tearful departure, he, Lurk, and Adam begin the trek back to the original home cave. Adam is accompanying them because Dr. Milky has one last idea to try, a final attempt to gather evidence he hopes will be convincing; he wants to retrieve a camera and some recording equipment from the cache of supplies Dr. Simian left behind for him.

Dr. Milky is amazed at how short the return hike seems with Adam leading the way. It is a long day, but they arrive with enough light left for filming.

He uses whatever materials and props he can find, attempting to capture the results in such a way as to avoid any appearance of trickery. He places Adam about two meters from the camera, facing away from the lens, and then holds up various objects in front of the camera, asking Adam to identify them. Adam gets everything right, 100 percent accuracy, even when Dr. Milky holds up two objects at once or holds up objects Adam has never seen before. In an attempt to demonstrate it is only necessary that Dr. Milky know the name of an object for Adam to name it, Dr. Milky opens, on camera, the package of long-term survival gear that was been left behind for him. He pulls out and holds before the camera a small, folded, aluminum rectangle. Adam, still facing away from the camera and gazing over the rolling moss hummocks of Mowdabb, says, "Solar stove" without hesitation. When Dr. Milky holds up a green triangular pendant fruit of the moss, Adam says "Earring," which momentarily puzzles Dr. Milky because he has never heard it referred to as an earring. When Dr. Milky asks Adam aloud, for the benefit of the camera, why he said earring, Adam says, "You were thinking 'green triangular pendant fruit,' but we call it 'earring.'" Dr. Milky is most impressed by this. Adam has read his thoughts and then translated them to the local vernacular. It is an impressive performance, exceeding anything Dr. Milky had ever read about telepaths, but he also knows that it is not enough to convince every skeptic. It could be said, for instance, that Adam might have been looking at a tiny mirror or at a hidden video monitor showing Dr. Milky's activities, or that the show had been staged, the voices dubbed, the answers memorized.

Dr. Milky is aware that more suspicious skeptics will fear the footage was staged for some nefarious purpose, to embarrass, or even to kidnap the council members. Of all the impressive demonstrations Dr. Milky captures on film, he knows there is nothing that will not be doubted in some way. In desperation, he asks Adam to stand close to the lens, about a meter away, and to send a message to the men that will be seeing the movie. Adam obliges, staring at the camera, his big dark eyes unblinking, for almost a minute. Dr. Milky cannot sense anything Adam might be sending, nor can he dream what the child might be saying to men he has never met and cannot possibly imagine. At the least, Dr. Milky hopes the footage might capture a little of Adam's confident intelligence.

There is nothing left to do. When Dr. Milky runs out of ideas to film and light to film them, it is time to call it a day. After a night's sleep in the home cave, they gather outside the cave at first light to say their goodbyes.

Without a word spoken aloud, Adam wishes Dr. Milky good luck and conveys the hope that he return to them soon with good news. Somehow, he is able to send these thoughts to Dr. Milky so Lurk can hear them too.

Lurk is, by now, better-tuned to the incredible abilities of his first-born son, having stood by through two days of experiments. He can see how fond Adam has grown of Dr. Milky, and how trusting. Adam, more than anyone else on Mowdabb (except perhaps the two oldest girls, who also demonstrate a shyer version of Adam's telepathic skills), has come to know Dr. Milky's earnest good nature and native intelligence. Lurk can only imagine the invaluable advantage it must be in judging the character and veracity of others to be able to read their thoughts directly. Since Adam seems certain Dr. Milky's motives are good, Lurk has to believe the New Mowdabbians will be well represented before the Federation Council.

With their goodbyes over, Lurk and Adam begin the trek back to the clan, leaving Dr. Milky to wait for the hovercraft to come and take him away.

Hiring

The transformation of the space that had once been The Planet of Love began after the majority of The Big Shuffle was finished. In Marilyn's preliminary planning, she had thought they could convert it to a bookstore. Jerry liked her idea, but took it one step further; he wanted to make it a Science Fiction bookstore. After many evenings of discussion, most often nose-to-nose in bed, often interrupted by prolonged lovemaking, they worked out the details: Science Fiction was what Jerry knew and loved, so even though it wouldn't likely make as much money as a bookstore not limited to Science Fiction, that's what it would be, and they would call it The Planet of Books. Furthermore, Jerry would *not* manage the store. They would hire someone to live in Jerry's old apartment and manage the new store for them. They had saved enough money from the furniture sale to pay someone until the store could earn enough to pay for its own operation. Instead, Jerry would keep writing. The novel was progressing nicely and he already had a sequel in mind.

Even as he lobbied for his idea that their new bookstore should specialize in Science Fiction, Jerry already knew who he wanted to manage it. He didn't know if it would work out, or even if it was possible, but he wanted to try to hire the only fellow he had ever met who knew more about Science Fiction than he did: Leif.

- - -

On the morning Jerry began his search for Leif, there was a light snow drifting outside the bedroom window. He bundled against the cold and stepped outside at 6:00 a.m. into four beautiful inches of fresh wet snow stacked high on everything in sight. The rare Seattle snowfall was still white, newly fallen, not yet blown into drifts or stirred into dirty slush by the city's inhabitants. He vividly remembered the bone-deep cold of life on the street. It added a sense of urgency to his search.

The bus going downtown was prudently chained up against the slick roads and right on time, not yet overfilled by those who had sense enough to abandon their usual commute by car. Jerry had no trouble finding an empty seat at the front of the bus and rode looking out the big front window at the city's magical transformation. Four inches of snow in Kilgore would not have warranted discussion among the potato farmers who started their day at Ray's Café, but four inches in Seattle was an event that monopolized the news media and prompted the local weathermen to provide hourly updates of the "storm." It transformed what would have been the usual hectic morning commute into a winter carnival of spinning tires and slow-motion fender-benders providing endless entertainment for those who took the bus. Those who could not deviate from their routine morning commute, or were without the requisite good sense to do so, were already attempting to drive the hills of Seattle. In another hour, they would fill the intersections with their dented cars, put at risk those cars sensibly left by their owners at curbside, and make it impossible for the busses to run on time. Jerry was glad to be up early and thankful his piece-of-shit car had been stolen.

Jerry had no way of knowing if Leif was still in town, but he had to make the effort to find him; his plan for The Planet of Books needed someone with Leif's expertise. He got off the bus at Pioneer Square and began his search by walking to some of the places where he knew the homeless found shelter, places where he had often chosen to spend the night. He began along the waterfront and worked his way around to the backside of the train station, looking in the usual places, checking under makeshift lean-tos, now snow-covered, around collections of dumpsters, inside abandoned cars, anywhere that might offer the minimum necessary shelter in such weather. There was no point in looking in any of the crowded, city-run shelters because he knew Leif never used them, always preferring to spend the nights alone, whatever the weather.

Jerry found lots of homeless men, one or two in each likely spot, but he kept a discrete distance, as much as possible, while he checked to see if Leif was among them. He didn't want to disturb the occupants because he knew how difficult it was to get comfortable, to stay warm, and to get a good night's sleep under such circumstances. Everyone he found was burrowed in deep, covered with blankets, coats, cardboard, newspaper, anything that might add another insulating layer to retain a little more precious body heat.

He spent most of the morning peeking inside shelters to study the occupants. He had to get up close and look for details, squatting low to peer under hats or hoods. Some of those he found could safely be eliminated from the search at a comfortable distance, those who did not have Leif's short, rounded Buddha body type, or those who had full, warm beards, and not Leif's wispy chin whiskers. But, it was time consuming. Every place he searched, he looked for books; he couldn't imagine Leif being far from a book. Jerry also looked for Leif's trademark yellow slicker; he had never seen Leif wearing anything else, though it occurred to him Leif might have lost it in the months since Jerry had last seen him, or he might have layered something over the top of it against the cold.

All the while Jerry searched, he knew it was possible his effort was in vain, that Leif might have gone back home to Bellingham, or somewhere south for the winter. He also knew he might walk right by him; Leif might be burrowed in too thoroughly to leave any part of himself visible. It was even possible Leif had found his own good fortune and was no longer on the street.

Having no luck in any of the usual spots closer in, Jerry headed east, toward the elevated I-5 freeway under which he knew Leif frequently sheltered. That's where he found him, under a southbound section of I-5 just a few blocks southeast of the train station, not far from where they had first met. Leif was asleep in the dark shadows, tucked so tight against the base of a freeway overpass Jerry might never have noticed him if it hadn't been for the Barney-purple, heavyweight, mummy-style sleeping bag. The drawstring was pulled tight, leaving only a three-inch circle out of which projected a cold, round nose that periodically emitted tiny twin vents of breath. It looked as if a purple, larvae-like creature had swallowed Leif. There was not enough of his face showing to provide positive identification and the yellow slicker was not in evidence, but even so, there could be no mistake Jerry had found his erstwhile street buddy because, balanced atop a small stack of paperback Science Fiction books near the head of the mummy bag was a pair of thick, dirty, wire-framed glasses.

Jerry squatted a few feet away, reluctant to disturb what appeared to be a sound sleep. For a few minutes, he watched his own breath dissipate in the chilled air and listened to the traffic race southbound overhead. There was still time to change his mind; he could walk away and Leif would never know he'd been there.

Jerry knew he would be taking a chance with Leif; he really didn't know anything about him except for his encyclopedic knowledge of published Science Fiction. Nevertheless, Jerry did not walk away from the purple, larvae-like creature; something told him he was about to do the right thing.

Leif had made his bed on the shelf of a giant concrete pad serving as a base for the overhead freeway span. He had arranged his sleeping bag on half a dozen layers of cardboard to keep out the concrete chill. Close overhead were the steel beams supporting the road surface above. A large aluminum-framed backpack leaned against the abutment near the pile of paperbacks. A small circle of rocks in the dirt below the cement pad contained the cold ashes of a fire. It would be the only evidence, after Leif was gone, of anyone having spent the night there.

Jerry had never liked sleeping under the freeways around the city because of the miasma of car exhaust pouring down from the incessant mechanical rush overhead. The fouled air, along with the engine roar and tire slap of traffic, always left him with a thundering headache in the morning. It was the memory of such a headache that provoked him to wait no longer before disturbing Leif's sleep.

Jerry yelled Leif's name over the traffic noise, but it had no effect. He had to prod him several times before getting a response of any kind, a deep sleeper indeed. The purple larva thing made a strange "Annnhh" sound that was part irritation and part alarm. After one more poke, Leif sat up, though still cocooned except for his nose. His purple-padded head just missed connecting with the overhead iron. Leif sat upright and was still for almost a minute before yelling "What?" out of the three-inch hole of his mummy bag.

Jerry leaned in close to yell, "I came to buy you breakfast."

Leif thought about that for a time, then lay back down so he could snake an arm up his chest to loosen the drawstring. He then reached out of the opening to retrieve his glasses, relying on memory for their relative location. He brought the glasses inside the bag to put them on. He then sat back up and expanded the opening of his mummy bag a little more, so he could look out.

"Harold," he said. It was the only name Leif had known for Jerry.

Jerry smiled and said, "Close enough for now," but he said it too quietly for Leif to hear above the commuter noise.

- - -

They each ordered a chiliburger and fries at a cafe across from the train station. They were content to eat without much conversation through the avid consumption of burgers and several cups of coffee, as the two of them warmed up. Jerry finished first and settled back to watch Leif eat, admiring the street-practical way Leif loaded each cup of his coffee with all the cream that would fit and with four packets of brown sugar. He slowly consumed the last of his French fries by thoroughly and carefully coating each one in a messy puddle of ketchup. Leif ate slowly by Jerry's standards but savored his food no less.

When Leif finished the last of his food and leaned back in the booth, the waitress removed the plates and then came back to give them each another refill of coffee along with another dish of little plastic half-and-half cups for Leif. Jerry decided he would give her a good tip.

She said, "Pie?"

Jerry raised questioning eyebrows at Leif, who asked, "Do you have apple?

She looked at Jerry and said, "Two?"

With a nod she was gone to get the pie.

Leif finished enriching his coffee and Jerry decided the time was right. He leaned his elbows on the table and began. "First of all, my name is not Harold."

Leif did not react to this news except to blink once behind his glasses, causing his big, magnified eyes to disappear momentarily.

"My name is Jerry Garcia Gustafson. Harold Gustafson, is the name you saw on my duffel bag. He was my uncle."

Leif still did not react except to blink once again. Jerry resisted the urge to reach across the table, take Leif's glasses off, and clean them for him.

"I have a business proposition for you," he said.

Leif blinked again, his mouth hanging open slightly. This was his usual aspect and Jerry knew Leif well enough not to have expected anything more animated, but he could tell he now had Leif's full attention. Jerry thought many people underestimated Leif based on his appearance.

"How would you like to manage a Science Fiction bookstore for me?"

Leif's eyes, normally appearing quite large behind the magnification of his glasses, increased their size considerably. He was fully awake now. His expression altered slightly, making him look almost fearful this might be a cruel joke.

"It comes with an apartment," Jerry said.

Leif scanned Jerry's face for any sign he wasn't serious. Further response was a long time coming, but he finally said, "Cool," and smiled for the first time in Jerry's memory.

Jerry was surprised to learn Leif had one gold incisor.

- - -

Over apple pie and yet more coffee (with a restroom break), Jerry described the good fortune that had befallen him. He began with his discovery of The Planet of Love and his hiring as its manager. He briefly told of his newfound relationship with Marilyn and of their serendipitous inheritance of the Serendip Corporation. He finished with an overview of the subsequent furniture sale, building renovations, and their plan to establish The Planet of Books where The Planet of Love had been.

Leif's eyes and mouth were open wide throughout the telling. He did not interrupt with questions. Even after Jerry laid out the details of the proposition, of having Leif help with the setup of the store and then to manage The Planet of Books in exchange for a free apartment and a small salary, Leif did not speak. Jerry was beginning to fear he might decline the offer, perhaps to reveal some bizarre truth about himself Jerry had never guessed, something that made it impossible for him to live indoors, or hold a job, or (and this was his biggest concern) to deal with the general public in a retail environment. But, he needn't have worried. A lone tear appeared below Leif's right lens and left a damp trail down his cheek.

"Thank you," he said.

- - -

"Marilyn, Leif. Leif, Marilyn" Jerry said after Leif had lowered his backpack to the floor of COPY/COPY. Marilyn interrupted the job she was doing to come around the front counter and offer her hand for Leif to shake. Instead, Leif held her hand gently while executing the faintest of bows.

"I understand you know a lot about Science Fiction," she said.

Leif revealed his gold incisor.

"Do you spell that L-E-I-F?" she asked.

"No," Leif said, "L-E-A-F."

Jerry could not believe it. All this time, he'd had Leif's name wrong. No, Jerry corrected himself, he'd had <u>Leaf's</u> name wrong.

"And what's your last name?" Marilyn asked.

"Walker."

This exchange between Leaf and Marilyn left Jerry's mind awhirl. He did not know this man at all! Neither of them had known the other's real name on the street. Jerry had never had a reason to dissuade anyone from calling him Harold, or, for that matter, from calling him anything else. There had never been a reason, either, for Jerry to ask Leaf to spell his name, or to ask for his last name. What kind of a name was that anyway, Leaf Walker? Who names their newborn Leaf? "Leif" might be understandably ethnic, but Leaf, as on a tree? And then there was the combination with the last name, "Leaf Walker!" Had his parents been ex-hippies, giving him a "cosmic" moniker? Or, were they Science Fiction nuts too, like their son, who might have chosen the name 'Leaf Walker' as an oblique homage to Luke Skywalker? Maybe it was something like a tribal name, given to him by his friends, or a name he had chosen for himself, like a street tag.

What had he gotten himself into? Jerry was afraid he might have just offered to bring a complete stranger into his home and business?

While Jerry dealt with his burgeoning anxiety, his only former street buddy was standing quietly at the counter in COPY/COPY, filling out the 1099 form Marilyn had given him.

Marilyn came back around the counter to Jerry while Leaf was writing.

"He's cute," she said, standing on her toes to whisper this in Jerry's ear. "I like him."

"Cute?" Jerry wondered. It was not a word he would have imagined anyone using to describe Leaf, but he was somewhat reassured by Marilyn's assessment.

"I think we might need to advance him a little cash," she said, continuing in a whisper, "so he can get some food and maybe some new shoes." She was looking at the worn and broken-down heels peeking out from under the damp cuffs of Leaf's baggy pants.

"OK," Jerry said, remembering Mr. Stamper had done the same for him. "We still want to put him in your old apartment?"

"Yes, at least until the painting is finished in your old place. You can get him started working on the painting first thing in the morning. The paint is already up there and I covered the furniture this morning with some old sheets."

"OK," Jerry said. "I'll work with him tomorrow, get him started, and make sure he does a good job." Jerry was still feeling a little apprehensive about their new employee.

"He'll be fine," Marilyn said. "You can probably get back to your writing after you get him started, just check on him now and then if you like, but he'll be fine."

She was smiling as she said it, watching Leaf struggle through his layers of clothing to extract his wallet, probably to find some information for the form. She obviously believed Leaf was going to work out, so Jerry relaxed a little, deciding to trust Marilyn's intuition.

- - -

The next day, Leaf and Jerry worked on opposite sides of Jerry's old apartment, Jerry rolling an eggshell white on the walls while Leaf applied a light teal blue to the woodwork around the doors and window.

"Have you got enough shelving?" Leaf had never been one to initiate much conversation, so the occasional question from him was a veritable chatter of excitement about The Planet of Books.

"No, we don't, but there's a little left over from the old store, though it's all different sizes and not nearly enough for what I hope the shop will need someday."

They painted quietly for a few minutes, there was only the sheesh, sheesh, sheesh of Jerry's roller until Leaf asked, "Where are you getting your inventory?"

"Anywhere I can. You got any ideas along those lines?"

Leaf took so long to answer Jerry stopped his roller to watch him work. He was doing a good job. He was not fast, but his hand was steady and he kept at it.

"I know all the used bookstores from Bellingham to Olympia," Leaf said at last.

It did not sound like bragging and Jerry believed him; he had never seen Leaf without three or four old paperbacks.

Jerry resumed painting and waited for more.

"Also," Leaf said carefully, "I have a friend with boxes of Science Fiction in his mother's basement. She's always giving him shit about it; I'm sure you could have them all if you offered to haul them away."

It was Leaf's longest discourse of the morning, so there was a necessary period of quiet after it was over.

Sheesh, sheesh, sheesh.

"Would you call your friend for me and ask if he's willing to let us have them?" Jerry asked.

"Sure."

Sheesh, sheesh, sheesh.

"I'd say your best place to start though," Leaf continued his oration, "would be at Red Books in Tacoma. Talk to Kevin. He's a good man with way too many books, and he's always threatening to go out of business."

Sheesh, sheesh, sheesh.

Jerry heard Leaf's stomach growl all the way across the room. "Hey, you probably didn't have any breakfast," he said.

No comment from Leaf.

"Let's break for an early lunch," Jerry said. "Stow your brush, we'll continue after we've eaten."

It was only 10:00, but Jerry could always eat.

- - -

After leading Leaf into the big apartment, Jerry began fixing them each a huge bowl of hot oatmeal into which he stirred walnuts, raisins, a few sliced almonds, and a heaping tablespoon of brown sugar. He topped it off with milk and a handful of blueberries. By that time, the coffee was done. They sat at the kitchen table and continued their conversation.

"After we're finished eating, I'll give you a key to get in the building, for the alley door. Then we'll go down to COPY/COPY so Marilyn can give you a cash advance. She handles all the money. That way you can go shopping after work today; get whatever food you'll need for the next few days. After you get the advance from Marilyn, you can continue with the painting on your own. I'll come in from time to time to see if you need anything, but I'm working on something else, usually every morning, so I'll leave you to work alone most of the time. OK?"

Leaf finished crunching through a big mouthful of oatmeal before saying, "Cool." Then, after another thoughtful mouthful, he asked, "What are you working on?"

It was an innocent question, but Jerry hesitated to answer. He did not know if he wanted to confide in Leaf on so delicate a subject as his writing, especially on the writing of Science Fiction. It made Jerry realize he was a little intimidated by Leaf's expertise on the subject. On the other hand, his novel was almost finished; he could not expect to keep such a thing private much longer and, what's more, he was becoming excited about it, busting to tell somebody besides Marilyn. Jerry screwed his courage to the sticking place.

"I'm writing a Science Fiction novel."

Leaf had just taken another spoonful into his mouth, but he had to say it anyway, "Cool."

There was oatmeal on his gold incisor when he smiled.

Leaf wanted to know more, but Jerry resisted; he'd wait to give Leaf a signed copy... if it ever got published.

Building the Inventory

After a good deal of coaching from Marilyn to prepare him for his new role as Businessman, Jerry took a bus to the underground terminal in downtown Tacoma. He headed uphill to the address Leaf had given him in the Hilltop district. There he found what he was looking for, or nearly so. He had expected to find a store named "Red Books," but the sign outside said, "Redd Books." The front door was propped open by a card table stacked with paperback books. A hand-written sign crookedly taped to the inside of the open door read, "$1 each, 5 for $3, 10 for $5." Just inside the door, Jerry saw a business card holder competing for space on a glass-fronted countertop with stacks of more paperbacks. Jerry took a card. It read:

Redd Books

"Read but still readable"

Owner: Kevin Redd.

There didn't appear to be anybody in the store. It was dark and quiet inside, a warren of overstuffed bookshelves covering most of the floor space. The shelves extended all the way to the high ceiling and served to absorb most of the sound from the street. Jerry looked around the front of the shop. Every shelf in the place was full of books in the way one expects to see shelves filled, and then some. Books were wedged into every available space. There was no apparent order to it. The "additional copies" shelves, those above the reach of most browsers, had there been any browsers, were stuffed even more hopelessly with jumbled genres. What's more, every other horizontal surface in the shop was covered with books. Even the quiet stereo and its wall-mounted speakers supported precarious stacks of yellowing paperbacks.

He began to wander among the shelves, delighted to see a great many Science Fiction titles scattered about, though in no apparent order. Many of their spines were turned the wrong way so the titles were upside down, forcing him to tilt his head the other way to read them. The deeper he went into the store, the darker and more cluttered it became.

At the back of the store, far from the last traces of natural light coming in the front windows, sitting under a low-wattage desk lamp illuminating an especially cluttered corner of the shop, was a man he assumed to be Kevin Redd. The man sat on the front edge of his chair so he could rest his elbows on the desk and his head in his hands. He was reading a book while his fingers combed despondently through the salt-and-pepper tangle over his ears. After a time, the man sensed he was being watched and turned a gloomy eye Jerry's way.

"Do you have any books for sale?" Jerry said as brightly as he could.

Kevin turned back to his reading and said, "You should see the storeroom."

"I'm looking for some Science Fiction."

Kevin gave him the eye again, pulled one hand away from his hair, and drew lazy circles overhead while shaking his head, as if in a hopeless search for organization. "Can you be more specific?"

"No," Jerry said. "I can't."

Kevin leaned back in his creaky old desk chair, the complaint of wood and springs reminding Jerry of Ms. Nervan's treacherous chair. Kevin rotated the chair to contemplate Jerry with both eyes, obviously wondering if this lanky visitor was pulling his chain or was just stupid. "I would dearly love to sell you every goddamn Science Fiction book in the place, or any subset thereof," Kevin said, "but if you're looking for some suggestions from me, you'll have to give me something to work with. What do you like, fantasy, the classics, hard science, virtual science? Do you like any particular authors, stuff from the golden age, what?"

Jerry smiled to hear Kevin voluntarily weaken his bargaining position when he admitted he would love to sell it all. It was time for him to drop the bomb. "How about quoting me a "per book" price for *all* your Science Fiction. Could you do that?"

Kevin's eyes slowly widened, going slightly out of focus as he tried to imagine how many Science Fiction books had accumulated in his shelves and then to calculate the unprecedented cash windfall their sale would bring at various multiples of "per book" prices. His eyes jittered with the effort. "You want *all* of them?"

"Anything in good condition, with spine and original cover intact, any title that doesn't stretch the definition of Science Fiction too far."

Kevin seemed unable to respond, so Jerry continued, outlining the conditions for a bulk purchase that had been worked out over a spaghetti dinner the night before with Marilyn and Leaf. "I'd need them counted, boxed, and delivered to my shop in Seattle. I don't have a car, so you'd have to take care of all the shipping. I would reserve the right to return any books I thought were too worn or damaged, or were too far outside of *my* definition of Science Fiction."

Kevin had taken on a shrewd expression, wary, looking for some reason to be suspicious of the offer, but his eyes still danced with the possibilities.

Jerry continued. "To serve as an earnest money deposit, I could pay you... let's say one third of the total sale, the agreed-upon price per book, multiplied by your rough estimate of the total number of Science Fiction books you can come up with. Once all the books have been delivered, I could pay you the second third of the price. Then, we'll sort and count them to arrive at the total number of acceptable books, after which, when you come to haul away those books that have been sorted out for refusal, I would hand you a final check to cover the adjusted amount."

"I can deliver; I have a pickup," Kevin said as if thinking out loud, obviously liking the idea of a bulk sale, but too stunned with the newness of it to say more.

"Before you quote me a price," Jerry hurried to say, "you should know I would be open to a standing arrangement with you, to take all the Science Fiction you get in the future, as customers bring it in for trade. So... think about this for a while, see if you have any questions, and then make me the best offer you can."

"This might take me some time to figure out," Kevin admitted. "I have no clue how many I have. Lots, but they're all over..." He waved a hand around, looking at the ceiling-high jumble as if seeing it anew. "I'll have to go through... and then I'll need to... how soon do you want them?"

"We can begin taking books from you as soon as we can strike a deal. I'm going to be in and out, shopping around for the next few days, looking for other sources of used Science Fiction, but my store manager will be there."

"Can I just call you with my per/book price?"

"Any time."

Jerry pulled out one of the business cards Marilyn had made for him on the big copier. It said:

The Planet of Books

"The Best Selection of Science Fiction in the Northwest"

Jerry Gustafson

Along the bottom of the card was the address and phone number.

"Jerry," Kevin said quietly, studying the card as if committing the name to memory. Then he looked up at him with a decision. "I'll call you by this time tomorrow."

Kevin stood up to shake Jerry's hand. The expression on his face was one Jerry liked. Kevin was excited about their deal and earnestly searching for reassurance in Jerry's eyes. Jerry nodded. "Nice to meet you Kevin." He started to leave and then turned back; something else had occurred to him, nothing that needed to be said, but rather something he wanted to say. His meeting with Kevin had put Jerry in a strange mood, feeling a combination of sudden confidence at having done well in presenting his first-ever business deal and a sense of largess he had never in his life been in a position to feel. He looked Kevin in the eye once again, waiting perhaps for some guidance from the weasel before he spoke. "Kevin," he said, "if this first deal works out well for both of us, I have some other ideas you might like too. If you send me good stuff at a good price on this first deal, I would be more inclined to sweeten the deal for you on a standing arrangement and on anything else we might do together in the future."

"I'll give you a good price," Kevin said, defiantly holding his gaze, obviously misunderstanding Jerry's intended message.

"I'm not saying this very well." Jerry hesitated even to try to say more, to articulate what he was feeling. After a time, he said, "I think you will give me a reasonable price. I'm talking about something else." Though, at this point he still didn't know what exactly. "I think I'm talking about abstract stuff, like fairness and honor, about things that might mean we could be doing business together for the rest of our lives."

Jerry left the store, leaving Kevin to chew on that.

Kevin called at 9:00 the next morning with a quote. Jerry almost didn't recognize Kevin's voice; the listless growl of the previous afternoon had become a breezy, euphoric chatter. "Hey Jerry," he began. "I'm a little goofy; I've been up all night drinking Red Bull and counting books. I haven't stayed up all night since college. But, while I counted, I boxed up about 800 books so far, some of my best stuff. It's ten moving boxes full. I stopped with ten boxes because I figure that's about all I can fit in my old pickup. I'm hoping you like my price because I sure don't want to have to put them all back on the shelves."

"Sounds good," Jerry said, just to be saying something.

"So here's the deal..." Kevin continued, "I figure I can do this kind of a bulk sale, if you take all I have, at 14 cents per paperback. That's all I'm working with right now, paperbacks. I have several hundred hardcover too, mostly anthologies, but I wasn't sure if you wanted hardcover too, so I've just been figuring paperbacks. It's hard to come up with a good estimate of how many I might have altogether because the stuff in the storeroom is still in boxes." He stopped for a breath. "So... just estimating, I kind of did a sample count and extrapolated from that, I'm guessing I must have at least 4000 Science Fiction paperbacks in what I would call good condition. Now, boxed up, that must be about five pickup loads, but as I said, it's hard to estimate, so my count could be over or under by several hundred. Anyway... we can start with a count of 4000. So, if you think 14 cents is a fair price, 4000 at 14 cents is $560 and a third of that, for the first shipment, is..."

Jerry interrupted him. "Let's make it 15 cents."

"What?"

"I said, let's make it 15 cents per book. It just divides out better."

Jerry had been expecting a price higher than 14 cents per book and, anyway, was still feeling that sense of largess he had liked so much from the day before.

Kevin was delighted. "Well, 15 cents it is! Hey, I like the way you do business. OK, so 4000 books at *15* cents is..." he could hear Kevin punching keys on his calculator. "$600! So, a third of that is... hey, you're right, 15 cents does work out better, two hundred bucks."

"When can you deliver?"

"I can bring the first ten boxes over tonight, say around six o'clock?"

"I'll have a check for $200 waiting for you," Jerry said. Then on an impulse, he added, "Why don't you plan to join us for dinner?" He was sure Marilyn would like the idea. Jerry could even do the cooking himself if she was too busy to cook extra for a guest and if she was willing to give him some guidance.

"Hey, I might just do that," Kevin said. "I'm real curious about your store anyway; give me a chance to look around."

- - -

Jerry was right; Marilyn liked the idea of having a guest. When he went into COPY/COPY to tell her about Kevin's call, she scribbled out a shopping list for him to fill when he finished writing for the day, everything they would need to make a ricotta stuffed pasta dish she had been wanting to try. Jerry went back to his writing, pleased with himself and with… well, with everything.

Book Buyer's Dinner

Marilyn called up to the main apartment from COPY/COPY. "Jerry, there's a truck parking at the front door with cardboard boxes in the back; I think our books are here."

By the time Jerry got down the stairs, through the empty store, and to the street, Kevin was out of the truck, leaning back to look up, hands on hips, admiring the new sign on the front of the store.

"Very nice, Jerry. I have to admit it."

They shook hands a second time, now more like old friends.

Jerry adopted the same stance as Kevin to look up at the sign. "Yes. It does have a certain flair doesn't it?"

The new storefront sign was in place. It was also a planet-rise, not too different from the old, faded-pink planet-rise that was now mounted behind Jerry's writing desk, but this new planet appeared to be covered by books. A literalist might have said it was a representation of the upper half of a sphere covered with a jumble of tiny rectangles, but to Jerry's eye, it was clearly a planet made up entirely of books, like an accretion of books around a magnetic core. The sign painter had done a good job. The name of the store, 'The Planet of Books' rested on the planet's horizon, arching around the curve of the sign. The sign painter also removed the old layer of green paint that had covered the front windows of the shop. This flooded the interior with natural light and allowed customers to see inside the store. Once the front windows were clean, Jerry asked the painter to paint some words along their bottom edge. The words were: 'The Best Selection of Science Fiction in the Northwest.' This was clearly a case of overreach on Jerry's part, the result of his recent happy state of mind, because the shelves inside The Planet of Books were still perfectly empty of Science Fiction.

They each grabbed a box of books from the truck and Kevin followed Jerry in the front door, stopping abruptly just inside. "It's empty!" Kevin finally noticed. "You're just starting? No wonder I've never heard of The Planet of Books." He looked all around, appraising the store, reading the newly painted signs that hung on chains from the ceiling, signs effectively dividing the store into sections, promising that The Planet of Books would eventually contain Fantasy, New Releases, Classics, Hard Science, Virtual Science, and Magazines. "You don't even have many shelves!"

Kevin slowly rotated on the spot to take it all in, nodding appreciatively, having forgotten about the weight of books in his arms. His survey was interrupted when Leaf came through the hidden doorway in the back wall, carrying a bundle of poster board and marking pens.

"Leaf!" Kevin looked back and forth from Jerry to Leaf several times before saying it again. "Leaf!"

"Kevin," Jerry said, "I guess you've met my store manager."

"Manager?" Kevin said.

Leaf displayed his gold incisor.

"Kevin. Isn't that getting heavy?" Jerry asked.

Kevin sat the box down and walked over to shake Leaf's hand. "Manager!" he said again, having been reduced to one-word responses.

Jerry was pleased to see there seemed to be an old rapport between them. They continued to shake hands and exchange pleasantries, with Leaf grinning unabashedly.

Jerry left them to their reunion and walked back to the truck for another box. When he came back, he said, "Leaf, Kevin is staying for dinner. Would you like to join us too? Marilyn is making a special pasta dish and I bought a couple of bottles of Chianti to go with it. We can talk a little business when we're through eating."

"Cool."

"Are you the one who suggested Jerry come to me for books?" Kevin asked Leaf. Leaf just continued to display his gold tooth.

While Leaf and Kevin walked out to the truck to continue the unloading, all the while discussing recent changes in their lives, Jerry eagerly opened the first box of books to see what Kevin had brought. At first, he just grabbed them by the handfuls and stood them on the nearest shelf, flipping and rotating them as necessary, but he soon slowed whenever he spotted one he hadn't seen before or recognized an author he especially liked. When the truck was empty Kevin and Leaf joined Jerry's slow-motion shelving efforts. When the boxes were empty, a colorful variety of paperbacks occupied a small section of shelving. Kevin and Jerry stepped back to take it all in, but Leaf kept going, straightening and arranging the books, pulling them from one location and inserting them in another, organizing them according to his own esoteric system. His eyes had taken on a sparkle his dirty glasses couldn't begin to hide. Jerry and Kevin grinned at one another, enjoying Leaf's enthusiasm.

Kevin turned to face the emptiness of the place. "So, you're starting a science-fiction-only bookstore and you've only got 800 books?"

"There's a lot of work ahead before we're ready to open, but we'll have at least 4000 from you when we finish our deal. And, Leaf's friend is going to donate three or four hundred more. I have some other ideas too, that we can talk about after dinner."

"What about shelving?"

Jerry surveyed the nearly empty store and admitted, "We could use more shelving."

"I might be able to help you out there," Kevin said, buzzing with potentials. "I know of a couple of places that might have some extra book shelving for sale. Maybe, if there was something in it for me, like a finder's fee, I could…"

Jerry turned to face Kevin squarely. "Kevin. Good business involves both parties benefiting. This evening, after we have shared dinner, we will talk of future business."

Kevin nodded and seemed to relax a little. "Message received; we'll talk about it after dinner."

Jerry nodded too and they turned their attention back to Leaf's efforts to organize their inventory. Conversation naturally turned to a debate of the best system for organizing their eventual inventory.

- - -

Leaf was the last to arrive for dinner. Jerry left Marilyn and Kevin, already talking in the kitchen like old friends, to answer Leaf's knock. When he opened the door, he found a new Leaf, one obviously fresh from a bath after his day of shelving and sorting. He was wearing a Mariners sweatshirt, the first evidence of his new income. He had even taken the time to clean his glasses.

When Leaf arrived in the kitchen, Marilyn said, "Hey Leaf, pour yourself a glass of wine."

Kevin said, "Go Mariners!" and pointed to Leaf's sweatshirt. Leaf smiled and pointed back at Kevin.

Marilyn returned to her grilling of a skillet full of chicken thighs in a thick tomato sauce and of her grilling of Kevin, peppering him with all kinds of personal questions, things Jerry would never have asked.

"Are you married?"

"I was for a few years."

"Any children?"

"No."

"How long have you been in the used book business?"

"Five years."

"Does your family live in the area?"

"My Mom is in Olympia. My Dad died a few years ago."

"Oh, I'm so sorry." Marilyn sounded truly saddened.

"Heart attack."

"Me, too," Leaf said.

That stopped the conversation; it was unusual to have Leaf volunteer anything, especially anything personal, and no one was sure what he'd meant by "Me too."

Marilyn most needed clarification.

"You mean your father died of a heart attack too?"

"A year ago today."

"Oh, I'm so sorry," Marilyn said again, sounding even sadder than before.

"Don't be," Leaf said flatly. His tone left no one wanting to pursue the subject, though Marilyn was near to bursting with questions. She looked to Jerry for some clue as to how to handle the moment.

Jerry gave her a faint head shake "No" and then raised his glass to say aloud, "To The Planet of Books."

When the three of them responded in kind and everyone saw the spontaneous expressions of pleasure on all their faces, they began to laugh at the abrupt change in mood. They clinked their glasses and started to drink, but Marilyn left her glass in the air and added another toast, "To a long and happy life."

They clinked again and Kevin left his glass raised this time, taking his turn.

"To good business for the rest of our lives," he said, looking Jerry in the eye.

They clinked once more and everyone turned to Leaf, giving him a turn to toast.

He studied each of their faces as he thought about what to say. "To my mother, wherever she is." At last they drank.

- - -

Kevin ate almost as much as Jerry did. The ricotta stuffed pasta shells were a big hit. Leaf had a good portion and thirds on the salad.

Marilyn smiled through the whole meal, obviously enjoying having so many hungry men to feed. "I grew up with three brothers," she volunteered at one point. "They enjoyed their food too, but you three have better table manners."

When everyone was too stuffed to continue eating and the second bottle of wine was gone, Marilyn and Jerry cleared away the dishes, readying the table for the evening's business, smiling at each other as they worked in the kitchen and listened to Kevin tease Leaf about becoming the manager of a store with no books. Leaf, who had been made relatively talkative by the wine, began to relay a brief account of Jerry finding him to offer the job.

While Leaf's narration continued, Jerry put his arm around Marilyn to get her attention. "This feels good doesn't it?" he asked quietly, so as not to interrupt the conversation around the table.

"I've never felt better," Marilyn said.

"Me either."

He gave her a kiss, which Kevin inadvertently interrupted by shouting an incredulous question across the kitchen. "You inherited the building?!"

"Yup, from the man who hired me," Jerry said, readily sharing in the amazement over such good fortune.

"So you have no overhead from rent?!"

Jerry shrugged his lucky shoulders.

"You just might be able to make this work," Kevin observed.

Jerry turned to Marilyn. "I think the business portion of the evening has begun."

- - -

After amicable negotiations, it was agreed that Redd Books would funnel all of its good quality Science Fiction trade-ins to The Planet of Books. They talked about standards for quality and a workable definition for the genre itself. When the subject of hardcover books came up, their progress slowed; they weren't able to decide how to handle them at a bulk rate.

"What if I found a real gem," Kevin asked, "maybe a rare comic, or signed copies, or even a first edition, something I knew was a good price, but didn't want to buy myself? Would you want me to bid on it in your name, like a purchasing agent?"

Jerry immediately liked the idea and said so. "We can work out some kind of commission-type arrangement, but we've probably had too much wine to put it together now."

Kevin grinned at that, looking over at Leaf to borrow his favorite response. "Cool."

"Cool," Leaf echoed.

"That's a done deal then;" Jerry said, "pending an agreement on how to handle bulk hardcover and on the commission for "gems," Kevin will be the purchasing agent for The Planet of Books. Leaf and I can concentrate on getting The Planet of Books ready to open."

"I gotta say," Kevin said, suddenly serious, "I like the way you do business."

"I'm just trying to keep everything right up front," Jerry said. "I won't promise to do anything I can't do and I'll do whatever I promise to do. You do the same, and we're golden."

"That's my boy," Marilyn said.

"Bunch of sci-fi geeks," Leaf said, his gold incisor on display again. Everybody smiled at everyone else around the table and they all broke into a round of wine-loosened giggling.

"I think the business meeting is over," Jerry said.

- - -

As Kevin and Leaf gathered at the door to say goodbye, Marilyn gave Leaf a hug. "I think Jerry made a good choice for store manager." She said it quietly, so no one else would hear, but they all did and pretended not to.

She gave Kevin a hug too. "I'd like to meet your mom sometime," she said, surprising them all.

"I think she'd like that."

Wrapping it Up

As Kevin and Leaf continued to build the inventory of The Planet of Books, Jerry was left free to spend each morning in his writing corner upstairs. He couldn't have been happier with the arrangement. While Jerry's mornings were dedicated to working on the discoveries of Mowdabb, he spent his afternoons helping to ready The Planet of Books for its day of dawning. Safely nested in the land of Serendip, his writing made rapid progress. He started early every day, making the deep dive into Mowdabb and not resurfacing until well after lunch. He returned to earth hungry and a little disoriented, just as if returning from a long space voyage. His immersion into the creative element was so absolute he was oblivious to the bustling projects underway one floor below.

With each return to earth, in corroboration of time's relativity, he would descend the stairs to find his world had been greatly transformed, another part of the building refurbished by Leaf (who had repeatedly proven himself quite capable of working with little direction from Jerry), or another section of shelving in The Planet of Books filled from the boxes of books that continued to arrive from their enthusiastic purchasing agent. Leaf's slow, persistent style as a painter had long since beautified the store and most of all three apartments, including the hallways outside the apartments and all three of the connecting stairwells, all done in accordance with a color scheme painstakingly chosen by Marilyn.

Jerry had never been more excited with his life, or more at peace. He was too happy even to worry (as he might normally have done) that his happiness might end, as if it was enough to have known such happiness. He would always have the memory of it, so why spoil it by worrying.

Much of the joy he felt came reflected back to him. Marilyn, the bubbling dynamo of his new, extended family, was effervescent with new ideas. The more they were together, the closer they became and the more he wanted to stay with her. She had quickly become the linchpin of his life, keeping him grounded and focused. When he told her just that, using those same words in his own careful way one night in their four-poster bed, she actually cried with joy. It was a transcendental moment for him, to learn how much Marilyn loved being his linchpin.

Leaf, too, was transformed. As the store opening approached, he dedicated every waking hour to readying The Planet of Books. When he wasn't organizing the rapidly growing inventory, he worked on an elaborate display for the store's front window involving a flock of flying books, which hung from thin, black filaments, pages spread wide. It reminded Jerry of having sent *Stranger In a Strange Land* flying so long ago.

Leaf would disappear into his apartment at the end of a workday. Jerry and Marilyn assumed he was simply luxuriating in his new home as they had done, but, then they began to see small, hand-lettered placards appear in strategic places around The Planet of Books as opening day approached. It was what Leaf had been doing in the evenings, making placards to guide customers in their search for books. They were an eccentric mix of good marketing recommendations and obscure sci-fi factoids, such as:

> "If you liked *The Fountains of Paradise* by
> Arthur C. Clark, then you should check
> out any of the "Heechee" series by
> Frederick Pohl."

or

> "Is evolution a gradual process, as Darwin
> believed, or can change occur suddenly
> as has been suggested by Stephen J.
> Gould? Find out what Greg Bear thinks by
> reading *Darwin's Radio*."

Thereafter, as Jerry entered the store for the first time each afternoon, his first activity was to search for the latest of Leaf's placards discreetly mounted on the walls or to the ends of shelves. Many of them offered esoteric Science Fiction facts that were new to Jerry, things that could only be loved by a real fan of the genre. An example:

> *Childhood's End* by Arthur C. Clark
> inspired a Pink Floyd song by the same
> name and probably the third verse to Neil
> Young's famous "After the Goldrush."

And some were just creepy:

> A creature called Demodex folliculorum, a
> tiny mite, lives head-down in the hair
> follicles of most humans on earth. What
> other creatures are we hosting?

More shelving continued to appear, some purchased through Kevin on behalf of Serendip Incorporated and some scavenged by Leaf from mysterious sources. The store still looked thinly stocked, but they were now confidant it would eventually be full and "The Best Selection of Science Fiction in the Northwest."

They had a "soft opening," accomplished by simply hanging an OPEN sign in the front window. A formal, publicized "Grand Opening" could wait until their growing inventory had more time to fill the shelving.

There weren't many actual customers for the soft opening; they were mostly just curious people who frequented the neighborhood, many of whom made a point of registering their pleasure that The Planet of Love was gone. Leaf showed every one of them his gold incisor. There were even a few who mentioned having heard of the new store from Kevin Redd. Even without advertising, word was beginning to spread among bibliophiles and the many avid Sci-Fi fans colonizing the Puget Sound.

During this same time period, along with everything else she was doing, Marilyn began interviewing applicants who might help her with the growing workload at COPY/COPY. Her idea was to find someone who could eventually take over the management of the store for her.

The general level of excitement and positive energy was unprecedented in all of their lives. It was so pervasive it was leaking back and forth between Jerry's two worlds.

Dr. Milky Returns

The months following Dr. Milky's departure revert to normal, pastoral Mowdabbian existence. The twins make the bittersweet announcement they are both pregnant and that Dr. Milky is undoubtedly the father. They are elated by the idea of bearing his children but fearful they will never see him again.

All three women are six months pregnant when Lurk's clan hears the steadily growing hum that announces the inevitable end of their time alone and the approach of a planetary shuttle. The sound comes at them from all directions until the clouds overhead part and a bright yellow shuttle lands without further ado about 200 meters from their new home cave, proving, as Dr. Milky had warned, that no one would have a problem in locating them.

At Dr. Milky's insistence, the landing is made far from the home cave in order to minimize blast damage to the moss in the immediate area and to reduce the chance of injury to any of the children that might be playing nearby. Otherwise, the landing is made as close as possible to the home cave because the three Federation Council members on board are quite elderly and have difficulty getting around.

When the shuttle's engines shut down and the doors open, Lurk's clan is already approaching, even though Lurk tries to hold them back because he is fearful Dr. Simian might be among the passengers. Dr. Milky is first down the ramp. His triumphant grin is visible from far away and is enough to reassure Lurk that Dr. Simian is not with them. The elders appear in the shuttle doorway one-by-one, each one looking like an ancient wizard in their colorful cloaks of office. While they make their way slowly down the ramp, Dr.

Milky abandons proper decorum to run, whooping, into the arms of the twins. There is no doubt of his joy.

Adam smiles at Lurk and steps forward to meet the elders at the bottom of the ramp. His confidence, like his body, has grown in the months Dr. Milky has been gone. Besides, he knows these important men have come to see him. He reaches up to shake the hand of each one of the elders as they step down onto Mowdabbian soil. With each handshake, he looks the man in the eye and puts the same thought into each of their minds: "Welcome to Mowdabb."

It is enough. Each of the three Federation Councilmen is similarly stunned by Adam's greeting and immediately convinced of his abilities. All else that follows during their visit is pomp and circumstance, polite ceremony and, in the end, some relatively easy negotiation.

It is an historic meeting, the only time that, not one, but *three* majestic members of the Federation Council have deigned to convene on such a remote and uncivilized planet. Thanks to Dr. Milky's relentless advance work, most of the results of that historic meeting are largely predetermined. Through his efforts, the council has agreed to approve the sovereignty of Mowdabb if two conditions are met on their arrival: First, of course, they would have to be unanimously convinced of Adam's abilities.

That condition is accomplished in the first minute.

Second, each of the adults on Mowdabb, Lurk and all three women, would have to approve, and agree to abide by, every word of the twelve-point list of conditions Dr. Milky has negotiated on their behalf during the many weeks of negotiations that took place back in the council's chambers.

The second condition is addressed when all the adults on the planet are seated in a circle of moss cushions arranged for them by the children. The older children stand all around outside the meeting circle to listen intently to what is said. The older children also serve to keep the younger children from bothering their impressive visitors as they curiously attempt to examine the fabric of their ornate robes and the other accoutrements of their high office.

Dr. Milky begins the meeting with something of an understatement. "I am delighted to know that our three distinguished guests are convinced of the telepathic abilities of the children of Mowdabb."

In truth, the three council members and their personal attendants are more than convinced; they are in awe of the children and have been talking of little else since their arrival. They have each had long, quiet conversations with Adam and with the two oldest girls, and they have also, unavoidably, explored the nascent telepathic abilities of the younger children, who have followed the progress of their exotic visitors everywhere, like a raft of ducklings. They pepper their guests with bold and pointed questions, which the elders attempt to answer when they can. None of the children have ever seen anyone as old as their guests, or as colorfully dressed.

The playfulness of the younger children has obviously infected the Federation Councilmen, whose smiles are evident all around the circle, making the elders look about twenty years younger than they did coming down the ramp.

Dr. Milky continues. "I am now pleased to present the twelve conditions that have been agreed upon by the Federation Council. In order to be granted planetary sovereignty, all twelve of these conditions must be agreed to by all four adult members of the New Mowdabbians. After I have read all twelve conditions, I will ask each of you if you approve of them as written and to pledge to abide by them. If you all answer in the affirmative, they will take effect immediately. Are there any questions?"

"Yes." Lurk has a question. "Are you saying that it's all or nothing, that all four of us must accept all twelve conditions?"

"Exactly."

"And if we accept them, we can stay?"

"Yes, under these twelve conditions."

Lurk looks at the women. They seem anxious but hopeful that the conditions might not be too bad.

Lurk turns back to Dr. Milky. "OK, let's hear 'em."

The now famous "list of conditions" Dr. Milky then reads to the group will eventually come to be known throughout the Federation of Planets as The Mowdabbian Rules. As soon as the list is read and explained, it receives unanimous approval from all four New Mowdabbian adults.

After the meeting, the council members and their entourage stay for another hour. They spend that time in intense conversations with Adam, with the two oldest girls, and with the other children. They are given tastes of some of the food that has kept the New Mowdabbians alive and well. The elders receive each example of Mowdabbian food as if it is a sacrament, assuming, as many would do in the years to come, it is the food that gives telekinetic abilities to children conceived and raised on that diet.

True to their word, upon return to the Headquarters of The Federation Council, the three members issue a proclamation, which formalizes the twelve tenets and thereby fixes the conditions under which all civilizations within The Federation of Planets must conduct any future interaction with the planet Mowdabb and with the New Mowdabbians.

The Mowdabbian Rules are as follows:

1. The four original adults comprising the "Rydgyd" party and their descendants born on the planet are sovereign inhabitants of Mowdabb.

2. The "Rydgyd" party members and their adult descendants shall comprise the voting custodians of the planet Mowdabb in perpetuity. They shall elect as many as twelve of their number to act as lifetime executors.

3. Dr. Adrian Milky shall have honorary citizenship and, as needed, will act as Mowdabb's first ambassador to the Federation for the duration of his lifetime, or until such time as he chooses to appoint his successor from among Mowdabb's executors, or until such time as he is voted out of that position by a majority vote of Mowdabb's executors.

4. Any scientific study of the planet will be at the behest of Mowdabb's executors and will be moderated by the Federation to enforce compliance with all the tenets and conditions of Mowdabb's Declaration of Sovereignty.

5. Anyone wishing to make a pilgrimage to Mowdabb must be pre-approved by the non-profit Mowdabbian Retreat Administration Service (MRAS), said service to be established within the offices of the Federation Council.

6. Visitors wishing to make a pilgrimage to the planet shall, upon acceptance, be allowed a maximum stay of thirty Mowdabbian days.

7. Pilgrimage fees will be used solely to finance the operations of MRAS and to maintain the required infrastructure in support of said pilgrimages.

8. The established airfield shall be the one geographical point of contact for the planet, the only point of ingress and egress.

9. Nothing can be brought to the planet: Visitors must undergo a thorough physical to determine they carry no communicable disease. They must arrive without possessions and naked.

10. Nothing can be taken away; visitors must leave naked.

11. There shall be no destruction, alteration, or defacement of the existing ruins and no new construction of any kind.

12. Nothing shall be done to harm the moss.

FINISHED!

Publishing Picnic

The novel was finished!

Jerry resisted the temptation to throw open the bedroom window and scream *Yaaaaahooooo* at the unsuspecting world, which he might have done if his elation was not momentarily restrained by a well-worn anxiety that the file of his finished novel might be lost if any one of a dozen catastrophes he could imagine were to occur, ranging from a simple hard disk failure to the more horrific eventuality of an apartment fire. First, he uploaded *Lurk on the Love Planet* to a secure online storage service. Then he hustled into the kitchen, where he stood on his toes to retrieve the memory stick he had long been using to allay his paranoid need for backup. It was way in the back between a can of Crisco and a cellophane package of rice noodles, on a shelf Marilyn could barely reach with her kitchen stool. He copied the file from the hard drive to the memory stick, completing the last step of his daily backup ritual. He considered making another backup copy somehow, one he could perhaps store in a safe-deposit box, but reasoned this would probably qualify him as obsessive.

With his anxiety appeased, Jerry could allow his elation to resurface. He clambered down the inside stairwell into COPY/COPY on a joyous galumphing descent to share the news with Marilyn. When he burst through the door at the bottom of the stairs, holding the memory stick overhead like a lightning rod, looking and sounding like a madman, he came face to face with a strange woman standing among the storage shelves. She appeared to be even more startled by his sudden burst out of the hidden door in the back wall than Jerry was to find a stranger in Marilyn's work area. She held a ream of paper in front of her like a shield and looked about to scream when Jerry smiled and transferred the memory stick he still held overhead into his other hand so he could offer his right hand to shake.

"Hi. I'm an author," he said as she tentatively reached out to shake his hand. "Sorry for the entrance."

"Jerry," Marilyn said from the other side of the shelves. He was still holding the stranger's hand when Marilyn rounded the corner to introduce them. "April, I see you've met Jerry. Jerry, I've just hired April to work with me in COPY/COPY."

"Welcome to the clan," he said, being still somewhat Mowdabbified in his thinking.

"I'm finished!" he said to Marilyn. He raised the memory stick and his eyebrows to show her what he meant. Jerry was still holding April's hand even while Marilyn jumped on him like a rowdy child, throwing her arms around his neck and her legs around his waist. She let out a joyous, uninhibited "Yeeeeeaaaaaouw!" similar to the Yaaaaahooooo he had been tempted to scream earlier. Her assault on his balance required him to continue holding April's hand to keep from toppling backwards into the recycle bins.

After a long kiss that must have made April begin to wonder about her recent commitment to work with these people, Marilyn asked him, "When shall we publish?"

"The first step would have to be making a printout of the manuscript," he said, "and we don't have a printer."

This stumped them for a moment.

"Maybe..." April said, hesitating when they both turned to look at her. "My ex-husband sells used computer equipment."

Marilyn and Jerry smiled at each other, enjoying yet another serendipitous connection. He could not resist the temptation any longer. "Yaaaaahooooo!" he yelled at the ceiling.

Hand Made

Collectors would one day seek after a first edition of *Lurk on the Love Planet*, one of the 100 "hand-made" copies Marilyn, April, Leaf, and Jerry made in COPY/COPY, in what was their first and last "Publishing Picnic." Everyone enjoyed the process of making the books by hand, but it was a lot of work and was the last time it was ever done that way; subsequent editions were printed across town at Emerald City Printing.

Apart from his trip to Safeway to buy wine and cheese for the picnic, Jerry's only real contribution to Marilyn's complex publishing process was to print the master pages on a used laser printer he bought from April's ex-husband. Following Marilyn's instructions, Jerry set it up to print landscape, but using only half of the page, odd numbered pages on the right half of the sheet and even numbered pages on the left. When he passed the printed master pages to Marilyn, he did so reverentially, as if it was a sacred relic and not just a stack of paper. He was relieved it was done, reluctant to let it go, and grateful that Marilyn was there to receive it. She gave him a kiss as a receipt and carried the master pages into COPY/COPY, where the publishing crew (April and Leaf) was standing by. Since Jerry had never dealt with a copying task any more complex than to lay paper on the copier glass, he was condemned to the role of fretful spectator for the balance of the process, uselessly peering over shoulders.

The first step was to manually separate the odd and even pages of the master into two piles. Then, Marilyn made 100 collated copies of the pile of odd pages. The resulting copies were turned over and the odd pages run through the copier again, this time using the even page pile as the master. As the 100, two-sided copies of *Lurk on the Love Planet* came off the copier, Leaf used the big, electric, paper-cutter to cut away the blank half of the sheets, resulting in finished 8½ by 5½ pages, ready for binding.

The bookbinding began by clamping the 156 sheets of paper comprising the body of one book into the book press, carefully aligning the edge that was destined to be the spine of the book. A special rubber cement was spread over the exposed clamped edge and it was set aside to dry.

When all 100 book bodies were thus assembled and drying, everyone turned their attention to the picnic. They spread a checkered tablecloth in the middle of the workspace floor. As Leaf was lighting the candles, Jerry and Marilyn went upstairs to retrieve their first course of wine, cheese, and crackers, and to cut wedges of fresh Washington apples. When they returned with the food and wine, Jerry saw April unwrapping the colorful book covers. She placed a glossy stack of them next to the book press, getting them ready for the final part of the publishing process to take place after the picnic. Jerry left the food on the tablecloth and hurried to April's side, momentarily unable to think even about a picnic at the sight of the covers. He hadn't yet seen them because Marilyn had taken Jerry's unique design for that first edition cover to Kinko's in order to use their large-format, color copier. He marveled at the reality of them, a high-altitude view of a mysterious world behind a pulp-fiction title font.

April stood by, watching Jerry. He was a little embarrassed by his wanton fondling of the covers in front of a woman he didn't yet know well, so he tried to get some conversation going.

"What does your father do?" he asked. Fathers had always been a particularly interesting topic to Jerry, and one he had found to be a good conversation starter, except in Leaf's case; Jerry knew Leaf well enough not to ask about *his* father.

"He works in a boat repair shop in Bellingham," April said, and then was quiet.

Jerry couldn't think of another conversation starter, so he stopped fondling the book covers, turned off the shop lights, and moved to fold his long legs under him around their candlelit, red-checkered picnic. While the food was passed around, Jerry remembered Leaf having said something about Bellingham while they were both staring at a campfire. "Leaf, didn't you say you were from up Bellingham way?" Jerry was merely trying to include Leaf in his attempted conversation with April, but Leaf whipped his head around, focusing his high-powered lenses on Jerry. It was almost an angry reaction, as if Jerry might have betrayed a confidence.

"No, Jerry," Leaf said, pointedly, "I don't believe I ever said that."

Jerry was sure Leaf was from Bellingham, but didn't argue; Leaf obviously resented the question as a clumsy matchmaking effort. Jerry just said, "Oh."

Leaf turned back to April and said, "But, he's right; I did grow up in Bellingham. Till I was thirteen."

"Really?" April said. "I'm always pleased to meet another 'B'hammer.'"

Leaf smiled ever so slightly, careful not to reveal his gold tooth.

The two had been painfully shy around one another to that point, so Jerry was delighted he had gotten them talking.

April asked Leaf, "Why did you leave?"

While April probably didn't pick up on it, Jerry could tell Leaf was conflicted, wanting to answer the question and to continue his conversation with her, but struggling with what, or how much, to say. In the end, he did not answer directly. What he said was: "My uncle still works on the docks up there."

They all munched crackers and cheese and sipped their wine while April digested what Leaf had said. When she reached the conclusion, as everyone else had, that Leaf must have left Bellingham to get away from his father's family, she graciously changed the topic. "It's a nice town," she said. "There's a lot of good local music."

"Lot of good bookstores too," Leaf offered, obviously relieved to have the conversation turn back to something he liked to talk about.

"For sure!" April said, "I love Village Books."

Their conversation was started: Bookstores, music venues, best pizza, etc. Jerry could not help but smile. When he looked over to Marilyn, he discovered she was staring at him, smiling a little too, but her eyes were wet with the stuff of tears, though none of it had ventured down a cheek, so far.

"What?" he asked. "Is something wrong?"

She took Jerry's hand in one of hers and reached out to take Leaf's hand on the other side. She looked at Leaf and nodded toward April. Leaf and Jerry got the message and reached out to take April's hands. When the circle was complete, Marilyn said, "This just feels so... good."

Jerry was expecting more from the ever-verbose Marilyn, but she just passed her tearful smile around the picnic table until he, too, began to appreciate how good it felt.

"You're right," he said. "I am a lucky man."

"We are all lucky," Marilyn said.

Leaf and April both gravely nodded their agreement.

- - -

During his nightly patrol of Seattle's streets, Officer Comstock noticed what appeared to be a flickering glow coming from inside the otherwise dark storefront of COPY/COPY, a glow that might be a burglar's flashlight or the start of a fire. The patrol car managed a U-turn at the end of the block in the early-morning emptiness and came back to park in front of the store. Officer Comstock left his partner in the patrol car and got out to look through the front window. He could see the usual night light on inside the shop, but there was another flickering light beyond that. By standing on his toes at the far corner window, he could see behind the big copier. People were sitting cross-legged on the floor around a red-checkered tablecloth, like picnickers. A guttering candle-in-a-wine-bottle stood in the center, providing the flickering glow he had seen from the street. The tablecloth was covered by the remnants of a wine and cheese party. Officer Comstock tapped his five-cell flashlight on the doorframe and watched the picnickers jump in unison.

Marilyn peeked around the corner of the big copier and bounced to her feet to open the door. Everyone else simply stood up.

"Good morning," Marilyn said.

"Everything OK here?"

"Oh, yeah. Everything's fine," she said, suddenly realizing how their behavior might have aroused suspicion. "Sorry to have taken up your time like this, but, yeah, we're fine."

"OK," Officer Comstock said, "But I gotta say it's a strange time and place for a picnic."

Marilyn smiled back and shrugged an apology just as Jerry joined her at the door.

"Officer," he said, "come on in for a second. I want you to meet some people."

"Sure," Officer Comstock said and turned to signal his partner, touching his flashlight to the bill of his cap.

He followed Marilyn and Jerry inside. Leaf and April were still standing in position around the picnic.

Jerry began the introductions, "we're celebrating, among other things, our two new employees."

"Jerry finished his book!" Marilyn quickly added to explain the 'other things' and bounced her shoulders and her eyebrows in unison as she said it, as if to show she wasn't quite finished celebrating.

April grinned and nodded a greeting, but Leaf remained motionless and wild-eyed.

Jerry continued, "This is April. She's working with Marilyn."

Officer Comstock nodded a greeting and returned her smile.

"And this is Leaf. He's managing our new bookstore."

Leaf did not react. He looked as if he was standing before a firing squad.

Officer Comstock walked right up to Leaf and extended his hand to shake. "Yeah, Leaf and I have met," he said.

Leaf looked down at the proffered hand as if it might be holding a gun.

"Congratulations on the job," Officer Comstock said.

Leaf slowly reached out to shake hands. "Thanks."

While still holding Leaf's hand, Officer Comstock said to all of them, "It's good to have a new store in the neighborhood." Then he turned back to Leaf. "It's always nice to see a fresh beginning." He released Leaf's hand and addressed all of them again. "And… I am glad to see the end of The Planet of Love."

"Yeah," Jerry said, "we hear that a lot."

"Business has picked up in this store already since the other one closed," Marilyn said.

"Lucky for me," April added with a big grin.

"Well, I better keep moving," Officer Comstock said and started toward the door. He saluted Leaf and April just as he had earlier saluted his partner. "Welcome to the neighborhood."

"Thanks for watching out for us," Marilyn said to him before she closed the door.

Leaf exhaled loudly and relaxed for the first time since the knock on the door.

"How did you know him?" Jerry asked Leaf quietly as Marilyn returned to the picnic floor.

"He woke me up a few times."

"Oh," Jerry said, and left it at that. He had been rousted out of a warm sleep on occasion himself.

April overheard their whispered exchange and was made curious. "Why would he wake you up?"

Leaf and Jerry exchanged glances. Leaf waited for Jerry to say something, but when he didn't, chose that moment to bring his past out in the open.

"I lived on the street for a while," he said, as though trying out the sound of it.

"Oh," April said, not yet knowing how to react to that.

Leaf seemed to realize his admission only created more questions, so he explained, "That Officer had occasion to point out I was sleeping on private property."

"I see," April said, giving Leaf a big smile, almost as if she thought it was brave and adventurous to live on the street. Leaf gave her a tentative smile in return, almost revealing his gold tooth, and stole a quick glance at Jerry, as if looking for a clue about how he should react to April.

- - -

When the bookbinding resumed, each book body was given a fresh application of cement along the now-dry spine and was married with the cover stock. This assembly was returned to the book press for a final squeeze that served to bond it all together, to fold the front and back covers around the body of the book, and to crimp the spine so it would lay flat. With that, it became a book, clearly and sufficiently, a book.

Jerry remained by the drying racks throughout the bookbinding process, marveling at the manifestation of his first, wondrous, finished novel, as fascinated by the last book to be placed in the rack as he had been by the first. He could not have been more pleased. He could hardly keep his eyes off it. Simply looking at the cover of "his book" was enough to generate a faint electric thrill and a soft tingle of pride. All those years of dreaming and all those months of writing had produced something he could hold in his hand. It looked like such a simple thing, but it felt like an intricate treasure, full of magic. He could thumb through the pages and recall where he was, both physically and mentally, when he wrote each section of the book. *Lurk on the Love Planet* was the nearest thing he had to a journal of his own epic odyssey.

- - -

When the work was done, as the last thing they did that night, Leaf and Jerry loaded the 100, custom-printed copies into two boxes and carried them up the inside stairwell and down again into The Planet of Books.

"Let's just set them right here for now," Jerry said, lowering his box of books to the floor. "Tomorrow you can put them on display on a rack by themselves just inside the door, so no one can miss seeing them." Jerry was excited to think that *Lurk on the Love Planet* would be on sale in The Planet of Books the next morning.

Leaf set down the box he carried and opened it. He pulled out a single copy and studied it for a moment, thumbing through the first few pages. "I can't wait to read it," he said, and meant it.

"I'd like to hear what you think," Jerry said. He meant that too.

Leaf then noticed the quotes at the front of the book. "Follow the weasel?" he asked.

Jerry smiled. "That's another story entirely."

Long-Lost

Jerry had been living with Marilyn in the big apartment for more than a year without sharing his theory regarding Destiny's manipulation of his life. He was finally made certain enough, and brave enough, to speak it aloud when he was confronted with yet another thunderous change.

They were in that beautiful old bed, a place that had become the center of their lives. It was after another early-to-bed evening of lovemaking when Marilyn asked, rather anxiously Jerry thought, if he loved her.

"I do," he said without the slightest hesitation or reservation. "I do, and I always will," he added for good measure.

Jerry had said this many times before and in many different ways, but Marilyn still had a need to hear it said regularly. He was happy to oblige. He didn't really understand her need for reassurance because, for him, Marilyn's daily presence in his life was enough, but he was absolutely certain of his answer to this oft-asked question and found the words easy to say. This time however, his answer did not have its usual effect on her; a noticeable trace of her anxiety remained. Jerry raised his eyebrows at her and tilted his head, as dogs will sometimes do at the puzzling behavior of humans (a habit he had picked up from her) his way of asking what was on her mind.

She got up on her knees beside him. Jerry folded his arms behind his head and enjoyed the wonderfully compact nature of her nakedness.

"How are you feeling about Alaska?" she asked.

"Alaska is the last frontier of romance and adventure on this planet," he said without hesitation.

"Yes," Marilyn said; she had heard him say this many times as well, "but do you still have a secret desire to live there?"

At that moment, he truly did not want to be anywhere other than where he was. He was warm and happy and deeply in love.

"Maybe…" he began, teasing her a bit, "Maybe I could make do with an occasional, short-term romantic adventure there."

She knew he was teasing her and was sufficiently pleased with his answer for her anxiety to lessen considerably, but it was still not completely gone. Jerry decided to give her the full honest answer. "I truly do not want to be anywhere other than where I am," he said. "I am warm and happy and deeply in love." Jerry was certain that moving to Alaska, or anywhere else without this woman, would be a grave mistake.

Jerry could see this was what Marilyn needed to hear. Almost all of her anxiety was gone now, but there was still something on her mind.

Jerry waited.

When she had, at last, worked up her courage, she watched his eyes closely while she said something that thrilled every part of him: "Jerry, I think I'm pregnant."

The joy of that news washed through him and across his face. His expression was easy for Marilyn to read. His eyes filled and then overflowed with tears, dissolving completely the last of Marilyn's anxiety and leaving an expression on her face Jerry would treasure forever, a gentle, happy smile he would always associate with the word "Love."

"Are you sure?" he asked.

"I'm regular as a clock," she said, "but I've now missed two periods and the drugstore test says yes."

"Have you seen a doctor?

"I have an appointment tomorrow."

"Are you happy about this?" he asked.

"I am," she said, "and all the more so now I know you are happy about it."

Marilyn began to cry too, matching him tear for tear. Jerry pulled her down to him and licked away her salty tears as soon as they appeared. He kept at it like a big, dumb dog until she began to laugh and could not cry anymore. He told her some more that he loved her. He assured her she would make a wonderful mother, that he would never leave her, and would do his damnedest to be the best father he was capable of being, even though he had grown up without one. He would operate on instinct, and love, and all the books about fathering he could find.

They talked well into the night, bandying ideas about and speaking of dreams for the future, where they would put the baby, what they might call him-her-it, how Marilyn would have plenty of time to get April ready to run COPY/COPY, and on and on.

Later, when they had both exhausted all other subjects for the time being, while they still basked in the glow of Marilyn's news, but long before they were calm enough to sleep, Jerry told her of his theory.

"Now I have something to share with you," he began.

She sat upright in bed once again, turning to face him and sitting on her feet, her hands clasped in her naked lap, in full listening mode.

"This is going to sound crazy."

Marilyn's wonderful news was the last validation Jerry needed of his theory. Destiny *had* led him here. In that moment, he had no doubt. He was, at last, exactly where he was supposed to be.

He just said it straight out. "I believe Mr. Stamper was my grandfather."

- - -

Marilyn was made mute. She started to form several different responses, abandoning each one in turn, before she finally said, carefully, "How did you reach that conclusion?"

Now that he'd said it right out loud for the first time, it sounded crazier than he imagined it would. Was he becoming like his Uncle Harold? Crazy people were probably the last to know they were crazy.

"I never knew my father," he began, then continued with the entirety of the Gustafson fable of his father, his Grandmother's version of that Wildly Romantic Weekend in San Francisco, her story of her daughter's tragic love affair with a soldier going off to war.

When he finished, Marilyn reworded it for her own benefit: "So, you think it was Mr. Stamper's son your mother met in San Francisco?"

"Yes, probably at a Grateful Dead concert. I think it could have been him. She definitely met somebody in San Francisco and I certainly look like Darren. We've both seen that. Mr. Stamper saw that too. And the timing is right." Jerry was rushing to present all his evidence before the woman he loved began to suspect he'd lost his mind. "I mean I checked the dates. I was conceived around the same time Darren Stamper would have been on leave before shipping out to Vietnam. He was killed ten months later, one month after I was born. And, the Grateful Dead were performing in San Francisco that month. I looked it up. Plus, many soldiers shipped off to war from the Alameda Naval Air Station, so Darren would have been in the area."

"OK… Wow. So, maybe you discovered your Grandfather."

"Yes, or he discovered me. It's spooky isn't it?"

"Wait, you said 'probably at a Grateful Dead concert.' How would you know that and… what's that got to do with it?"

"Oh, right… you don't know about… It's nothing really. I mean it's not proof of anything. It's just that my Mother was a big-time Deadhead. She hitched all over the western states for their concerts. And, I haven't told you one other thing about me. I haven't told anyone really, but my middle name is Garcia."

Marilyn blinked a few times to tuck these new facts away and tried out Jerry's name, "Jerry Garcia Gustafson. OK… so you might have been Jerry Garcia Stamper."

"It's a strange and tangled world we live in."

"And your mother never mentioned your father's name?"

"Well, she died when I was only five, so maybe she mentioned something that I don't remember. But, I doubt it. If she ever said his name to my Grandma, it didn't get passed on to me."

"That is so sad."

"My Grandma's account of it was always tinged with romance, but that was probably her own spin on her daughter's illegitimate pregnancy, a way to cope with the narrow minds in conservative little Kilgore, Idaho. She would have done all she could to make it sound less… unseemly. I think the more likely truth of my Mother's Wildly Romantic Weekend was that it was nothing more than a one-nighter after a rock and roll concert, maybe just a drunken quickie. Maybe she never got his name."

"That is so sad," she said again.

"Anyway, romantic weekend or drunken quickie, the result is the same. So... after seeing the resemblance in the photo with the '57 Chevy... and after putting together all the facts I know, or think I know, and with the timing of everything..."

"Why hadn't you ever mentioned this?" she interrupted.

"Well... it all sounds pretty crazy and there's no real evidence except for the resemblance and the timing, so I didn't think there was any reason to make myself look crazy in your eyes. Now though, and this part doesn't make much sense either, the moment I heard you were pregnant, I was even more certain that I had met my grandfather. Whether or not it's true doesn't matter to me. It feels as if a missing piece of my life has fallen into place."

Marilyn's bottom lip began to quiver.

"My whole life has felt like an incomplete jigsaw puzzle. For a long time, I was finding puzzle pieces here and there, but nothing fit together. When you said you were pregnant, it was as if you had handed me the central piece of my puzzle, the one that completed the picture."

"Oh Jerry." Tears were forming.

"I now know, deep in my heart and without a doubt, that I am exactly where I'm supposed to be. This, all of this," he stretched his long arms across the bed to indicate the good fortune of their new home, "and Mr. Stamper and you and now our child..." he touched that magical place just below Marilyn's navel, where their child was growing. "*This* is my destiny. I believe I was meant to come to Seattle to find my last living relative, and to find you."

"To find me?"

"Sure, I think when Mr. Stamper brought us together, whether he knew it or not, he was acting like some kind of an agent."

"But he was just picking us out because we looked like his family."

"Maybe that's all there is to it," Jerry admitted. He knew it would sound even crazier to tell her about following the weasel.

Marilyn thought about Jerry's mystical view things. "Maybe," she said, putting her hands on her belly, "you and I were brought together to create this child."

- - -

EPILOGUE

Just as Carlos Castaneda eventually found his spot on Don Juan's porch, Jerry has found his spot on the earth. He has no doubt he is precisely where Destiny had in mind for him when she goosed him out of Ms. Nervan's chair at the Kilgore Library almost five years ago. The center of his new universe is his bedroom/office where he sits each day as he writes. That old, weatherworn, pink sign from The Love Planet, still mounted on the wall behind his desk, serves as a constant reminder of the great distance he has traveled beyond the life he might have known in Kilgore. It lends a sense of otherworldly romance to his bedroom/office that pleases him immensely.

Jerry struggles to write his third and most ambitious novel, this one inspired, at least in part, by the discoveries he made during his improbable odyssey. He thinks of it as his "imagined autobiography." It contains characters he likes to contemplate: There is a businessman who owns a furniture store and likes to read Shakespeare, but is struggling to keep his troubled family together. He has a rebellious son who chases after women, driving them around in a 1957 Chevy, until he is drafted and sent off to war. The businessman has a desperate wife who tries to keep her own demons at bay as she waits each day for another letter from her soldier son.

His "imagined autobiography" is a fiction that feels like truth, but it is not Science Fiction (and therefore a real stretch for him). By some mechanism he doesn't understand, writing it reinforces his thankful wonderment at his good fortune. Although, he need only look out any window to see walking reminders of just how badly his life might have turned out.

As he sits in the center of his universe, still wondering how the story will end, a gentle knock on the door interrupts his writing.

"Come in," he says, already knowing from the knock and from the hour that it is one of two people; he doesn't know which one it will be because he cannot remember whose turn it is to come and get him today.

The door creaks open and the small, blond head of a three-year-old appears around the corner.

"Mommy says 'Lunch is ready.'"

"Thanks Mandy, I'll be right there." Jerry is pretty sure it is Mandy, but she came and went so quickly it might have been Mindy. It really doesn't matter; they are used to people getting their names wrong.

The door is closed carefully; they have been taught by their Mommy not to disturb their Daddy when he is working.

"How could anybody have it better than me?" Jerry wonders yet again.

As the result of another cosmic fold in the universe, Marilyn turned out *not* to be carrying their child; she was carrying their children.

Twins.

There is a bewildering degree of wonderment for Jerry in that too. The first twins he ever saw boarded the bus out of Idaho. They caused him to include the "Doublemint" twins in his first novel. The same twins are pivotal characters in Jerry's second novel, *Mowdabbian Rules*, where the nature of their "twinness" plays a big role in the evolving mental abilities several generations later on Mowdabb. But the most stunning wonderment of twins in Jerry's life is in the fact that Mr. Stamper had been a twin. When he researched twins for writing *Mowdabbian Rules*, he learned that the likelihood for conceiving twins is carried in the father's genetics and that it occurs most often in every second generation. Score another point for his Grandpa Stamper theory.

- - -

When Jerry arrives at the kitchen table, Mindy and Mandy are already working on their baloney sandwiches. Mandy is chewing on a huge mouthful, evidenced by the size of the bite missing from her sandwich, while Mindy is still involved in using her newly acquired skills with a knife and fork to cut the crusts off her sandwich. Jerry can see he and Marilyn are having toasted cheese sandwiches and chicken soup.

"How's it going, Love?" Marilyn asks, meaning his writing.

"Real well," he says, meaning, with all his heart, his writing, his life, all of it.

"Author In Prime Tackles New Challenge." Marilyn says this as a suggestion for a headline for a future newspaper article about him. This is an old game between them now, one that started after an article about him and about The Planet of Books was published in the Seattle Weekly.

Jerry countered with a headline for an article about Marilyn's life. "Business Dynamo Settles for Nurturing Hack."

She closes her eyes and performs a little head-bow to acknowledge his compliment of her business prowess and then says with a smile, "I would change 'Settles for' to 'Finds Happiness with' but that still leaves a problem with your modifier; you are *not* a nurturing hack."

"True," he concedes. "You are the nurturing one, I am the hack."

"My love, of course I mean to say *you are* nurturing *and* you *are not* a hack. You are a wonderful storyteller. Isn't that so girls? Isn't your father a wonderful storyteller?" Both twins nod soberly to their mom in perfect unison and turn their big eyes on their father, waiting for his response in this bewildering adult conversation. Once again, Jerry basks in the attention of the Beautiful Young Women in his life. Having three pairs of deep, dark eyes focused on him dissolves the faintest trace of unrest that might have sprouted in his gypsy soul. Jerry is awash with happiness. It is almost enough to bring tears.

"Tonight, I'll tell you a story about a furry E.T. that was raised by Alaskan grizzlies," he suggests. "OK?"

The twins nod again with wide-eyed sobriety, fully prepared for yet another bizarre bedtime story.

"Don't forget," Marilyn reminds him, "You should spend a few minutes with Leaf before he gets off work at 6:00."

"Wilco."

"What's 'Wilco'?" Mandy asks, her mouth finally clear of baloney sandwich.

"That's short for 'Will comply'," he says.

"What's 'comply'?" Mindy asks with her mouth still full, not to be left out.

"That means 'obey'," he says.

"Obey means 'Do it right now!'" Mandy volunteers this, with emphasis.

"I'm not going to tell you again," Mindy adds.

"Your mother is a good teacher," Jerry says.

The twins look at each other across the table in a kind of mind-meld thing as they eat, perhaps digesting 'wilco' and 'comply' for future use, or deciding how to proceed with the next line of questioning.

Mandy turns out to be the designated questioner. "Will Leaf feed the birds?"

"Yes," Marilyn intervenes. "I've already talked to Leaf about that, and he'll also water the plants and feed your fish. Now no more questions; your father has to finish his lunch so he can get back to work." She grins at him, having rescued him again from another merciless inquisition by the twin information sponges.

As Jerry leaves the lunch table, he bows with silly drama. "I thank you ladies for the delicious lunch and for the fine conversation." He finishes with an Elizabethan flourish, indicating the door. "I must away."

Marilyn graces him with a stylized kiss, blown from her fingertips. The twins watch their mother and then attempt the same, Mandy first planting a messy kiss in the center of her palm, showing Jerry her palm, and leaving a few breadcrumbs on her cheek. Mindy watches her sister, then takes her turn to perform the same gesture, except remembering to blow.

- - -

They are planning a vacation, their first as a family. It will also be the first time Leaf is left alone to run The Planet of Books. This is worrisome for Jerry. When he attempts to get back to his writing, he is instead thinking about the trip, about talking to Leaf, and about all that needs to be done before they go. He leaves his preferred spot in the world and goes down the stairs to appear through the unnoticeable door at the back of The Planet of Books.

- - -

"How's it going today?" he asks Leaf.

"Sold one this morning," Leaf says, knowing it is something Jerry will ask about.

"Cool!" Jerry says, an expression he never uses with anyone except Leaf. "Which one?"

"Lurk," Leaf says, abbreviating the title to allow as few words as possible in conversation.

Leaf sits and reads, as he does all day, every day, on the stool behind the glass-topped counter. He never seems to tire of it. Like the inscrutable Buddha he still resembles, Leaf sits peacefully upright, holding in his pale, soft hands one of the many thousands of Science Fiction books that now line the store's shelves. The Planet of Books has truly become "The Best Selection of Science Fiction in the Northwest."

Jerry stops to inspect the wire rack that holds a display of his books just inside the store entrance. His second novel *Mowdabbian Rules* fills every space on the right side of the rack and *Lurk on the Love Planet* dominates the left side. When he notices a few empty spaces in the left side of the rack, he cannot help but say, "This rack isn't full."

Leaf does not react at all.

"Books sell better from a full shelf. That's a marketing fact," he tells Leaf, yet again, knowing he's being obsessive even while he's doing it.

Jerry had considered putting a sign behind the counter so it would always be in Leaf's view: "BOOKS SELL BETTER FROM A FULL SHELF." This is really about all Jerry understands about the business of running a bookstore, so it has become his personal bookselling mantra.

"OK." Leaf says as neutrally as humanly possible.

"You know these two books are very special to me," Jerry continues shamelessly, "I want them always on the rack right here in front, so it's the first thing the customer sees, and I want the shelves always kept full, so it looks like it's a fresh shipment from the publisher."

Leaf is a little miffed at Jerry's condescension. He stares blankly through his thick and dirty glasses, pretending to listen; he has heard it all before. It is his way of being relatively polite since he can't read while Jerry is talking anyway. It is also literally the least he can do.

He says "OK" one more time, flatly, in a way that will tell Jerry he is being an asshole and tuned out.

- - -

From its opening day, business in The Planet of Books had improved steadily, largely due to Leaf's infectious enthusiasm for Science Fiction and his conscientious store management (despite the nagging empty rack issue). It also helped business that the store was owned, and sometimes attended by an author of Science Fiction. Word of Jerry's book spread among rabid Sci-Fi fans in the area (there turned out to be many more than he could have imagined around the Puget Sound) and *Lurk on the Love Planet* became a local, minor-league, cult favorite. Fans sometimes came to the store to meet the new author in town and buy a signed copy. Jerry was always willing to appear through the magical, invisible door at the back of the store to meet a fan. He would often also sell a copy to people who had never heard of him. "Have you seen my novel?" was his unabashed opening line. The resultant interaction with an idle browser often culminated with Jerry humbly offering to sign a copy for them and then composing an elaborate, personalized dedication on the flyleaf.

Jerry's big break as a writer of Science Fiction came after *Lurk on the Love Planet* was favorably reviewed in an article in the Seattle Weekly section of the Seattle Times. The article was really about The Planet of Books, saying there was a new independent bookstore in town at a time when most independents were closing down, but it also made brief mention of him and his novel, describing it as "a fresh first-vision of another world." The article also made much of the fact that it was self-published *and* self-printed in COPY/COPY right next-door. This mention of COPY/COPY resulted in a healthy boost to business there as well. The article ended with a plug for The Planet of Books echoing the store's own advertising copy, that it offered "The Best Selection of Science Fiction in the Northwest." Marilyn had that article framed and mounted in both stores.

Jerry's writing career was on its way. *Mowdabbian Rules,* Jerry's second novel, was published just as his twins had their second birthday. "Rules," as Leaf referred to it, was based on the twelve rules listed at the end of *Lurk on the Love Planet.* It chronicled the next eight generations of Lurk's decedents as their telepathic powers evolved on Mowdabb's peculiar diet.

While "Rules" was well-received by hardcore Sci-Fi fans, it did not sell as well as his first book. After "Rules" was published, Jerry realized it was a bit tedious and over-long, focusing too much on the administration of the pilgrimages of those who dared the grueling, month-long Mowdabbian retreat. But, it sold well enough that Jerry was able to justify continuing to think of himself as an author.

He entertained no delusions about his novels; he knew he would likely never have been published by conventional means. (Leaf once referred to Jerry's novels as "light-weight," which was true of course, but stung nonetheless.) Marilyn had made it all possible. She was the beginning of everything. She was the source of his miraculous family and of every shred of his happiness. These truths he would often publicly espouse by paraphrasing Shakespeare (with apologies to Silvia):

> Then to Marilyn let us sing
>
> That Marilyn is excelling.
>
> She excels each mortal thing
>
> Upon the dull earth dwelling.

The Two Gentlemen of Verona, act 4, sc. 2.

Jerry taught the twins this quote in lieu of another extemporaneous bedtime story, for which the twins then devised a simple melody. Marilyn thought it was embarrassing to have her girls wandering around singing praise of their mother (she was afraid people would think she had taught it to them), but she was secretly pleased.

- - -

"Look, Leaf, I have to go," Jerry said. "We still have some packing to do. So... do you have any questions?"

Leaf looks around the store as if he is trying to remember where he is and then shakes his head, as if to confirm he does not have a clue; playing dumb is his way of getting even, knowing now Jerry will have to worry during the whole time he is gone about having left Leaf in charge.

- - -

Even after knowing Leaf for over five years, Jerry still found him to be alien and inscrutable; he could be alternately stoically dense and stunningly brilliant, a sci-fi geek and a reliable store manager. Jerry was still able to see both the street bum and the Buddha. It was an ongoing challenge for an anxious man named Jerry Garcia Gustafson to relate to a placid man named Leaf Walker.

- - -

"Here's the number of the lodge where we'll be staying." Jerry wrote the number down for Leaf, pinning the note to a shelf by the phone. "Call me if you run into any kind of problem. OK?"

"OK."

"So, don't call just to tell me a guppy died."

"OK."

"On the other hand, if something *is* going wrong, don't hesitate to call. OK?"

"OK."

"We'll see you in two weeks."

"OK."

- - -

Convinced nothing short of a direct meteor impact on the building would cause Leaf to call and that there is nothing more he can do about it, Jerry leaves to help Marilyn with the last of the packing, resigned to the fact Leaf was, and would always be, a thoroughgoing mystery.

In the middle of his claustrophobic climb back up the narrow stairwell, a passage he normally made three steps at a time, Jerry is brought to a complete stop. He has suddenly remembered applying those same words "a thoroughgoing mystery" to Mr. Stamper. He is immobilized in the quiet of that darkened stairwell, just as he had been following the collapse of Ms. Nervan's chair in the Kilgore Library. What has stopped him now, though, is different from the epiphany that rocked his quiet life to the core so long ago; it is more like a humbling realization that he had been glibly labeling people as mysteries and moving on, plodding through his days, dismissing those he could not understand, and abandoning any chance to know them better. He had labeled Mr. Stamper as a senile old coot, so all the questions he might have asked his grandfather would remain forever unanswered. For the rest of his life, Jerry was condemned to wish he had done more to *solve* the thoroughgoing mystery that was Mr. Stamper.

Jerry had to change this; he would never get to know anyone well at this rate (except for Marilyn, around whom all his barriers were down). Despite his penchant for dismissing those he could not understand, everyone he had come to know well had somehow enriched his life. Kevin was a good example. Every real human interaction had evolved in unexpected ways into something more, often with incomprehensible repercussions. If he were to give up trying to solve the thoroughgoing mystery of Leaf, he would be repeating the mistake he made with his grandfather.

Another angle occurred to him in his moment of clarity: Perhaps he might now be serving as an agent for change in Leaf's own odyssey, somehow unknowingly playing a role that would be as pivotal for Leaf as Mr. Stamper's role had proven to be for him. He hoped so, but there was no way of knowing and that was the whole point. Even though Leaf was a little spacey, and an exasperating conversationalist, he was a friend, and had been for over five years now. There might be a good reason for that.

Jerry felt as if there had been a major change in his world once again, as if his grandfather might have indirectly taught him a major life lesson. This practice of his, of labeling people as mysterious (or "narrow-minded," as had been the case in Kilgore), tended to close the door on the unknowable potential most people represented. Life was too short for that; its peculiar twists and turns needed to be monitored continuously for the subtle tell-tales of Destiny's hand. It was integral to the art of following the weasel.

He turned around and headed back down the stairs. He opened the doorway at the bottom and hollered the length of the store. "Hey Leaf, my friend," Leaf is startled from his reading, mouth hanging open as usual, which made him look even more startled. "I'm glad you're here," Jerry says.

Before he turns to go back up the stairs, he sees the gleam of Leaf's gold tooth.

- - -

Marilyn has two large suitcases open on the bed and is carefully folding her clothes into them. Amazingly, at the same time, she is also directing the twins as they do their part to pack a third, smaller suitcase they have open on the floor, precisely in the middle of the highest traffic area of the bedroom.

"I don't think Boo Bee will fit, dear," Marilyn is saying as Jerry steps into the room, "You'll have to carry him on the plane."

"Boo Bee wants to ride in the suitcase," Mandy responds. A little distraught over being unable to accommodate Boo Bee's wishes, she is tamping the unfortunate stuffed creature with both fists into the limited available space in her half of the suitcase.

"You talk to Boo Bee about it," Marilyn suggests. "He might want to ride with you so he can look out the window too."

Mandy thinks about this, pulls the battered doll out of the suitcase by its ears (or by its horns or its antennae, who could tell anymore) and takes it to the corner of the room where a long, whispered conversation begins.

Meanwhile, Mindy is squatted on the floor, carefully folding her socks and lining them up for later placement into the already-neat collection of clothes in her half of the suitcase.

Jerry is again amazed how two otherwise-identical people can be so different.

"Hi, Babies," he says, so they will notice his arrival. The twins drop what they are doing, launching themselves into their usual squealing race to be the first to hug him. The race turns out to be an obvious tie, but they are able to hug a knee apiece. Work is over now; Daddy is home to play.

"Hi, Love," Marilyn says. "Did you get Leaf ready to go?"

"Oh sure," Jerry answers, while walking into the room, swinging his legs wide to accommodate a child riding each of his legs, "He'll be fine unless absolutely anything out of the ordinary is required of him."

"Leaf will rise to any challenge," she says.

"He'll go whichever way the wind blows, more likely."

Marilyn laughs. She still laughs in all the right places. "He'll be fine," she says, already knowing Jerry is going to worry about it during the whole trip no matter what.

"I hope you're right, because we're betting the farm on it."

"There's always April," Marilyn points out. "He can consult with her if he's unsure what to do."

"Damn! I should have reminded him of that."

Mindy and Mandy exchange a look, registering yet another "damn" from their father.

April lives in Marilyn's old apartment and manages COPY/COPY for them, now that Marilyn is a full-time mom. April has turned out to be a real treasure, solid as a rock. It has lately become suspected that April occasionally invites Leaf to her apartment for dinner.

"Is your laptop ready to travel?" Marilyn asks.

"Yup. The battery's charged, the AC adapter is in the carry-case, I have my backups, the works."

"You've already made your backups?"

"Yup."

"Writer Tackles Alaskan Wilderness," she suggests with a smile. Marilyn knows how much this trip means to Jerry.

He knows she is mostly doing it for him.

"Woman Makes Family Possible," he responds. It would make a lousy headline, but it gets a smile from her and that is all he is after.

- - -

Also by Larry Sherrer

Zigzag Men is a work of historical fiction that captures the dark humor of an unruly cadre of loosely led, overworked helicopter pilots. They are reluctant warriors who commute into combat from a remote airfield in Vietnam, zigzagging over the jungle, around one another, and through the indelible intensity of war. Quan Loi is their staging-point for flight operations during the day and a disreputable haven for hardcore, drug-altered malcontents during the long hours of darkness. When Newbies arrive at Quan Loi, the inevitable friendships and animosities become amplified by exhausting hours of combat flying, followed by immoderate revelry, into a bizarre distortion of military life, where unlikely friendships, inconsolable grief, and surprising heroism are stirred into a unique and unexpected brew.